W9-CCX-780

DISCARD

American Folklife

American ican Folk life

Edited by Don Yoder

UNIVERSITY OF TEXAS PRESS

AUSTIN AND LONDON

Library of Congress Cataloging in Publication Data
Main entry under title:

American folklife.

Includes index.
1. Folk-lore, American—Addresses, essays,
lectures. 2. United States—Social life and
customs—Addresses, essays, lectures.
I. Yoder, Don.
GR105.A6   390'.0973   75-16073
ISBN 0-292-70308-2

Copyright © 1976 by the University of Texas
Press
All rights reserved
Printed in the United States of America

Design / Eje W. Wray
Typesetting / G&S Typesetters
Printing / Edwards Brothers
Binding / Universal

Contents

Preface

With the growing focus upon American experience in creating New World cultures, this volume on the folklife approach to our traditional cultural patterns will, we trust, take its place in the academic world beside its many European counterparts. It is our hope that it will stimulate research that will help us all to understand the American experience and, in doing so, to understand ourselves.

The volume presents a variety of offerings. Ward Goodenough's essay is an introduction to the broadest possible setting for folklife studies—the anthropological and ethnological sciences—and lays stress on the place of folklife data in the very contemporary American search for personal and group identity. James Marston Fitch's article, growing out of his work in historic preservation at Columbia University, sets folk or vernacular architecture against a world-wide research setting, while Warren E. Roberts gives us a detailed approach to the architectural history and setting of one folk-culturally significant building from rural Indiana. Fred Kniffen, leader of the folklife wing in American cultural geography, during his long teaching career at Louisiana State University fathered some thirty doctoral dissertations, most of them in the area of American folk-cultural patterns as studiable in geography. We are happy to include in this volume Dr. Kniffen's essay on the relation of cultural geography to folklife studies, as well as the Knipmeyer-Glassie article on regional boat patterns of French Louisiana (originally part of a Kniffen dissertation).

The article by Leslie P. Greenhill, director of the American Archive of the *Encyclopaedia Cinematographica*, reports on the world-wide ethnological filming mission of the encyclopaedia's sponsor, the Institute for Scientific Film at Göttingen, West Germany, and its possibilities for recording American traditional activities on film. Two excellent examples of historical ethnography at its scholarly best are the papers by David J. Winslow on turnpikes and turnpike lore in New York state and Walter Lee Robbins on the custom of shooting in the New Year among the Germans of the southern states. They combine data from the widest possible network of historical source materials with interviews of current informants. The paper by Gerald L. Davis on coil basketry in the Sea Islands is likewise a model of the interview approach to a living craft and points to new dimensions in black studies, emphasizing material aspects of black culture. The paper by James L. Evans points up what one can learn of the historical origins of ethnic tensions, in this case those between Hispanos and Anglos in the lower Rio Grande Valley in the nineteenth century. The method is historical but the focus is on contemporary ethnic problems. Finally, the closing paper of the volume, that by Jacob D. Elder on Yoruba ritual in Trinidad, directs us to a wider horizon for American folklife research, which will necessarily include the study of Caribbean traditional cultures.

Finally, a word of gratitude is expressed to all those who have aided me in the production of this volume—the contributors, who represent among them not only colleagues in research but also, in some cases, former students; the American Folklore Society, whose committee on material culture contributed some of the drive for the project; the Folklore and Folklife Department of the University of Pennsylvania, which encouraged the project from its inception in 1968; the University of Texas Press; and, finally, Scott Hambly, my editorial assistant at the University of Pennsylvania, whose able aid has facilitated the progress of the volume at the copy-reading and galley stages during the past year and a half.

Don Yoder

American Folklife

1. Folklife Studies in American Scholarship

Don Yoder

Folklife studies (regional ethnology) is a subject of recent development in the United States. Essentially it is the application to the American scene of the European discipline called *folklivsforskning*, or regional ethnology, in the Scandinavian lands (particularly in Sweden where the term *folkliv* was coined) and *Volkskunde* in the German-speaking areas of Europe. Folklife studies, or folklife research, has penetrated American academia both directly from the Scandinavian sources and indirectly from the British Isles, where the term *folklife* is used for scholarly journals, societies, and university programs.[1]

The concept of folklife studies was developed in Europe to study the native European cultures, focusing on the traditional aspects of these cultures. As an academic migrant it has come to the American scene at an unusually favorable moment in the development of American scholarship. With the present concern of Americans, particularly American youth, to determine their identity as it relates to ethnic, national, and world loyalties, we are witnessing at our universities a growth of ethnic studies programs, which focus on the experience and acculturation of the diverse groups that make up the American people. Ethnic consciousness is certainly one of the motivating forces for the search evident in the lives of the student population for their meaning in the larger picture. While black consciousness is the most conspicuous of these movements toward self-understanding on the American human landscape, the focus on civil rights and the rights to ethnic heritage and language have aroused many of our ethnic enclaves from the Mexican Americans of the Southwest to the French Canadians of the Northeast. What we are witnessing is in a sense a re-ethnicizing of America, a final ground swell of denial of the old "melting pot" concept of American history, and in its stead a vigorous vote of confidence for the concept of cultural pluralism.[2]

America will soon be celebrating the two-hundredth anniversary of her political birth. The cultural conception of America is of a much earlier date and involves the acculturation of three elements without which America cannot be explained—the native American Indian cultures, the European cultures of the emigrants (Oscar Handlin's "uprooted"), and the African cultures of the blacks. These are the peoples that have made the American people, and as such they are, in Ward Goodenough's phrase in the first essay in this volume, the proper focus of American folklife research.

By "American" folklife we mean essentially the regional cultures of North America with principal focus upon the United States, but with attention also to our neighbors in the North American experience of organizing New World cultures out of native American and European and African components. These are, in particular, Canada, Mexico,

3

and the Caribbean island nations. Canadian culture is an especially valuable check on American studies, since some of the same ethnic ingredients produced different cultural results there than in the States. Mexico, indeed all Latin America, is of increasing cultural importance to the United States for the understanding of our entire southwestern Spanish culture from Texas to California. The Caribbean, closer to us psychologically in the days of the clipper ships and the triangular trade, which left a deposit of Caribbean street names in our seaport towns and Caribbean foods on our urban tables, has become important once again, among other reasons, as providing additional keys to black acculturation in the United States.

At the present moment, it is difficult to define the terms *folklife* and *folklife studies* to the satisfaction of all elements interested in the subject matter.[3] There are those who, starting with *folklore* in its usual Anglo-American sense, define *folklife* by default, as material culture only. This is not the boundary set for it by its European creators. To Sigurd Erixon, folklife research was "the science of [European] man as a cultural being."[4] As such Erixon saw it as a regional branch of general anthropology, and in fact he often preferred to call it regional ethnology or, in its wider reaches, European ethnology. Its subject matter involves material, social, and spiritual culture, thus including what in the Anglo-American world has usually been called *folklore*. In its methodology "historical, descriptive, and reconstructive studies alternate with functional studies of culture, society, and the individual." The most useful British manual of folklife research defines it broadly as the study of the interaction of man (in this case British man) with his environment, hence, "British ethnography."[5] And Richard Weiss of the University of Zurich in 1946 defined *Volkskunde*, the continental European parent of American folklife studies, as "the study of the interrelationships between the folk and folk-culture, in so far as they are determined by community and tradition."[6] Weiss differentiates folk culture from mass culture, but locates "the folk-cultural," that is, traditionally mediated attitudes and beliefs, within the mind of the individual, where it coexists alongside other elements from different cultural levels. Thus Weiss prefers to speak not of "folk" levels of society or "folk" classes as wholes, but essentially of the folk-cultural element in the individual. It all goes back, of course, to that thorny word *folk* and the difficulty one faces in attempting to define it. The important point to note in all these definitions is that, in distinction to Anglo-American folklore studies, which have been until recently genre oriented, folklife research is oriented toward holistic studies of culture regionally delimited and toward "life," the life of the society under study and of the individual within that society.

If definitions of the subject matter of folklife studies were difficult in the opening stages of its development as a university discipline, it was equally difficult—as is the case with every developing discipline—to relate the new study to already existing sciences. Richard Weiss, whom we have already cited, was one of the shapers of folklife studies in Europe. In his model ethnography of Switzerland, *Volkskunde der Schweiz*, he wrestled with the interdisciplinary character of his subject. He marveled at the great range of subject matter involved in folklife monographs and asked whether there is a common bond that unites all these different approaches. "Is there such a spiritual bond, which makes a unified science of folklife studies? Or is folklife studies a product of addition, made up of research on settlement patterns, house types, costumes, customs, folksongs, tales, legends, legal aspects, and folk piety? Are these disciplines simply fringe fields in other sciences—geography, cultural history, and the sciences of literature, law, and religion? Or can folklife studies bring them all into fruitful and necessary cooperation?"[7]

Obviously, the focus on the regional and national cultures of Switzerland combined the tributary disciplines into a unified scientific study. With their more fully developed sense of homeland and heritage—national, regional, even local—and their recognition of national character, the European nations began early in the nineteenth century to develop archives, academic programs, and, finally, museums to record and study the traditional aspects of regional European existence. In a distinguished series of research institutions from north to south, from Nordiska Museet in Stockholm to the Museo Nazionale dell'Arte e Tradizione Popolari in Rome, and in a chain of ethnographic museums from Moscow and Bucharest on the east to Dublin and Lisbon on the west, European folklife scholarship has analyzed the traditional genius of Europe. But what began as by-product of the Romantic Movement with its focus on cultural nationalism developed gradually into the cooperative science of European folk-cultural studies. National boundaries were early seen as nondeterminative in folk-cultural phenomena, as the European atlases of folk culture make clear. Folklife studies, under whatever name it is known, has developed within its European perimeters into a university discipline in almost every European nation, and in the understanding of European life it is a potent ally of the historical, sociological, and anthropological sciences.[8]

In general, folklife studies stands particularly close to cultural and social anthropology, and, as we have suggested, in many European countries it is referred to as European ethnology. The major difference between the disciplines is that folklife studies insists on historical as well as ethnographic methodology. In the American academic world, folklife studies shares subject matter not only with cultural anthropology but also with the two historical disciplines, the older American history and the newer American civilization or, as it is frequently called, American studies. In the academic locales where it is taught in the United States, folklife studies is most closely associated with folklore and folkloristics, a division reminiscent of the Scandinavian distinction between *folkliv* and *folkminne* and in the distinction between *folklore* and (regional) *ethnology* in the Europeanist organization Societé Internationale d'Ethnologie et de Folklore (SIEF). In the Anglo-American world a minority of folklorists prefer to stretch the word *folklore* to include *folklife*. I prefer to follow Åke Hultkrantz[9] and the Arnhem Congress[10] of 1955 in subsuming *folklore* (defining it after William Bascom[11] as the verbal arts of a society) under *folklife*, as only one aspect of folk culture.

Among the other disciplines that are related to folklife studies in sharing subject matter and that, in analyzing American culture, are potential allies of folklife studies in the academic world are agricultural history, rural sociology, human relations, ethnohistory, oral history, ethnomusicology, social psychology and parapsychology, medical history, art history, architectural history, history of diet and nutrition, cultural geography, medieval studies, historical archaeology, industrial archaeology, history of technology, and dialectology and linguistic geography.

In focusing upon traditional forms of life, folklife studies thus far in its development in Europe and the United States has offered three essentially different approaches: (1) the study of the historical past, (2) the study of the past as surviving in and influencing the present, and (3) the study of the ethnographic present. Let us look at these approaches one after the other.

Historical Folklife Studies.

A great many researchers in traditional culture, particularly those in Europe, prefer to approach their subject matter completely oriented to past levels of the culture, reconstructing them through the use of the tried-and-true, if conservative, methods of analyzing historical texts and material artifacts. Europeans, more so than Americans, have turned to their abundant historical source materials to reconstruct the past levels of their own cultures. State and local archives are developed to a higher degree, and in most cultures the scholar has available every possible historical source from medieval charters to the present-day newspaper. What the Germans call *rechtliche Volkskunde* (legal ethnology) is a good example of this approach. The laws and edicts, the sumptuary legislation, the criminal and civil codes comprise one fruitful source of dated material on folklife from the early Middle Ages to the present that Europeans have thoroughly studied.[12] Church records, almost entirely neglected here as a source even for social history, have been abstracted and used not only for local history and genealogy, as here, but also for the highest level of social and regional history.[13]

What is called for in this country is a democratizing of historiography. The strongest rationale for such a democratizing of American history has come from Theodore Blegen, whose work, based at the University of Minnesota, on ethnic studies (concentration on Norwegian Americana) and regional history (with focus on Upper Mississippi Valley cultures) has put him in the forefront of American historians in our field. "The pivot of history is not the uncommon," writes Blegen, "but the usual, and the makers of history are 'the people, yes.' . . . This is the essence of grass roots history. It grapples, as history should grapple, with the need of understanding the small, everyday elements, the basic elements, in large movements. It recognizes, as maturely conceived history should recognize, the importance of the simple, however complex and subtle the problem of understanding the simple may be."[14] This broadening of historiography to include the life of all classes has still not been completely achieved even in social history. Lynn White, Jr., writing of medieval history, makes the point that, "from its beginnings until very recently, written history has been a history of the upper classes by the upper classes and for the upper classes." Our culture is not completely democratic, because of our long-inherited tradition of aristocratic scholarship. We need, he insists, "the history of all mankind including the hitherto silent majority, and not merely that of the tiny vocal fraction which dominated the rest." In his own field of medieval studies, this means new concentration upon peasant life, using every source available from medieval literature to agrarian archaeology.[15]

Historical folklife studies has great potential for our discipline because, when our historical source materials are abstracted and archived, we will at last have on hand some basic diachronic documentation for our ethnographic studies. This "accumulation of micro-regional-ethnological studies," as Alexander Fenton puts it, will in time allow a comparative view of the development of the country under study, as well as providing material of international comparative value.[16] Every area of folklife research and many of the related disciplines will profit from such documentation. To give one example, the historical dictionaries of American English were constructed on the policy of using only printed citations in tracing the history of American words.[17] In the case of many Americanisms, earlier datings than those in Mathews turn up constantly in manuscript source materials. The wills and inventories, one widespread manuscript source, that exist by the hundreds of thousands in the courthouses of the older settled parts of the country need to be abstracted systematically for early American culture and its vocabulary. The wills and inventories, which are dated and official yet intensely personal documents, shed light on every aspect of regional folk culture in the United States.[18] The full range of historical source material—travel accounts, newspapers, diaries, autobiographies, collections of letters, local histories—will eventually have to be plowed through and abstracted if we are to understand the full development of our regional cultures.

Of the regional file systems set up thus far to archive historical materials, three deserve special mention: (*a*) the Index of American Cultures, dealing with colonial urban America (Boston, 1675–1725, and Philadelphia, 1725–1775), directed by Dr. Anthony N. B. Garvan at the University of Pennsylvania in connection with the Human Relations Area Files;[19] (*b*) the Index of American Folk Belief (including folk medicine), initiated by Dr. Wayland D. Hand at the University of California at Los Angeles; and (*c*) the Pennsylvania Folk-Cultural Index of the Pennsylvania Folklife Society, now on deposit at the Myrin Library, Ursinus College, Collegeville, Pennsylvania. The first represents an urban area study, the second a topical research area within folklife studies, and the third a regional cultural approach.

Folklife Studies and Survivals.

For those who define folk culture as the culture of preindustrial, pre-urban groups in Western civilization, the approach has been to look at the present but to focus upon existing remnants of the "true" folk cultures of the past.[20] *Survival* is a suspect word these days from its earlier overuse, but one literal survival from all our regional pasts is our older architecture—man's most visible alteration of his environment. Unfortunately, this is now rapidly disappearing from sight and memory, giving way to the bulldozer, the superhighway, and the suburban developer (as well as less permanently to the Permastone salesman). The necessity of preserving at least some of America's earlier architectural forms is recognized by scholarly groups the nation over, from the Society for the Preservation of New England Antiquities to the National Trust. Much education is still needed in the local field to encourage appreciation of local and regional examples of architecture. Preservation efforts should involve not only the George-Washington-slept-here types of houses, important because of their historical associations, but also the best surviving examples of regional types—not only homes, but also civil, ecclesiastical, and farmstead architecture. Such examples serve literally as "landmarks" in our culture, as way stations to the present and to our own understanding of ourselves.

In the long run the historical environment may be as important to us psychologically as the natural environment. Regional architecture has teaching value in orienting us to the meaning of our own situation in the cultural-historical spectrum. European cultures have seen this value most intelligently, both in preservation programs and in teaching institutions, such as the open-air museums that developed out of folklife studies. Unfortunately, the American ethos has a built-in derogation of the past, from the Pilgrims' rejection of Europe to Henry Ford's classic evaluation, "History is bunk." Unfortunately, too, the American business motto that "progress is our most important product," as well as our "conspicuous consumption" and "planned obsolescence" syndromes, have long been blinding forces in preventing preservation. A kind of passive barbarism, as Iorwerth Peate puts it, has developed in the West, just as destructive of heritage as what he calls the active barbarism of the East.[21]

The past is important, and our historic man-made environment of rural and village architecture, of farmstead and town layouts, of settlement patterns in general is important for Americans to recognize as part of their heritage, as keys to self-understanding.

Folklife Studies and the Ethnographic Present.

The third approach to folklife scholarship is the ethnographic, focusing on the present and scientifically describing the contemporary forms of American traditional culture. Field work is the method of this approach, and field work in fact is the primary need in American folklife scholarship today.

When American folk-cultural scholarship is compared with its European model, one of the gravest complaints is that we are half a century behind Europe in gathering the raw materials for understanding our own traditional cultures. In only a few areas of traditional culture, for example folksong and folktale, do we have even a relatively complete national selection. It is true that the European university and museum worlds have been recording their own cultures since the beginning of the nineteenth century. My favorite example of the many European folk-cultural research institutions is Nordiska Museet in Stockholm, founded in 1871 to record Scandinavian and, in particular, Swedish culture. One single research department of the museum, the Archive of Swedish Folklore directed by Dr. Carl-Herman Tillhagen since 1945, has today a staff of over two dozen persons and several million references in its catalogue, derived from field work and informant questionnaires from every area of Sweden.[22] Sweden is an especially good example of the academic cooperation that has developed in Europe to study traditional cultures of a national area. Supplementing the Folklore Archive of Nordiska Museet are the equally impressive Folklife Archive at the University of Lund and the Dialect Archive at the University of Uppsala.

The common quest for social relevance in scholarship has in the last decades brought new emphases in folklife studies. The new, or "contemporary folklife," approach arose largely in Germany since World War II, in part through the necessity of coming to grips with the acculturation problems of resettled German-speaking groups from Eastern Europe. The lore and customs of these displaced persons were immediately forced into acculturation with the customs and lore of the new settlements. The important focus of research was recognized as not the Germanic "survivals" but the contemporary patterns of human life in an industrialized and urbanized world. Not peasant cultures as such, but the impact of the industrial revolution as social process, in which both traditional culture and individual are caught up inexorably, was seen as the proper focus for folklife scholarship.[23] The modern locus of both folklore and folklife was seen as the city, and the concepts of "urban folklife" and "industrial folklife" have already taken their place beside the concepts of peasant, regional, and ethnic cultures. In Germany the work of Hermann Bausinger at Tübingen,[24] of Walter Hävernick and Herbert Freudenthal at Hamburg,[25] and of Gerhard Heilfurth and his associates at Marburg[26] point folk-cultural scholarship in this direction.

An example of this updating of European folklife research methodology is the recent criticism of the folk-cultural questionnaire technique. According to Rudolf Schenda of Tübingen, questionnaires have made no substantial progress since the nineteenth century, when they were based on the ideas of "primitive uniformity" of the groups studied, the concept of "cultural relics," and the principle of "continuity" from past to present.[27] Questions and answers were directed not at the reality of today, the social facts as they exist, but at an ideal picture, a projection of the vanished past. Finally, the folk-cultural questionnaires have been material oriented rather than problem oriented. In general they need to be geared into the research methods of the social sciences. Instead of focusing on the remnants of primitive culture "still alive today," we need to focus on the individual in the midst of social conflict, the present, and the future.

This would seem to be a widespread new orientation in European folklife research. In his inaugural lecture at the University of Lund, Professor Nils-Arvid Bringéus in 1967 called for what amounts to a complete updating of folk-cultural research method. Following Erixon's lead, he played up the necessity of observing the present. "Our only opportunity of obtaining an all-round study of folklife is still and always will be the present way of life itself." And again:

In the future we must not simply be content with reminiscences instead of testimonies, we must also study what is alive. We must learn to find easier ways of getting into homes, not just old people's homes, to densely populated areas instead of to the sparsely populated ones. The ethnologist is looking for the normal situation.

Superficially this may mean that ethnology becomes less historical. But its objectives in the study of society must still be to demonstrate the part played by tradition as the mortar in our culture. Consequently, a historical perspective is needed in an analysis of the present and in planning the future.[28]

In many areas of everyday life, what is now increasingly called "popular culture" turns out to be an extension of or development from the older traditional forms of culture.[29] This is brought graphically to focus in the folklife films in the series Deutsche Volkskunde, edited by Dr. Ingeborg Weber-Kellermann of the University of Marburg. One of the films deals with the concept of *Volkslesestoff*, or everyday reading matter. In the eighteenth century the average Germans read chapbook lives of saints and legends of popular heroes. In the nineteenth century they read the "trivial romance," in installments in the newspapers and the family periodicals.[30] In the twentieth century their descendants read comic books and look at TV westerns. The forms and manners of distribution have changed—from market stalls, peddlers, *Bänkelsänger*, and colporteurs—but the function in the group involved and in the individual life remains the same.

It seems clear that we continue to need both the historically oriented reconstructions of earlier stages of our present culture and the sociologically and anthropologically oriented analysis of present-day forms of culture, urban or rural, that are equivalent or analogous to the earlier folk forms. Which emphasis will take priority in North American scholarship remains to be seen.

In conclusion, let us take a brief overview of the ways in which folklife scholarship is represented in the American academic world today.

Courses in American folk culture, its regional versions and branches, are offered at the State University of New York at Oneonta-Cooperstown, Indiana University, University of California at Los Angeles, University of Pennsylvania, University of Texas at Austin, University of North Carolina, Vanderbilt University, Pennsylvania State University, Utah State University, Western Kentucky University, and others. Several of the institutions mentioned offer folklife programs as such, while others offer folklife courses under the aegis of folklore, anthropology, American studies, cultural geography, and other departments. In some cases, branches of folklife studies or specialties within folklife are featured. For example, courses in folk art are offered at the University of California at Los Angeles, folk architecture and architectural preservation at Columbia, and cookery and foodways at the Capitol Campus of Pennsylvania State University. Area studies in European and American ethnography, regional culture courses, and work in ethnic and immigration history are given at an increasing number of American universities and colleges.[31]

The research programs and folk-cultural archives of many of these institutions accent, as was done in Europe, the local regional cultural materials as well as comparative materials from other cultures both here and abroad. For example, the University of Maryland has an archive that deals with Maryland materials, the University of Maine has one that deals heavily though not exclusively in materials from Maine, Western Kentucky University channels Appalachian materials into its archive, and UCLA features California and western materials. In addition, the larger university programs sponsor research in particular phases of folklife studies. The Institute of Urban Ethnography at the University of Pennsylvania has sponsored research in the cultures of many American ethnic enclaves. The Center for Comparative Folklore and Mythology at UCLA has sponsored the *American Dictionary of Superstitions and Popular Beliefs*, edited by Wayland D. Hand on the model of the *Handwörterbuch des Deutschen Aberglaubens*, and is the principal research institution in the United States at the present time for folk medicine.

In addition to these academic institutions, museums conduct much folklife research, particularly the open-air museums that have been founded in the United States and Canada on the Scandinavian model.[32] The principal examples here are Colonial Williamsburg in Virginia, Old Sturbridge Village and Plimoth Plantation in Massachusetts, the Farmers Museum at Cooperstown, N.Y., the Pennsylvania Farm Museum at Landis Valley in Pennsylvania, Mystic Seaport in Connecticut, and the Black Creek Village and Upper Canada Village in Ontario. Old Sturbridge Village, for one example, has a staff of some thirty full-time researchers working on various phases of New England life in the period of the museum, 1790–1840, on every subject from religion to agriculture and from cookery to rural dress. In addition, specialized museums, such as the Du Pont Museum at Winterthur, cultivate specialties that are useful to folklife studies, such as Winterthur's emphasis on early American decorative arts. Its sister institution, the Hagley Museum, also founded by the Du Ponts, specializes in early American crafts and technology. The American folk arts are represented in major collections in many of the fine arts museums of the country, as, for example, the Karolik Collection of the Boston Museum of Fine Arts and the Garbisch Collection in the National Gallery in Washington, while American and other folk arts are featured in the Museum of International Folk Art at Santa Fe.

Of the national museums of Canada and the United States, the National Museum of Man in Ottawa and the Smithsonian Institution both express increasing interest in folklife materials. The Canadian Centre for Folk Culture Studies at the National Museum of Man is essentially a collecting institute for ethnographic data, artifacts, and audiovisual materials from all of Canada's current ethnic populations.[33] The Smithsonian Institution has several divisions that are working in folklife materials—the Center for the Study of Man, the Division of Preindustrial Cultural History, the Division of Agricultural History, the Division of Ethnic and Western Cultural History, and the Division of Performing Arts. Out of the latter's interest in American crafts has come the Festival of American Folklife,[34] now in its eighth year, which is reflected on the state level by such newer festivals as the Texas Folklife Festival founded in 1972 by the Institute of Texan Cultures at San Antonio. While festivals are attempts at displaying folk culture to the public in a different way than is possible in the older museum format, what is most exciting is the solid research preparation that goes into them. For example, in connection with the Smithsonian festival entire states have each year been surveyed to determine the current status of folk craftsmanship. Particularly healthy also in this newer movement is the Smithsonian festival's emphasis not only upon rural crafts but also upon the contemporary urban labor union craftsman as the modern equivalent of the older village artisan.[35]

In the new world of ethnic studies in the United States and Canada, contributions are being made to folklife scholarship by the various ethnic institutes and historical societies, some of them connected with academic institutions, others independent.[36] Four examples out of many that could be cited are the American Swedish Historical Foundation in Philadelphia, as well as its homeland counterpart, the Emigrant Institute at Växjö in Sweden; the Norwegian-American Historical Society in Minneapolis, which under the leadership of Theodore Blegen revived ethnic history of the best sort in the twentieth century and provided a model for all ethnic historiography; the work of the various Pennsylvania German organizations headed by the Pennsylvania German Society founded in 1891; and the Yivo Institute in New York for the study of Jewish immigrant culture and, principally, the Yiddish language culture of the Eastern European Jews in America.

On the national level, two general institutions now exist in the United States with the broad purpose of surveying all ethnic groups. These are the Center for Migration Studies located on Staten Island, which has begun a distinguished series of ethnic bibliographies, and the Balch Institute in Philadelphia, which is becoming the depository for records of historical societies of many ethnic groups. Equally promising for their breadth of purpose are two statewide organizations, the Institute of Texan Cultures at San Antonio, organized under the University of Texas, and the Ethnic Culture Survey of Pennsylvania at Harrisburg, organized under the Pennsylvania Historical and Museum Commission.

In the American academic field, there are also many journals, mostly quarterlies, that publish, at least occasionally, articles of folk-cultural interest. These range from folklore (e.g., the *Journal of American Folklore* and the various state and regional folklore journals) through anthropology, ethnology, ethnohistory, sociology, agricultural history, and the history of technology to geography. Museum publications, such as the *Winterthur Portfolio*, carry folklife articles along with others.

Many state and county historical society publications show increasing interest in folk-cultural data, everyday life—in other words, the historical ethnographic approach.

From this point on, statewide programs and national coordination of folklife research will be increasingly necessary. National vision demands national programs, here as in Europe. Plans for an American Folklife Foundation reached the stage of hearings before the Ninety-first Congress (1971), and, as the American Folklife Center to be established under the aegis of the Library of Congress, the project is marshalling support in the Ninety-second Congress (1973).[37] Plans for an atlas of American folk culture have also been broached.[38]

Folklife studies, in conclusion, is a newer holistic approach that analyzes traditional cultural elements in a complex society—whether these elements are defined as folk, ethnic, regional, rural, urban, or sectarian—viewing them in the context of that larger unifying society and culture of which all subgroups and traditions are functioning parts. It can focus upon the individual, the group, single cultural traits or complexes, or the culture as a whole. As the regional ethnology of North America, American ethnology in the widest sense of that term, it takes its place beside European ethnology in researching the continuing role of tradition in Western civilization.

NOTES

1. For the history of folklife research, see Sigurd Erixon, "European Ethnology in Our Time," *Ethnologia Europaea* 1, no. 1 (1967): 3–11; Ronald H. Buchanan, "A Decade of Folklife Study," *Ulster Folklife* 10 (1965): 63–75; Ingeborg Weber-Kellermann, *Deutsche Volkskunde zwischen Germanistik und Sozialwissenschaften*; and Don Yoder, "The Folklife Studies Movement," *Pennsylvania Folklife* 13, no. 3 (July 1963): 43–56. The best manual of the subject thus far, although unfortunately not available in English, is Sigfrid Svensson, *Introduktion till Folklivsforskningen*. For the history of the terms *folkliv* and *folklivsforskning*, see Sigurd Erixon, "Benämningen på Sven Lampas docentur och den svenska folklivsforskning," in *Kulturspeglingar*, ed. Ernst-Folke Lindberg, pp. 67–74.

2. For recent summaries of the "melting pot" and "cultural pluralist" theories, see Milton M. Gordon, *Assimilation in American Life*.

3. The best collection of definitions thus far is included in Åke Hultkrantz (ed.), *General Ethnological Concepts*, pp. 126–144.

4. Erixon, cited in ibid., pp. 133–134. See also Åke Hultkrantz, "The Conception of 'Folk' in Sigurd Erixon's Ethnological Theory," *Ethnologia Europaea* 2–3 (1968–1969): 18–20.

5. J. W. Y. Higgs, *Folk Life Collection and Classification*, pp. 4–7.

6. Richard Weiss, *Volkskunde der Schweiz*, p. 11.

7. Ibid., pp. 45–49: "Die Volkskunde und ihre Nachbarwissenschaften."

8. The most recent report on the academic organization of folklife studies in Europe is "The Academic Position of European Ethnology," *Ethnologia Europaea* 1, no. 4 (1967): [243]–323.

9. Hultkrantz, *General Ethnological Concepts*, pp. 133–134.

10. *Actes du Congrès International d'Ethnologie Régionale.*

11. William R. Bascom, "Folklore and Anthropology," *Journal of American Folklore* 66 (1953): 283–290; idem, "Verbal Art," *Journal of American Folklore* 68 (1955): 245–252.

12. For a brief summary in English, with German references, see Hermann Baltl, "Folklore Research and Legal History in the German Language Area," *Journal of the Folklore Institute* 5, nos. 2–3 (1968): 142–151.

13.   Historical ethnography is highly developed in Europe. One model example that can be cited out of many is the work of Karl-Sigismund Kramer, *Volksleben im Fürstentum Ansbach und seinen Nachbargebieten (1500–1800)*, which draws upon every available type of historical source. My two favorite examples of historical ethnography on a regional basis from the United States are Guion Griffis Johnson, *Ante-Bellum North Carolina*, and Solon J. and Elizabeth Buck, *The Planting of Civilization in Western Pennsylvania*.

14.   Theodore C. Blegen, *Grass Roots History*, p. vii.

15.   Lynn White, Jr., "The Life of the Silent Majority," in *Life and Thought in the Early Middle Ages*, ed. Robert S. Hoyt, pp. 85–100.

16.   Alexander Fenton, "Historical Ethnology in Scotland," *Ethnologia Europaea* 1, no. 2 (1967): 125–129.

17.   Mitford M. Mathews (ed.), *A Dictionary of Americanisms on Historical Principles*.

18.   Unfortunately, the abstracts of wills in our historical societies were done mostly by and for genealogists, and they lack the materials needed by the folklife scholar. The best published collection of American inventories thus far is Abbott Lowell Cummings, *Rural Household Inventories Establishing the Names, Uses and Furnishings in the Colonial New England Home, 1675–1775*.

19.   For the Human Relations Area Files, see George P. Murdock et al., *Outline of Cultural Materials*. For the Index of American Cultures, see Anthony N. B. Garvan, "Historical Depth in Comparative Culture Study," *American Quarterly* 14, no. 2, part 2 (Summer 1962 Supplement): 260–274.

20.   For a series of models illustrating the relation of historical reconstruction of past levels of a culture and ethnographic research into its present level, see Nils-Arvid Bringéus, "Probleme und Methoden ethnologischer Nahrungsforschung im Lichte jüngster schwedischer Untersuchungen," *Ethnologia Scandinavica* 1 (1971): 20–23.

21.   Iorwerth C. Peate, "The Study of Folk Life and Its Part in the Defence of Civilization," *Advancement of Science* 15, no. 58 (September 1958): 86–94.

22.   Carl-Herman Tillhagen, "Folklore Archives in Sweden," *Journal of the Folklore Institute* 1, nos. 1–2 (1964): 20–36. For the program of Nordiska Museet in general, see Mats Rehnberg, *The Nordiska Museet and Skansen*.

23.   The volume by Rudolf Braun, *Industrialisierung und Volkskultur*, dealing with the impact of the Industrial Revolution on the Zürcher Oberland, is a model of research using precisely this concept. For more general perspectives on this whole problem, see Hermann Bausinger, *Volkskultur in der technischen Welt*.

24.   Hermann Bausinger, "Folklore Research at the University of Tübingen: On the Activities of the Ludwig-Uhland-Institut," *Journal of the Folklore Institute* 5, nos. 2–3 (1968): 124–133.

25.   Walter Hävernick, "The Hamburg School of Folklore Research," *Journal of the Folklore Institute* 5, nos. 2–3 (1968): 113–123.

26.   Gerhard Heilfurth, "The Institut für mitteleuropäische Volksforschung at the University of Marburg," *Journal of the Folklore Institute* 5, nos. 2–3 (1968): 134–141.

27.   Rudolf Schenda, "Einheitlich—Urtümlich—Noch Heute: Probleme der volkskundlichen Befragung," in *Abschied vom Volksleben*, ed. Klaus Geiger, Utz Jeggle, and Gottfried Korff, pp. 124–154.

28.   Nils-Arvid Bringéus, "Det etnologiska perspektivet. Installations-föreläsning vid Lunds universitet den 9 mars 1968," *Rig*, 1968.

29.   In the field of American popular culture, the works of Carl Bode and Russell B. Nye have pioneered. The *American Quarterly* has published articles on this subject, and more recently Ray B. Browne has established the useful *Journal of Popular Culture*. For boundaries and relations between "folk" and "popular" cultures, see Henry Glassie, *Pattern in the Material Folk Culture of the Eastern United States*.

30.   On these genres of popular culture, see Dorothee Bayer, *Der triviale Familien- und Liebesroman im 20. Jahrhundert*; and Hermann Fischer, *Volkslied—Schlager—Evergreen*.

31.   A selective listing of institutions, personnel, and specialties taught is given in Paul Leser, "The Academic Position of European Ethnology in North America," *Ethnologia Europaea* 1, no. 4 (1967): 320–322.

32.   *The Official Museum Directory: United States–Canada, 1971* lists open-air museums under history, agriculture, and other categories. For agricultural museums, see Darwin P. Kelsey, "Outdoor Museums and Historical Agriculture," in *Farming in the New Nation*, ed. Darwin P. Kelsey, pp. 105–127. For the new concept of the "living historical farm," see the article by John T. Schlebecker, "Curatorial Agriculture," in ibid., pp. 95–103.

33.   For the Centre's program, see Carmen Roy, *Canadian Centre for Folk Culture Studies: Annual Review 1972*.

34.   The seven printed programs of the Festival of American Folklife provide an excellent record of the geographical areas, craft specialties, and ethnic groups featured in the seven years since the festival's foundation in 1967. For the philosophy of the festival as a "living museum," see the foreword by S. Dillon Ripley in the *1973 Festival of American Folklife*, p. 4. Starting in 1973 the festival has been jointly sponsored by the Smithsonian Institution and the National Park Service, which has in its many historic sites museums over the country featured for decades the concept of "living history."

35.   See the section "Working Americans" in the *1973 Festival of American Folklife*, pp. 38–43. The emphasis on industrial folklore and folklife was pioneered in this country by such scholars as George Korson and Archie Green, whose volumes on miners' songs and their context are models of their kind.

36.   For ethnic historiography in the United States and the various movements that have shaped it, see John J. Appel, "Immigrant Historical Societies in the United States, 1880–1950," Ph.D. dissertation.

37.   *American Folklife Foundation Act. Hearing before the Subcommittee on Education of the Committee on Labor and Public Welfare, United States Senate, Ninety-First Congress, Second Session, on S. 1591: To Establish an American Folklife Foundation, and for Other Purposes. May 18, 1970.* For the current bills (S. 1844, H.R. 8770, H.R. 8781), to provide for the establishment of an American Folklife Center in the Library of Congress, see the *Congressional Record*, May 17, 1973, and June 18, 1973.

38.   William F. H. Nicolaisen, formerly of the School of Scottish Studies, Edinburgh, now at the State University of New York, Binghamton, addressed the November 1970 meeting of the American Folklore Society on the possibilities of an American folklore atlas, and at the 1971 and 1972 sessions he conducted panel discussions of the atlas plans. He is at present organizing a national committee to consider the steps necessary to establish such an atlas research program. Unfortunately, there are no prior regional atlases here as in Europe, except for the linguistic atlases, of which the most useful is Hans Kurath's *Linguistic Atlas of New England.*

BIBLIOGRAPHY

"Academic Position of European Ethnology." *Ethnologia Europaea* 1, no. 4 (1967): [243]–323.

Actes du Congrès International d'Ethnologie Régionale, Arnhem, 1955. Arnhem: Rijksmuseum voor Volkskunde, 1956.

American Folklife Foundation Act. Hearing before the Subcommittee on Education of the Committee on Labor and Public Welfare, United States Senate, Ninety-First Congress, Second Session, on S. 1591: To Establish an American Folklife Foundation, and for Other Purposes. May 18, 1970. Washington, D.C.: U.S. Government Printing Office, 1970.

Appel, John J. "Immigrant Historical Societies in the United States, 1880–1950." Ph.D. Dissertation, University of Pennsylvania, 1960.

Bach, Adolf. *Deutsche Volkskunde.* 3d ed. Heidelberg: Quelle & Meyer, 1960.

Baltl, Hermann. "Folklore Research and Legal History in the German Language Area." *Journal of the Folklore Institute* 5, nos. 2–3 (1968): 142–151.

Bascom, William R. "Folklore and Anthropology." *Journal of American Folklore* 66 (1953): 283–290.

———. "Verbal Art." *Journal of American Folklore* 68 (1955): 245–252.

Bausinger, Hermann. "Folklore Research at the University of Tübingen: On the Activities of the Ludwig-Uhland-Institut." *Journal of the Folklore Institute* 5, nos. 2–3 (1968): 124–133.

———. *Volkskultur in der technischen Welt.* Stuttgart: W. Kohlhammer, 1961.

———. *Volkskunde: Von der Altertumsforschung zur Kulturanalyse.* Das Wissen der Gegenwart: Geisteswissenschaften. Berlin-Darmstadt: Carl Habel Verlagsbuchhandlung, 1970.

———, ed. *Populus Revisus: Beiträge zur Erforschung der Gegenwart.* Volksleben, no. 14. Tübingen: Tübinger Vereinigung für Volkskunde, 1966.

Bayer, Dorothee. *Der triviale Familien- und Liebesroman im 20. Jahrhundert*. Volksleben, no. 1. Tübingen: Tübinger Vereinigung für Volkskunde, 1963.

Blegen, Theodore C. *Grass Roots History*. Minneapolis: University of Minnesota Press, 1947.

Braun, Rudolf. *Industrialisierung und Volkskultur: Sozialer und kultureller Wandel in einem ländlichen Industriegebiet*. Erlenbach-Zurich: Eugen Rentsch Verlag, 1960.

Bringéus, Nils-Arvid. "Det etnologiska perspectivet: Installations-föreläsning vid Lunds universitet den 9 mars 1968." *Rig*, 1968. Reprinted in *Artikelsamling i folklivsforskning*, pp. 33–41. Lund: Studentlitteratur, 1970.

———. "Probleme und Methoden ethnologischer Nahrungsforschung im Lichte jüngster schwedischer Untersuchungen." *Ethnologia Scandinavica* 1 (1971): 19–36.

Brunvand, Jan H. *The Study of American Folklore: An Introduction*. New York: W. W. Norton & Co., 1968.

Buchanan, Ronald H. "A Decade of Folklife Study." *Ulster Folklife* 10 (1965): 63–75.

———. "Geography and Folk Life." *Folk Life: Journal of the Society for Folk Life Studies* 1 (1963): 5–15.

———. "The Study of Folklore." *Ulster Folklife* 1 (1955): 8–12.

Buck, Solon J. and Elizabeth H. *The Planting of Civilization in Western Pennsylvania*. Pittsburgh: University of Pittsburgh Press, 1939.

Carvalho-Neto, Paulo de. *The Concept of Folklore*. Translated by Jacques M. P. Wilson. Coral Gables: University of Miami Press, 1971.

Cocchiara, Giuseppe. *Storia del Folklore in Europa*. Turin: Einaudi, 1952.

Cummings, Abbott Lowell. *Rural Household Inventories Establishing the Names, Uses and Furnishings in the Colonial New England Home, 1675–1775*. Boston: Society for the Preservation of New England Antiquities. 1964.

Dalton, George. "Peasantries in Anthropology and History." *Current Anthropology* 13 (1972): 385–415.

Dégh, Linda. "Folklore and Related Disciplines in Eastern Europe." *Journal of the Folklore Institute* 2 (1965): 103–119.

———. "Survival and Revival of European Folk Cultures in America." *Ethnologia Europaea* 2–3 (1968–1969): 97–107.

Dorson, Richard M., ed. *Folklore and Folklife: An Introduction*. Chicago: University of Chicago Press, 1972.

———, ed. *Folklore Research around the World: A North American Point of View*. Port Washington, N.Y.: Kennikat Press, 1973.

Erich, Oswald A., and Richard Beitl, eds. *Wörterbuch der deutschen Volkskunde*. 2d ed., revised by Richard Beitl. Stuttgart: Alfred Kröner Verlag, 1955.

Erixon, Sigurd. "Benämningen på Sven Lampas docentur och den svenska folklivsforskning." In *Kulturspeglingar: Studier tillägnade Sam Owen Jansson 19 mars 1966*, edited by Ernst-Folke Lindberg, pp. 67–74. Stockholm: Nordiska Museet, 1966.

———. "European Ethnology in Our Time." *Ethnologia Europaea* 1, no. 1 (1967): 3–11.

———. "Folklife Research in Our Time: From a Swedish Point of View." *Gwerin* 3 (1962): 275–291.

———. "An Introduction to Folk Life Research or Nordic Ethnology." *Folkliv* 14–15 (1950–1951): 5–15.

"Erixoniana: Contributions to the Study of European Ethnology in Memory of Sigurd Erixon." *Ethnologia Europaea* 2–3 (1968–1969); 4 (1970).

Fél, Edit, and Tamás Hofer. *Proper Peasants*. Viking Fund Publications in Anthropology, no. 46. Chicago: Aldine Press, 1969.

Fenton, Alexander. "Historical Ethnology in Scotland." *Ethnologia Europaea* 1, no. 2 (1967): 125–129.

———. "Material Culture as an Aid to Local History Studies in Scotland." *Journal of the Folklore Institute* 2 (1965): 326–339.

Fenton, William H., L. H. Butterfield, and Wilcomb E. Washburn. *American Indian and White Relations to 1830: Needs and Opportunities for Study*. Chapel Hill: University of North Carolina Press, 1957.

Fife, Austin, Alta Fife, and Henry Glassie, eds. *Forms upon the Frontier: Folklife and Folk Arts in the United States*. Monograph Series, 16, no. 2. Logan: Utah State University Press, 1969.

Fischer, Hermann. *Volkslied—Schlager—Evergreen: Studien über das lebendige Singen aufgrund von Untersuchungen im Kreis Reutlingen*. Volksleben, no. 7. Tübingen: Tübinger Vereinigung für Volkskunde, 1965.

Garvan, Anthony N. B. "Historical Depth in Comparative Culture Study." *American Quarterly* 14, no. 2, part 2 (Summer 1962 Supplement): 260–274.

Glassie, Henry. *Pattern in the Material Folk Culture of the Eastern United States*. University of Pennsylvania Monographs in Folklore and Folklife, no. 1. Philadelphia: University of Pennsylvania Press, 1968.

————. "The Types of the Southern Mountain Cabin." Appendix to *The Study of American Folklore: An Introduction*, by Jan H. Brunvand, pp. 338–370. New York: W. W. Norton & Co., 1968.

Gordon, Milton M. *Assimilation in American Life: The Role of Race, Religion, and National Origins*. New York: Oxford University Press, 1964.

Haug, Jörg. *Heimatkunde und Volkskunde*. Volksleben, no. 22. Tübingen: Tübinger Vereinigung für Volkskunde, 1970.

Hävernick, Walter. "The Hamburg School of Folklore Research." *Journal of the Folklore Institute* 5, nos. 2–3 (1968): 113–123.

Heilfurth, Gerhard. "The Institut für mitteleuropäische Volksforschung at the University of Marburg." *Journal of the Folklore Institute* 5, nos. 2–3 (1968): 134–141.

Higgs, J. W. Y. *Folk Life Collection and Classification*. London: Museums Association, 1963.

Hultkrantz, Åke. "The Conception of 'Folk' in Sigurd Erixon's Ethnological Theory." *Ethnologia Europaea* 2–3 (1968–1969): 18–20.

————. "Historical Approaches in American Ethnology: A Research Survey." *Ethnologia Europaea* 1, no. 2 (1967): 96–116.

————, ed. *General Ethnological Concepts*. International Dictionary of Regional European Ethnology and Folklore, no. 1. Copenhagen: Rosenkilde and Bagger, 1960.

Jenkins, Geraint, ed. *Studies in Folk Life: Essays in Honour of Iorwerth C. Peate*. New York: Barnes and Noble, 1969.

Jenson, Merrill, ed. *Regionalism in America*. Madison: University of Wisconsin Press, 1965.

Jocher, Katharine, ed. *Folk, Region, and Society: Selected Papers of Howard Washington Odum*. Chapel Hill: University of North Carolina Press, 1964.

Johnson, Guion Griffis. *Ante-Bellum North Carolina*. Chapel Hill: University of North Carolina Press, 1937.

Kelsey, Darwin P. "Outdoor Museums and Historical Agriculture." In *Farming in the New Nation: Interpreting American Agriculture, 1790–1840*, edited by Darwin P. Kelsey, pp. 105–127. Washington, D.C.: Agricultural History Association, 1972.

————, ed. *Farming in the New Nation: Interpreting American Agriculture, 1790–1840*. Washington, D.C.: Agricultural History Society, 1972.

Kramer, Karl-Sigismund. "Volkskunde jenseits der Philologie." *Zeitschrift für Volkskunde* 64 (1968): 1–29.

————. *Volksleben im Fürstentum Ansbach und seinen Nachbargebieten (1500–1800): Eine Volkskunde auf Grund archivalischer Quellen*. Würzburg: Kommissionsverlag Ferdinand Schöningh, 1961.

Kurath, Hans, ed. *Linguistic Atlas of New England*. 3 vols. Providence, R.I.: Brown University Press, 1939–1943.

————. *A Word Geography of the Eastern United States*. Studies in American English, no. 1. Ann Arbor: University of Michigan Press, 1949.

Leser, Paul. "The Academic Position of European Ethnology in North America." *Ethnologia Europaea* 1, no. 4 (1967): 320–322.

Lindberg, Ernst-Folke, ed. *Kulturspeglingar: Studier tillägnade Sam Owen Jansson 19 mars 1966*. Stockholm: Nordiska Museet, 1966.

Lutz, Gerhard. "Volkskunde, 'Lehre vom Volke' und Ethnologie: Zur Geschichte einer Fachbezeichnung." *Hessische Blätter für Volkskunde* 62–63 (1971–1972): 11–29.

Maget, Marcel. "Problèmes d'Ethnographie Européenne." In *Ethnologie Générale*, edited by Jean Poirier, pp. 1247–1338. Encyclopédie de la Pléiade, no. 24. Paris: Éditions Gallimard, 1968.

Marden, Charles F., and Gladys Meyer, eds. *Minorities in American Society*. 3d ed. New York: American Book Company, 1968.

Mathews, Mitford M., ed. *A Dictionary of Americanisms on Historical Principles*. Chicago: University of Chicago Press, 1951.

Murdock, George P., et al. *Outline of Cultural Materials*. 4th rev. ed. New Haven, Conn.: Human Relations Area Files, 1961.

Murphey, Murray G. "An Approach to the Historical Study of National Character." In *Context and Meaning in Cultural Anthropology*, edited by Melford E. Spiro, in honor of A. Irving Hallowell. New York: Free Press, 1965.

Niederer, Arnold. "Zur gesellschaftlichen Verantwortung der gegenwärtigen Volkskunde." In *Kontakte und Grenzen: Probleme der Volks-, Kultur- und Sozialforschung. Festschrift für Gerhard Heilfurth zum 60. Geburtstag*, edited by Hans Friedrich Foltin, Ina-Maria Greverus, and Joachim Schwebe, pp. 1–10. Göttingen: Verlag Otto Schwartz, 1969.

Odum, Howard W., and Harry E. Moore. *American Regionalism: A Cultural-Historical Approach*. New York: Henry Holt and Co., 1938.

The Official Museum Directory: United States–Canada, 1971. New York: American Association of Museums and Crowell-Collier Educational Corp., 1970.

Peate, Iorwerth C. "The Study of Folk Life and Its Part in the Defence of Civilization." *Advancement of Science* 15, no. 58 (September 1958): 86–94; reprinted in *Gwerin* 2 (1959): 97–109.

————. *Tradition & Folk Life: A Welsh View*. London: Faber and Faber, 1972.

Poirier, Jean, ed. *Ethnologie Générale*. Encyclopédie de la Pléiade, no. 24. Paris: Éditions Gallimard, 1968.

Rasmussen, Holger. "Classification Systems of European Ethnological Material." *Ethnologia Europaea* 4 (1970): 73–97.

Redfield, Robert. *Peasant Society and Culture: An Anthropological Approach to Civilization*. Chicago: University of Chicago Press, 1956.

Rehnberg, Mats. *The Nordiska Museet and Skansen: An Introduction to the History and Activities of a Famous Swedish Museum*. Stockholm: Nordiska Museet, 1957.

Riedl, Norbert F. "Folklore and the Study of Material Aspects of Folk Culture." *Journal of American Folklore* 79 (1966): 557–563.

Roy, Carmen. *Canadian Centre for Folk Culture Studies: Annual Review 1972*. Mercury Series, Canadian Centre for Folk Culture Studies, Paper no. 6. Ottawa: National Museum of Man, National Museums of Canada, 1973.

Saintyves, P. *Manuel de Folklore*. Paris: Librairie Émile Nourry, 1936.

Sanderson, Stewart F. "The Work of the School of Scottish Studies." *Scottish Studies* 1 (1957): 3–13.

Schenda, Rudolf. "Einheitlich—Urtümlich—Noch Heute: Probleme der volkskundlichen Befragung." In *Abschied vom Volksleben*, edited by Klaus Geiger, Utz Jeggle, and Gottfried Korff, pp. 124–154. Volksleben, no. 27. Tübingen: Tübinger Vereinigung für Volkskunde, 1970.

Schlebecker, John T. "Curatorial Agriculture." In *Farming in the New Nation: Interpreting American Agriculture, 1790–1840*, edited by Darwin P. Kelsey, pp. 95–103. Washington, D.C.: Agricultural History Association, 1972.

Smithsonian Institution, Division of Performing Arts. *Festival of American Folklife*. Annual Programs. Washington, D.C.: Smithsonian Institution, 1967–1973.

Svensson, Sigfrid. *Introduktion till Folklivsforskningen*. Stockholm: Natur och Kultur, 1969.

Thomas, Charles. "Archaeology and Folk-Life Studies." *Gwerin* 3 (1960): 7–17.

Tillhagen, Carl-Herman. "Folklore Archives in Sweden." *Journal of the Folklore Institute* 1, nos. 1–2 (1964): 20–36.

Trindell, Roger T. "American Folklore Studies and Geography." *Southern Folklore Quarterly* 34, no. 1 (March 1970): 1–11.

Utley, Francis Lee. "A Role for Folk Life Study in the United States." *Ethnologia Europaea* 4 (1970): 150–154.

Varagnac, André. *Civilisation traditionnelle et genres de vie*. Sciences d'aujourd'hui. Paris: A. Michel, 1948.

Wagner, Philip L., and Marvin W. Mikesell, eds. *Readings in Cultural Geography*. Chicago: University of Chicago Press, 1962.

Weber-Kellermann, Ingeborg. *Deutsche Volkskunde zwischen Germanistik und Sozialwissenschaften*. Stuttgart: J. B. Metzlersche Verlagsbuchhandlung, 1969.

Weiss, Richard. *Volkskunde der Schweiz: Grundriss*. Erlenbach-Zurich: Eugen Rentsch Verlag, 1946.

White, Lynn, Jr. "The Life of the Silent Majority." In *Life and Thought in the Early Middle Ages*, edited by Robert S. Hoyt, pp. 85–100. Minneapolis: University of Minnesota Press, 1967.

Whitten, Norman E., Jr., and John F. Szwed, eds. *Afro-American Anthropology: Contemporary Perspectives*. New York: Free Press, 1970.

Wiegelmann, Günter. "Möglichkeiten ethnohistorischer Nahrungsforschung." *Ethnologia Europaea* 1, no. 3 (1967): 185–194.

Yoder, Don. "The Folklife Studies Movement." *Pennsylvania Folklife* 13, no. 3 (July 1963): 43–56.

———. "Historical Sources for American Foodways Research and Plans for an American Foodways Archive." *Ethnologia Scandinavica* 1 (1971): 41–55.

———. "Pennsylvania German Folklore Research: A Historical Analysis." In *The German Language in America*, edited by Glenn G. Gilbert, pp. 70–105, 148–163. Austin: University of Texas Press, 1971.

———, ed. "Symposium on Folk Religion." *Western Folklore* 33, no. 1 (January 1974): 1–87.

2. Folklife Study and Social Change

Ward H. Goodenough

Folklife studies and the term *folklife*, itself, have been closely associated in Europe with ethnography and ethnology, the branches of
anthropology that deal with the description and comparative study of
customs, beliefs, and institutions. Indeed, the name for ethnology in
German (*Völkerkunde*) is the plural of the name for folklife or folklore
(*Volkskunde*). The difference has been essentially one of locus of immediate interest. Ethnology has been comparatively oriented, and
ethnographic description has concentrated on alien peoples, peoples
with whom the investigator felt little ethnic kinship. Folklife, by contrast, has concentrated on peasants and regional groups that were an
integral part of a larger social body with which the investigator identified himself. Interest in folklife, indeed, emerged after the consolida-
tion of modern nation states in Europe and the growth within each of a
large middle class, or bourgeoisie, with a distinctive culture (or several
regional cultures) of its own. National identity and pride have been
compounded with antiquarian sentiment, all reflecting a concern with
self, to stimulate both a scholarly and a popular interest in folklife. In the
United States, given the end of massive immigration and the later
generations' sense of secure membership in national middle-class
American society, folklife should become an increasingly popular
subject of study for much the same reasons that have made it popular
in Europe.

In the study of custom, attention naturally is drawn to things that
differ from what the investigator is used to. Folklife students have concentrated on the features of peasant and regional culture that differed
from their national bourgeois culture. Cultural anthropologists have
done much the same. Because anthropologists have dealt with peoples
all over the world—many with little or no ties to European cultural
traditions—they have faced a much broader spectrum of cultural differences. Consequently, they have dealt with a wider range of topics than
have most students of folklife. On the other hand, students of folklife
have gone more deeply into such topics as popular arts and crafts.
Their work in oral literature has strongly influenced those anthropologists who have pursued this subject among non-Western peoples.
Despite these differences of approach, cultural anthropology and folklife
study have been concerned with the same kinds of phenomena. The
processes by which customs and institutions come into being, are
maintained, and fade away are of equal interest to both disciplines, as
are the methods by which customs and institutions are to be described
and the theoretical issues regarding the very nature of custom and
culture.

The separation of cultural anthropology and folklife study, then, is not
a reflection of an intrinsic difference in their respective subject matter;

rather, it is a reflection of how Euro-American scholars have identified themselves with the peoples whose customs and cultures they study. Anthropology—because of its early interest in human evolution and because of its early concentration on peoples with hunting and horticultural economies, on the mistaken assumption that they were fossilized relics of a general past human state—has come to be associated popularly with the study of so-called primitive peoples. But the designation "primitive" hardly fits the people who produced the civilizations of Central and South America, of West Africa, and of the Orient. Consequently, anthropology has come to be viewed more recently as the study of non-Western peoples. The disciplines of rural sociology and folklore in the United States and of folklife in Europe, on the other hand, dealt with Western peoples. There is nothing wrong with such a division of labor on practical grounds. What has been wrong is the false assumption by some that it represented a basic difference in the kinds of phenomena studied, an assumption following from an ethnocentric conceit of the sort expressed in the idea of "the white man's burden."

In the second half of the twentieth century, this conceit has become an anachronism. Anthropologists have taken to studying the same communities that have been the preserve of sociologists and students of folklife, approaching them successfully in much the same manner they have approached non-Western communities. The peasant community, moreover, has come to assume a major place in theoretical discussion in anthropology. In addition to these developments, anthropologists are now actively engaged in the study of complex modern institutions, such as hospitals, and of modern urban communities. In practice, the distinction between folklife and cultural anthropology is rapidly disappearing. We are reaching a point where we can say that folklife represents that aspect of cultural anthropology which concentrates on the study of one's own national cultural heritage. When an American studies a Japanese community he is doing anthropology, whereas his Japanese colleague is studying folklife. When a Japanese anthropologist studies an American community, he is doing anthropology, but an American working in the same community is studying folklife.

If folklife refers to the study of one's own national cultural heritage, then it properly encompasses all of that cultural heritage as represented by all the different cultural groups within its national boundaries. If the Japanese were to call it anthropology when they study the Ainu and folklife when they study rural Japanese, they would be making an invidious comparison between themselves and an ethnic minority within their national boundaries. We in America would be doing the same thing, if we said it was anthropology when we studied the Navaho and folklife when we studied the Amish. The same invidious distinction holds if we exhibit Navaho culture in a museum of ethnology together with exhibits of ethnic groups outside the United States and reserve exhibits of ethnic minorities of European origin for a separate museum of national folklife. Such distinctions serve no scientific purpose, nor do they serve any useful social purpose; they serve only to indulge popular ethnocentrism and desires for racial exclusiveness.

I dwell on this distinction because it seems only a matter of time before a growing interest in folklife will lead to the establishment of folklife institutes, folklife museums, and academic programs and degrees in folklife studies (of which last there are already a few). Such development is to be encouraged, but not in a form in which expressions of ethnocentrism and racial exclusiveness receive academic and national institutional blessing, for such can only aggravate the feelings of social discrimination and the second-class citizenship that a number of ethnic minorities within the United States are struggling to overcome. Their struggle, moreover, is part of a world-wide effort to break down a global system of social caste that is part of the heritage of conquest and colonial expansion. This caste system was rationalized and justified in terms of an ideology of racial and cultural superiority that had pseudoscientific authority (the doctrine of social Darwinism). The ideology fed the sense of worth and inflated the egos of those in privileged positions in the system, but it added insult to the injuries sustained by the conquered and the colonized. Desire for a sense of worth and for a renewed self-respect is perhaps the most important single motivation for popular support of revolutionary ideologies and the many revolutionary movements of our time.

Sense of worth and self-respect relate directly to questions of who and what one is and how the particular who and what are to be valued. Important among these features of a person's identity are his group affiliations—the groups with which he identifies himself and with which he is identified by others. When I travel abroad, I like to be identified as an American in places where Americans are respected, and I do not enjoy it where Americans are despised. One of the most precious things in life is to be able to stand up and say who I am, knowing as I do it that people are not going to think the worse of me for it.

Closely identified with social groups are the customs of their members. A group's customary practices are, like its language or dialect, a badge of identity for its members. If a person can take pride in the customs and traditions of his group, he can feel good about himself; but he can take pride in them only as others with whom he deals show respect for them—especially those others whose respect, or lack of it, is likely to make the most difference in his fortunes in life. If a person is a member of a politically dominant group, he is likely to make competent use of his own customs and dialect (or language) a precondition for according respect and social or political advancement to members of other groups within the larger polity. In this way, he places a higher value on his own customs and cultural tradition, and he assigns to an inferior place the customs and traditions of the less powerful groups. Insofar as members of the other groups wish to advance themselves, they are bound to accept this valuation, at least in practice. And acceptance in practice inevitably leads to acceptance in habit of mind.

This process by which one of a number of different traditions becomes elevated in people's estimation leads, in a culturally plural society, to the emergence of what Robert Redfield has called a "great tradition." A great tradition, being that of the power elite of the dominant group, is the one that has provided the medium within which the bulk of a society's creative artistic and intellectual talent has worked. Thus, it has become the object of elaboration. Knowledge of and competence in the great tradition is the mark of sophistication, of being "civilized" and "cultured" (the original sense of these terms). What Redfield called the "little traditions"—here more appropriately called folk traditions—continue alongside the great tradition, influencing it and being influenced by it. As the members of a plural society come to see themselves as part of a larger social entity with which they all identify themselves, such as a national state, they begin to view their folk traditions as a part of their society's heritage, also, and to see them as contributing to the emerging national identity. The folk traditions become objects of romantic attention, attracting scholarly notice, providing new sources of artistic inspiration, and sometimes giving rise to an assortment of popular fads. The development of folklife studies, historically, is itself a product of this process.

When social change alters the relative power relations of people with different cultural traditions, a former folk tradition may give rise to a new great tradition. The most common effect of change in recent times, however, has been of another kind, one in which people find that their own tradition, in which they formerly took pride, has less value. This experience has regularly accompanied colonialism. In spite of the economic and political benefits that many people in colonial areas came to enjoy, colonialism was hated because of the devaluation of ethnic identity and cultural heritage universally experienced by colonial peoples. Everywhere these people have felt a strong need to restore their self-esteem.

Efforts to restore self-esteem may take the form of trying to adopt and master the cultural tradition of the dominant power. In the Trust Territory of the Pacific, for example, there is currently a wide demand by the local people for improved Western education, for Western education is seen as an avenue to status, recognition, and power in what is now a part of a social world dominated by Americans. This is a natural response by people who find themselves increasingly drawn into a larger political and economic arena. They want to know what they need to know in order to live in it successfully.

Efforts to restore self-esteem may go in the opposite direction. People may reject the culture and values of the dominant power and insist on having nothing to do with anything but their local tradition. Some Pueblo Indian communities have taken this course.

Neither of these approaches is likely to be entirely successful in the long run. Those who would fiercely seek to keep their local tradition uncontaminated by the culture of the dominant power cannot succeed forever in keeping their children from desiring to compete in a larger arena. On the other hand, even when people have been successful in taking on the dominant culture, as with many immigrant populations in the United States, their descendants come to feel a need for a meaningful link with their ethnic past of which they can be proud. The children of immigrants, responding to the pressures of school- and age-mates, are eager to disassociate themselves from their derogated ethnic backgrounds and become the ardent devotees of Americanism. The grandchildren, safely American, seek to know and take pride in their ethnic heritage, because they see this as a special part of their identity, one that makes them something more than faceless, homogenized products of the melting pot. Similarly, the increased concern of black Americans with their place in American history and with their African heritage is a natural outgrowth of their changing social identity and sense of self.

But this concern with ethnic heritage as a distinctive aspect of one's identity is more easily productive of social and psychological capital for some people than for others. For what will count as such capital has been controlled by the historically dominant groups within our society. The way history is written for and taught in our schools, for example, makes it easier for a child of French ancestry to take pride in his French heritage than for a child of Polish or Sicilian ancestry to take pride in his. Poland and Sicily occupy smaller places in our history books by comparison with France, because the history books deal mainly with the development of America's English heritage and because England was more intimately involved politically and culturally with France.

For American Indians, of course, our history books are impossible. But the years of ethnographic study, promoted so well by the Bureau of American Ethnology in the Smithsonian Institution, has produced a wealth of material that treats the Indian heritage with greater fairness, understanding, and appreciation. The monographs written by anthropologists have become the textbooks through which many American Indians are seeking to make authoritative contact with their own past. The monographs were not written with this object particularly in mind; they were addressed to other audiences. But they remain the one best resource to which concerned American Indians can now turn. And they are turning to it, albeit with mixed emotions, for much the same reasons that other Americans and Europeans have been interested in the reports of folklife study.

American Indians are not the only people turning to the reports of anthropologists. Micronesians are beginning to do so, also. Even where contact with their own past has not been interrupted, people are concerned to know what is being written about them.

As this discussion makes clear, anthropologists and students of folklife have social as well as scholarly and scientific responsibilities. The stuff of their scholarly and scientific interests, folk traditions and customs, are also the stuff from which people derive their self-respect and with which they associate social and psychological gains and losses. Morally, therefore, anthropologists and folklife students are accountable to the people whose customs they describe as well as to their professional colleagues.

Purely practical considerations accompany the moral ones. Cultural scientists can add to their existing knowledge only as they enjoy the cooperation of the ethnic groups whose traditions they wish to record and study. What they publish and the spirit in which they publish it affect the kind of cooperation they are likely to enjoy in the future. Their disciplines are also dependent for their existence in our universities and museums on lay support, and much of the financial part of that support is channeled through the power elites of their home communities. The interests of the different lay publics whose cooperation anthropologists and folklife students must manage to maintain are not always compatible. Anthropologists have found it necessary to treat portions of their research data as privileged communications that could not be made public, at least during the lifetime of certain individuals.

A major problem of professional ethics, both as to its definition and its implementation in practice, has been that of reconciling the interests of these lay publics and the interests of fellow scholars and scientists in a way that is morally acceptable.

At times this is very difficult to do. The sensitivities of living persons may be such as to make postponement of publication advisable. Some materials are better deposited in an archive for scholarly consultation only, at least for the immediate future. Usually, however, it is possible to publish one's findings in a way that violates neither the facts nor the feelings of interested parties. Descriptions of the results of personality testing, for example, can be presented jarringly in the language of the clinic with its inevitable overtones of pathology, giving offense to many, or they can be expressed in humanly more acceptable terms. The same facts can be stated either in a way that exhibits respect for others and sensitivity for their concerns or in a way that exhibits lack of respect and concern.

Often lack of respect and concern results from the scholar's failure to think of the people he has studied as being a part of his audience. He thinks of himself as writing for members of his own ethnic group, for members of the "establishment," or for his professional colleagues. He forgets that an "in" way of putting something for one audience may be offensive to another, forgotten one. He likes to use the "in" way because he feels it helps to validate his professional status or enhances his rapport with his audience. But in this approach, he may be unthinkingly seeking to score identity points for himself at the expense of the feelings of the people he has studied. The scholarly and scientific professions that deal with fellow human beings must follow a conscious policy to discourage such reporting. The facts should be published, but in a way that is in keeping with the basic respect that all men owe to their fellow men.

The implications of our social responsibility as anthropologists and folklife students go beyond the manner in which we report our research findings. They have to do with the way we handle our museums, the content of the courses we teach, and our institutional and academic divisions of labor. Departments of religion in our universities, for example, too often give courses in comparative religion that leave the impression that only a religion that has become associated with the great tradition of a large and complex society is worthy of serious consideration or even of the name "religion." Other religions are "primitive" and in the domain of anthropology. It would be easy for us to develop museums and curricula of folklife that implied that only the cultural traditions of ethnic groups that were historically a part of complex societies with great traditions are to be considered suitable for folklife study, and that other traditions are to be regarded as primitive and left to anthropology. Such divisions of labor are without scientific or scholarly justification. They, too, help to give us a sense that we are "in"—at the expense of others. As such, they are unnecessarily offensive and are bound to make cultural sciences suspect in the eyes of the people whose cooperation they require. And, in any case, as I have already indicated, anthropologists are already engaged in the study of all kinds of cultural traditions, in our own as well as in other societies. The study of folklife—of folk traditions—is already an integral part of anthropology in the United States.

The term *anthropology*, however, has acquired some unfortunate connotations that need correction. Its association with what have been miscalled primitive peoples has linked it for some people with Western snobbery. In newly independent nations, for example, some persons react sensitively to having anthropological research done in their countries. They prefer sociology, the discipline that they associate with national self-study in European countries. Folklife, also associated with national self-study, is freer of unpleasant connotations. It seems appropriate, therefore, that wider use of this term be made by anthropologists as a convenient synonym for many aspects of cultural anthropology. The terms *ethnography* and *ethnology*, also, have been spared unhappy connotations. They have the advantage, moreover, of being well established as scientific terms among English speakers. The important point, whatever terms we use, is that laymen be encouraged to perceive the study of the customs and traditions of non-Western peoples as indissolubly connected with the study of the customs and traditions of Western peoples. The unity of cultural studies, already scientifically recognized, needs popular emphasis in every possible way.

From this point of view, if we apply the term *folklife* to our institutional handling of all traditions that are represented in the United States, we shall be forced to include American Indian, Pacific Island, Asiatic, and African traditions as well as European ones within its compass. If the Smithsonian Institution, for example, should establish a museum of folklife, I would like to see the ethnological exhibits now in the Natural History Museum transferred into the new museum of folklife. If a national folklife program is established within the Smithsonian Institution without a separate museum, on the other hand, that program should be set up in conjunction with the existing program in anthropology, and national folklife exhibits should be added to the ethnological exhibits now in the Natural History Museum. Most suitable would be the establishment of a national museum of anthropology (or ethnology) and folklife. Its creation, with the active participation of all the ethnic groups involved, would be a positive act of recognition by the government of the United States of the equality as citizens of all members of our national community.

I have been saying that the changes now going on in our own national life, as well as in the world at large, require a change in our institutional stance in relation to the handling of folk traditions at home and abroad. A change is needed in order to help the development of a healthier national community. Growing interest in folklife study offers an opportune resource for helping to promote such change.

BIBLIOGRAPHY

Deloria, Vine, Jr. *Custer Died for Your Sins*. New York: Macmillan, 1969.

Fenton, William H., L. H. Butterfield, and Wilcomb E. Washburn. *American Indian and White Relations to 1830: Needs and Opportunities for Study*. Chapel Hill: University of North Carolina Press, 1957.

Goodenough, Ward H. *Cooperation in Change*. New York: Russell Sage Foundation, 1963.

————, ed. *Explorations in Cultural Anthropology*. New York: McGraw-Hill, 1964.

Hofstadter, Richard. *Social Darwinism in American Thought, 1860–1915*. Philadelphia: University of Pennsylvania Press, 1944. Revised edition, Boston: Beacon Press, 1965.

Koentjaraningrat. "Anthropology and Non-Euro-American Anthropologists: The Situation in Indonesia." In *Explorations in Cultural Anthropology*, edited by Ward H. Goodenough, pp. 293–308. New York: McGraw-Hill, 1964.

Officer, James E., and Francis McKinley, eds. *Anthropology and the American Indian: A Symposium*. San Francisco: Indian Historian Press, 1973.

Redfield, Robert. *The Little Community and Peasant Society and Culture*. Phoenix Books. Chicago: University of Chicago Press, 1960.

3. Uses of the Artistic Past

James Marston Fitch

Historic Attitudes toward the Artistic Past

An appreciation of the material culture of preindustrial societies has grown in the Western world in almost exact proportion to the ever-intensifying industrialization of the West itself. For centuries, this interest has been so powerful and persistent that it would be a serious mistake indeed to dismiss its motive forces as being merely sentimental, romantic, or obscurantist. Good and evident reasons have always existed for this ever-growing concern on the part of some of the best informed and most sensitive sectors of Western society; and these apply with special force today.

As a conscious act of exploration, the discovery of the architectural past involved the progressive liquidation of all the concentric shells of self-centeredness and parochialism that had encapsulated European thought since late Roman times. The first aspect of the past that the West began deliberately to explore was, of course, its own: classic antiquity—first the Roman, because that was closest in time and space; then the Greek. Architectural response to these investigations was prompt (indeed, many of the investigators were themselves architects). Brunelleschi's Ospedale dei Innocenti, begun in Florence in 1421, is commonly regarded as the first expression of a passionate interest in the past—an interest that was to extend through five centuries and spread across the whole Western world. The rediscovery of classic architecture furnished the basic alphabet and grammar of the idioms of the Renaissance, Baroque, Rococo, and Neoclassic revivals. The prestige of classical architecture was so great and its ideological utility so apparent that it was adopted by Peter the Great, who, with great difficulty, employed it to extirpate precedent idioms and to remold at least urban Russia into a facsimile of the classicized West.

The discovery by the West of cultures foreign or eccentric to its own course of development—Near Eastern, Far Eastern, New World, and Egyptoid-African—came as the direct consequence of European imperialist implosion into those continents from the fifteenth century on. The stimulating effect of these extra-European cultures can be directly traced in Western art and architecture. The discovery of China is expressed in the popularity of Chinese motifs in Rococo design (chinoiserie). A little later, Chinese and Japanese landscape painting played a decisive role in the development of the English naturalistic garden. English penetration of India and the Near East led to such "Hindoo" styles as that of the Royal Pavilion at Brighton by the court favorite, John Nash, in 1818.

Naturally, the first information brought back to Western designers from the early voyages of discovery was inexact and garbled. But new

27

concepts of historical development and new techniques of investigation were developed with surprising speed. In exploring her own past, Europe perfected new methods of analyzing documentary materials (art history) and artifacts (archaeology). Both methods had reached essentially modern forms by the latter half of the eighteenth century when Johann Joachim Winckelmann published his famous *History of Ancient Art*,[1] which was a pioneer effort to apply to the fields of art and architecture the already well developed historiographical methods of the day. This immensely influential work brought to public attention the first real information on the current excavations at Pompeii and Herculaneum, where the basis was being laid for modern archaeology. In Athens, meanwhile, Englishmen James Stuart and Nicholas Revett were using modern methods of surveying and drafting to prepare accurate measured drawings of the Acropolis.[2] These works were to be but the first rather crude beginnings of what has since become an enormous corpus of literature and a rich tradition of professional expertise on the art and architecture of classical antiquity.

But in exploring the material culture of the outside world, the Europeans had necessarily to develop other techniques for observing and recording what was found. Peoples, customs, and terrains were strange, and languages (at least at first) incomprehensible. The early explorers, therefore, prepared illustrated accounts of what they found—laying the base, thereby, for cultural anthropology. The need for such reports was understood quite early. Spanish officials reported with tolerable accuracy the magnificent cultures they were extirpating in Mexico; these accounts began to be published as early as 1517. The French expedition of 1564 to Florida included what today would be called a staff artist, Jacques Le Moyne. Even allowing for the liberties that engravers later took with them, his drawings of the Indians, their customs, architecture, and agriculture must have been models of careful observation.[3] John White, head of the English expedition of 1585–1587 to Virginia, returned with a remarkably broad and accurate set of drawings of the men, flora, and fauna of the Virginia seacoast.[4] French and Portuguese missionaries to the Far East published many volumes on the customs, art, and architecture of the Orientals.[5] And, of course, the French were the authors of that paradigm of scientific reports on a foreign culture, the many-volumed study of Egypt commissioned by Napoleon.[6]

From the point of view of the Western metropolis, all of the peoples, customs, and artifacts uncovered by the explorers were more or less historical oddities—eccentric, that is, to the main orbits of European ambitions. Whether they represented contemporaneous societies (e.g., the Aztecs and the Chinese mandarins) or ones from the historical past (e.g., Egyptians and Sumerians), they were assumed to be, by definition, inferior to the West: slated, as we would say today, for "modernization," for being "brought up to date." It was not until the very end of the nineteenth century that Europe was able to break through the last shell of cultural chauvinism and bring herself to face the possibility that many other cultures might well be qualitatively the equal of her own.[7]

And yet, with the exception of aboriginal peoples like the North American Indians or the South Sea islanders, the newly discovered

societies were complex, class structured, and urbane. Their architecture and gardens reflected this fact—urbanized, high style, the idiom
of palace and temple. The vernacular building of these societies went
almost unnoticed by early European reporters. Apparently because
it was rural, modest, and impermanent, they dismissed it as of no more
significance than their own peasant building at home.[8]

The first indication of an upper-class interest in folk or vernacular
architecture appears, paradoxically, in the most aristocratic circles of
European absolutism: the court of Louis XVI. In the 1780's Marie
Antoinette commissioned architect Robert Micque to build a little re-
treat in a corner of the palace grounds at Versailles. It took the form
of a three-dimensional facsimile of a Normandy farm group. One of the
buildings was actually habitable, and here, in warm weather, the king's
mistress could dally with her intimates. The motivation is sufficiently
clear—escape from the boredom and rigid protocol of the court to a
putatively "simpler" life. But why specifically that of a Norman peasant?
We know, of course, that rising dissatisfaction with life under the
monarchy took many forms. Rousseau had already published his prize-
winning essay on the noble savage in 1750; Abbé Laugier, in his *Essai
sur l'architecture* of 1753, had formulated his functionalist credo:
"Tenons-nous au simple et au naturel"; and painters like Chardin had
already turned away from the frivolity of court life to celebrate sober
middle-class virtues. Such new conceptualizations must have penetrated even Versailles, thus making acceptable the folk art of the noble
peasant, if not yet that of Rousseau's noble savage.

One of the very earliest evidences of an educated understanding of
the aesthetic quality and functional significance of primitive art comes
from American sculptor Horatio Greenough. While on a visit to Washington in 1843, he went to see an exhibition at the Patent Office of
"curios" brought from the South Seas by American whalers. He admired
these artifacts for the formal elegance with which they met the demands of functional necessity. He recognized this aesthetic quality as
resembling that of archaic Greek and Etruscan sculpture; and then—in
a brilliant leap of intuition—he saw its extension in the design and
craftsmanship of the American clipper ship. In all three aesthetic
idioms, drawn from such widely disparate climes and cultures, he saw
the common thread of functionalism and saw, moreover, that they were
the end result of evolutionary process.[9]

However, Greenough's intuitions were to have no immediate impact
upon American architectural theory. It would be half a century before
Louis Sullivan would postulate his theorem *form follows function*, and
even longer before Western artists began to discover the aesthetic
merits of primitive art. Meanwhile, of course, an enormous expansion of
ethnographic and anthropological work on primitive societies occurred.
Americans could read a remarkable series of papers by Lewis H. Morgan
on the domestic architecture of the North and Central American Indians during the 1870's—papers that, when published in book form are
supposed to have had a profound effect on Marx and Engels, among
others.[10] Simultaneously, the great French architectural theoretician,
Eugène Viollet-le-Duc, published his *Habitations of Man in All Ages*.[11]
Responding to the new concepts of evolution propounded with such

stunning effect by Charles Darwin, Viollet-le-Duc applied evolutionary theory to architecture. He not only attempted to trace historic architecture back to its prehistoric roots, but also took the position that the contradiction between formal and functional elements, always immanent in man's constructions, was best resolved by primitive societies —that is, when stern necessity restrained and disciplined formalistic conceits.

Of course, the grandest and most sustained polemic in favor of pre-industrial handicraft production was that carried on during the last three-quarters of the nineteenth century by A. W. N. Pugin, John Ruskin, and William Morris. Their field of interest was almost completely ethnocentric, however, seldom extending beyond medieval England and never beyond Western Europe. Nor did they often make any clear distinction between the art of usually literate and always highly skilled guildsmen, working for urbane ruling-class institutions, and that of the illiterate peasantry, working only for itself. Nevertheless, they contributed mightily to the growing European interest in folklore, especially folk song and folk dance. And they certainly helped to prepare the way for the contemporary prestige, throughout the Western world, of every facet of preindustrial art and architecture, whether it be of vernacular, folk, or authentically primitive origin.[12]

It is thus apparent that the changing perspectives through which the Western world viewed the artistic past sprang from diverse and often contradictory motivations. Though in early Renaissance times, and again in the epoch of Jefferson and the French Revolution, antique idioms were put to progressive or even revolutionary uses, they served quite different interests, too.[13] The true keepers of the past, from classic antiquity onward, have often represented the most conservative interests of their society. Their motivations were either pietistic or patriotic, and they employed art and architecture to buttress the institutions of church and state. This was true in Pausanias's day, as is clear from his *Description of Greece* with its endless lists of graves, shrines, and temples to be visited.[14] It is equally true today: when the DAR acts at all, artistically, it acts to preserve the shrines of its own eponymous heroes.

It is not surprising, then, to find that the West's inexhaustible fascination with its own and other peoples' past gave rise to many and contradictory attitudes among artists and architects themselves. In fact, by 1875, after four and a half centuries of artistic exploration, it might have been argued that any further fruitful studies were impossible. And this was just the way that it appeared to the radical artists and intellectuals of the times. Painters, poets, musicians, and architects felt themselves being suffocated by the sheer massive presence of the past, everywhere—in the landscape around them, in the attitudes of institutions and individuals who peopled it. This generation demanded that the way be cleared for wholly new artistic idioms that would be congruent with the new potentials seemingly promised by science, industry, and political democracy. If architecture lagged a few years behind painting or poesy, it was only because it was an incomparably more costly and obdurate medium of expression. But from the Chicago of Louis Sullivan to the Weimar Republic of Walter Gropius, the battle was on to liberate building and landscape alike from thralldom to the corrupt and ineffectual past.

It was a development historically long overdue; but it had implications that the radical architects of the Bauhaus generation were unable to anticipate. (Who could have dreamed, in 1925, that the time would come when *old* buildings would be in short supply?) As it turned out, their attack on the eclectic use of historic idioms did not occur in "normal" times. On the contrary, it began just when science and technology were accelerating along an exponential curve; when absolutely unprecedented technical means of construction and destruction were beginning to appear; and when even popular taste, historically so fundamentally conservative, was being radicalized by planned obsolescence and the annual model. As a consequence of such developments, especially since World War II, man now runs the literal risk of losing all the past, man-made and natural—either piecemeal to the bulldozer or instantaneously to nuclear weapons.

This revolutionary reversal of man's historic relationship to his environment suddenly imbues all material evidence of the human past with new significance. It is the cause of legitimate concern to all environmental scientists—ethologists, ecologists, conservationists, public health specialists, and so on—but it is an issue of special poignancy to those who are entrusted with the care of the artistic patrimony. The frantic efforts of archaeologists, anthropologists, and art historians to keep ahead of the technological manipulation of the landscape is unfortunately a world-wide phenomenon. The great monuments at Abu Simbel may have been saved, thanks to an international campaign. Here and there, an occasional monument or settlement is being, if not saved, at least recorded before it disappears forever. But the general tendency of urban redevelopment authorities and dam and highway engineers is to dismiss as romantic or sentimental the efforts to protect historical impediments to their special brand of "progress." The comprehensive protection of such monuments and artifacts and the scholarly examination of the theories and techniques that produced them thus become of central importance to our cultural future.

New Uses of the Artistic Past

We have seen that the material culture of the past has been useful to the West for a wide spectrum of reasons—ideological, aesthetic, and technical. But the past now has a significance of quite a new and different order. This can be demonstrated very readily in architecture and urbanism, as I hope to show: a broad, truly scientific examination of traditional building—especially folk and primitive building—is one of the field's most urgent tasks. Such a program should proceed at two levels: one rather narrowly technical and professional, the other broadly cultural. The first would involve an *intensive study of the theories and practices* of the past, with special emphasis on folk and primitive cultures. The other would imply the development of a comprehensive system for the *protection of the forms* of the entire artistic patrimony, with special attention to folk and vernacular forms (if for no other reason than that they have been most neglected to date). The first program would be international in scope: that is, all building technologies whether extant or historical. The second would presumably be built up of national or regional components: for example, New England folk architectural and artistic expression would be best preserved and enjoyed in its native habitat, Cajun and Creole in lower Louisiana, Navaho in the Southwest. Many projects of the latter type are of course already in operation in Europe and America.

With the growing industrialization and urbanization of the West, the contemporary architect displays an increasing tendency to ignore or minimize the natural world and the precariousness of man's position in it. Not only is this architect largely insulated against any stressful exposure to climatic and geographic cause and effect, but he also seems persuaded that climate and geography no longer play a significant role in our life. The disastrous consequences of this attitude (which of course he shares with all the decision makers of urban development and industrial expansion) are everywhere apparent. They are expressed in his consistent underestimation of the scale of environmental forces that play upon him, his buildings, and his cities; in his failure to grasp their ineluctable unity; and in his own persistent tendency to overestimate his technological capacities for overriding or ignoring them.

The preindustrial architect, whether folk or primitive, could never have been under such misapprehensions.[15] As a result of the controlling conditions under which he works, the margin for error allowed him is far narrower; at the same time, permissible factors of safety are far smaller. The consequence of this is that the preindustrial architect often shows a more precise comprehension of experiential reality and a more elegant response to it than does his modern colleague. Two qualities characterize his work, both of them significant for modern practice: (*a*) the canny exploitation of building materials and structural form to maximize environmental control (e.g., the Eskimo igloo); (*b*) the ingenious development of unit and communal plans to extend and consolidate environmental control (e.g., the troglodyte villages of Honan). The first set of characteristics is more easily studied in primitive architecture, the latter in the relatively more complex and stable folk communities. This is a necessary oversimplification, since many primitive tribes build quite sophisticated complexes (e.g., Zambian herdsmen in Africa, cliff dwellers in southwestern America), while folk architects sometimes build individual structures of great functional purity (e.g., corncribs of Lindoso, Portugal). But the distinction is useful and will be followed here.

In all his structures, the primitive architect always faces one supreme and absolute limitation: the impact of the environment in which he finds himself must be met by his own efforts, using the building materials that environment affords.[16] The environment itself is scarcely ever genial; and the building materials available to him would appear to modern man as appallingly meager in supply or restricted in kind. The Eskimo has only snow and ice, the Sudanese mud and reeds, the Siberian herdsman hides and felted hair, the Melanesian palm leaves and bamboo. Yet the architecture of these peoples reveals a sophisticated grasp of the problem, not only when viewed in the light of their own theoretical and material resources but also when analyzed in the light of modern scientific knowledge. Primitive practice reveals a precise and detailed understanding of local climate, on the one hand, and a remarkable grasp of the behavioral characteristics of local materials, on the other. However, the modern architect must make allowances for two contradictory limits to any approach to primitive art and architecture. If, on the one hand, he views primitive artifacts in the context of a cosmopolitan museum, he must remember that skillful curators have removed them from their context and rearranged them in an aesthetic environment, every dimension of which has been manipulated in favor of artifact and gallery visitor. If, on the other hand, he has the good fortune to actually visit living primitive communities, his urban sensibilities will be assaulted by a range of strange (and hence probably offensive) sights, sounds, and smells of the primitive community at its daily work. To properly appreciate the viable wisdom of primitive life, he must balance each experience against the other.

It is not hard to understand the appeal of primitive art to modern urban man; house or totem pole, war canoe or grain bin, wooden bowl or hair ornament—all these display harmony, clarity, an integrity of form and function that represents high levels of artistic accomplishment.[17] But it would be a mistake to assume that these qualities can be imported and added to our artifacts, like nutmeg or pepper. One must neither overlook nor oversimplify the cultural milieu that endows primitive art with its attractive properties. Spiritually or psychologically, the culture is no less complex than our own. The exact path of the primitive artist, from aspiration to finished artifact, is no less mysterious. His architecture, like his agriculture or medicine, will often have a rationale that only anthropologists or psychologists can interpret. But his practice—that is, how things are done as opposed to the reasons for doing them—is often astonishingly perceptive and sensible.

The primitive architect is the captive of an economy of scarcity. His resources in energy, time, and materials are strictly limited. At the same time, the conditions of life afford him little room for error in coping with environmental stresses; disaster lurks behind even small miscalculations. Without the formal organized knowledge of literate civilization to rely upon, his practice is always subject to check and modification by direct sensual experience. Primitive practice affords hundreds of examples that architects could study with profit, but two will suffice our purpose here—the Eskimo igloo and the mud-walled houses of the African and American deserts.

Of all environmental components, heat and cold are the most critical to human existence and the ones that confront the primitive architect with his most intricate architectural problems. Since thermal comfort is a function of four separate factors (ambient and radiant temperatures, air movement, and humidity) and since all four are in constant flux, any effective manipulation requires real analytic ability on the part of the designer of shelter. The Eskimo displays such ability in his igloo: from a purely theoretical point of view, it would be difficult to formulate a better design for protection against the Arctic winter. Its performance is excellent: with no mechanical equipment, it achieves a performance

33

level that modern engineers might envy (3.1). This performance is a function of both its geometry and its substance. The hemispherical dome offers maximum stability under winter gales from all compass points while, at the same time, exposing the minimum surface to their chilling effect. As a form, the dome has the further merit of enclosing the largest volume with the least material; and it also yields that volume which is most effectively heated by the radiant point source of a blubber lamp.

In terms of thermal response, the intense and steady cold of the Arctic dictates a wall of the lowest possible heat-holding capacity. Dry snow meets this criterion most admirably. Though at first glance snow might seem the least likely structural material conceivable, the Eskimo unlocks the paradox by constructing a dome of snow blocks (18 in. thick, 36 in. long, and 6 in. high), laid in one continuous in-sloping spiral. He makes the finished dome both stronger and more windproof by forming a glaze of ice on the interior surface. When, finally, he drapes the interior with skins and furs, thereby minimizing body chill from either radiant or conductive heat loss to cold floor or walls, the Eskimo architect has completed a most admirable instrument for thermal control (3.2).

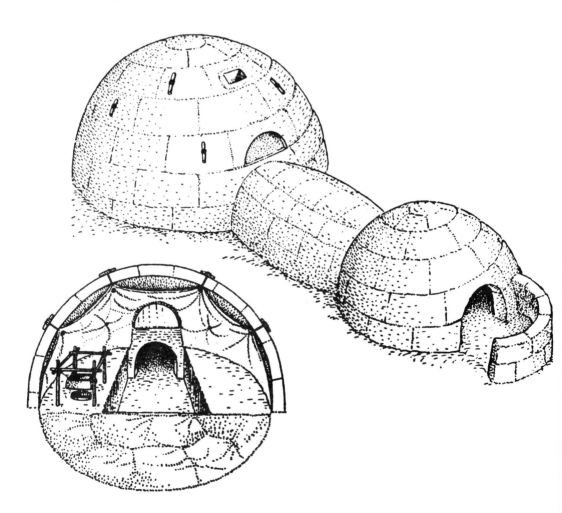

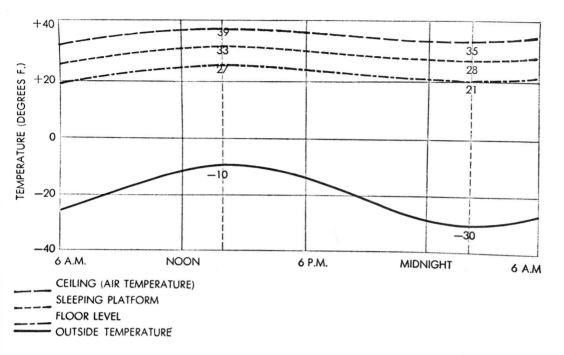

CEILING (AIR TEMPERATURE)
SLEEPING PLATFORM
FLOOR LEVEL
OUTSIDE TEMPERATURE

3.1

Igloo of Baffin Island type with airlock and antechamber for dogs, sleds, and outer clothing. Interior of igloo is draped in skins to act as radiant reflective insulation, thereby reducing heat loss from body to cold walls. (From "Primitive Architecture and Climate" by James Marston Fitch and Daniel P. Branch. Copyright © 1960 by Scientific American, Inc. All rights reserved.)

3.2

Diagram shows effectiveness of igloo as a thermal control device. Curves show air temperatures only; effective temperatures are higher, due to radiation from cooking fire and human inhabitants. (From "Primitive Architecture and Climate" by James Marston Fitch and Daniel P. Branch. Copyright © 1960 by Scientific American, Inc. All rights reserved.)

For the civilized Western nostril, olfactory conditions may be less than optimal, but odor preferences are notoriously culturally conditioned; and ventilation inside the igloo has proved adequate for family and fire alike for millennia. Space inside the dome is certainly limited; but the Baffin Island Eskimos build igloos of several domes, connected by barrel-vaulted tunnels and airlocks, to house dog teams, extra food, and surplus equipment. The life span of the igloo is short (it begins to collapse when outside temperatures rise above freezing), but, like most primitive building, it favors performance over durability. In any case, it lasts exactly as long as the Eskimo requires it. The lesson here is clear. Housing quality in the American Arctic today is low, even for Americans, in terms of American potentials: for the native Eskimos, living conditions are scandalous, according to a report by Abrams.[18] It may no longer be practicable to house even native populations in the igloo; but it seems improbable that a better functional prototype than the igloo can be evolved for comparable efficiencies in the future, no matter what the shape or material employed.

If we turn to another thermal regime, that of the great deserts of the

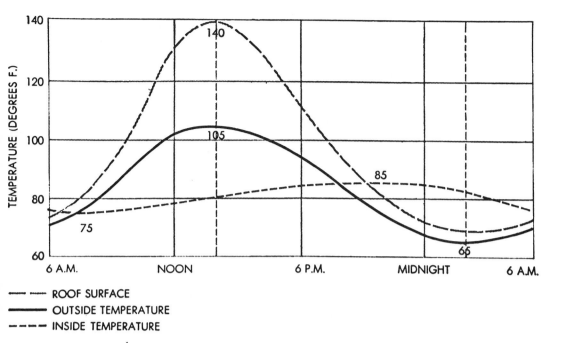

3·3

Typical of the mud-walled, mud-roofed construction of desert peoples, this idealized Southwest American Indian house shows characteristic features—thick walls and roof for heat storage, few windows and doors, rooftop for hot-weather sleeping and drying of foodstuffs. (From "Primitive Architecture and Climate" by James Marston Fitch and Daniel P. Branch. Copyright © 1960 by Scientific American, Inc. All rights reserved.)

3·4

Temperature curves for structure in figure 3.3 show how heat-storage capacity of mud walls flattens out diurnal temperature extremes of the desert. Since the atmosphere is very dry, effective temperatures inside the structure would be lower than those shown. (From "Primitive Architecture and Climate" by James Marston Fitch and Daniel P. Branch. Copyright © 1960 by Scientific American, Inc. All rights reserved.)

lower latitudes, we find another kind of response from the primitive architect, equally appropriate to radically different conditions. Here the designer confronts a climate of extremely high daytime temperatures, intense solar radiation, and very low humidities alternating with much lower temperatures at night. Sometimes, as in the Algerian mountains or the American Southwest, these diurnal fluctuations are super-imposed upon comparably severe seasonal ones (3.3). The main requirement for thermal comfort in this situation is a building with a very high heat-holding capacity—one that can absorb solar radiation all day, when air temperatures are high, and release it to the interior all night as temperatures fall. The mud-walled, mud-roofed constructions that desert peoples all over the world have evolved exploit this principle quite effectively, as temperature measurements will reveal (3.4).

Since humidities are very low, daytime ventilation is not mandatory. Indeed, at mid-day in mid-summer, most desert temperatures are so high that a breeze passing over the skin adds more heat by conduction than could be dissipated by the evaporation of sweat. Thus, the typical desert form is closed, with a limited number of small openings to cut down heat and glare. Shade is important to mid-day comfort; often primitive settlements will be so densely developed with huts and compounds that the whole complex shades itself. (This is standard town-planning practice in all civilized desert societies, as we shall see.) In some desert areas, rainfall is so scanty that dead flat mud roofs are practicable, even in such civilized urban societies as southern Morocco and the Nile Valley. In others, seasonal rains will compel the primitive architect to build his house against an overhanging cliff (Mesa Verde in Colorado) or to protect his mud huts with conical parasols of thatch (Dogons, Sudan).

Although the folk architectures of civilized societies display the same kind of pragmatic sagacity as do the primitive, they are of a qualitatively different order. The iron tools and mensuration systems of civilization immediately introduce such factors as modular building elements (brick, tile, dimensional lumber) and repetitive structural systems (Roman arcade, Gothic vaulted bay), which are antithetical to the plasticity of primitive forms. Literacy, on the other hand, introduces the disconcerting concept of choice in ways of building—an inconceivable situation to the primitive architect, to whom it never occurs that there is more than one way to build—that of his own inherited tradition.[19]

Unlike his primitive counterpart, the folk architect has to build for a much more complex social process. This requirement introduces complexities into his plans (i.e., size, scale, and compartmentalization of space) that limit his structural and environmental options. Thus, the exigency of organized warfare will impose moat and wall upon a plan that, experientially, calls for exposure to sun. Or an institution like polygamy and purdah leads to the harem, with sexual segregation and a consequent duplication of facilities. All such factors work against that "purity" of primitive response to sheer environmental forces so admired by Viollet-le-Duc. Obviously, all the folk architectures of civilization are phylogenetically derived from earlier primitive practice, though the line of descent may no longer be visibly traceable. Thus, the American log cabin can be traced back through historic Scandinavia and Moravia to its prehistoric origins in both regions. Thus, too, the conical trulli of modern Apulia are related to the prehistoric nuraghi of Sardinia; the skeletal wood carpentry of Japan has its origins in earlier lashed-together wood frames of aboriginal peoples; and the mud architecture of the Moslem towns of northern Nigeria is built on earlier pagan Negro expertise.

On the other hand, precisely because of immensely greater material and intellectual resources, folk architecture is able to solve with skill and imagination many problems of environmental manipulation that beset us today. This is why folk planning—at the level of village and town, of garden, orchard, and farm—is of extraordinary interest to cosmopolitan designers in the industrially advanced parts of the world. Folk architecture is remarkable for its exploitation of the building site, a quality it shares with preindustrial architecture in general but that is more marked in folk than ruling-class practice because resources are always more limited and ideological and ceremonial requirements more modest. Many nonarchitectural factors govern the selection of the site: closeness to food and water supplies, trade and transportation routes, defense against enemies, and so on. But the exploitation of the site, once selected, involves manipulation of two sorts of environmental forces, topographic and climatic. Both involve the expenditure of energy, animal or human; and, since such energy is notoriously inefficient and expensive, all sorts of stratagems are employed to minimize its application and to facilitate its tasks.

If, for example, the local problem is the mosquito pest—as it was after the Romans allowed Etruscan irrigation and drainage of the maremma to fall into disuse—then later Italians will be forced to move their villages to new sites along the hilltops, away from the coast.[20] In doing so, they face a new set of problems. The topography affords opportunities for exploitation of sun and wind. The builders will attempt to orient all the houses for shade and breeze in summer, for sun and wind protection in winter. But the street patterns thus theoretically indicated will, in real life, be strictly conditioned by topography. Above a given angle of ascent, gravity and not heat becomes the dominant force in establishing the street patterns; and many houses will consequently be left with orientations less than ideal because the thermal factor has been canceled by the topographic. Italian hill towns are a marvelous demonstration of this sort of experiential equilibrium between forces of varying types and magnitudes.

In other situations, such as the deserts of Africa and the Middle East, the overwhelming environmental force is an absolute excess of solar heat and light. If the culture is riverine, the topography will be relatively level and will impose few restrictions upon the layout of villages and towns. Street patterns may be regular or random. In either case, protection from sun is more important than exposure to breeze. Streets will be narrow, squares small, and both will be shaded by trelliswork and awnings as well as by the buildings along them. And the dense compartmentalization of the city will be intensified if the culture is Moslem with its requirements of purdah and harem. In such urban situations, vegetation is normally scarce; shade-creating devices are man-made. But in many peasant villages of the Nile delta, where irrigation makes it possible, the entire settlement will be sheltered under a high parasol of nut palms—high enough to permit ventilation, dense enough to parry the thrust of the noon sun, and yielding an important food crop as well.

Other types of desert or semiarid climates dictate other sorts of architectural and urbanistic response. There are situations, for example, where air temperatures, while high, are still low enough to make ventilation desirable, and where winds are reliable enough to make it practicable. Here we find folk architecture responding with such extraordinary inventions as the wind scoops of the towns of the Persian Gulf and the Sind of West Pakistan. Here the size, shape, and orientation of the scoop is oriented toward the source of comfort as precisely as any radarscope on a modern ship or plane.

The Yemenites of southern Algeria build in a somewhat similar temperature regime. But they build around oases and wells, and this location, together with the need for defense, dictates fortifications and high densities (3.5). The folk builder responds with mud-masonry skyscrapers, five and six stories in height. Windows in the upper stories admit light and air (and presumably permit detection of the enemy far away), but their relatively small size and thick jambs exclude most direct sunshine. Here again a number of functions are made to approach without interfering with one another.

No one who travels through these parts of Africa and the Middle East can fail to be struck by the qualitative differences between the response

of the folk architects and their modern Western-educated descendants to these overriding environmental realities. The latter are mindlessly replicating the wide shadeless streets and unshielded glass walls, the negative spaces of gridiron blocks and outward-facing centrifugal plans of American cities. The resulting architectural and urbanistic dysfunction is grotesque. No one, today, would expect Cairo or Baghdad to revert to the low-built, congested, and squalid state of the Mamelukes and the Janissaries. The physical deficiencies of the slums of South Cairo, for example, are grave and readily apparent: lack of toilet facilities, sewage systems, and plentiful pure water for drinking and bathing; lack of adequate street cleaning and garbage removal; lack of insect and rodent control; lack of parks and playgrounds; and on and on. These

3·5
Mud-walled masonry megastructures, like this one from southern Algeria, maintain much better metabolic balance with their environment than would isolated structures. Although the high degree of compartmentalization is a response to danger of attack and Moslem segregation of the sexes, it also yields a settlement that shades itself.

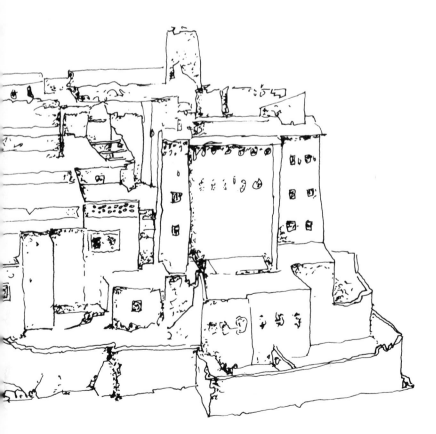

are ills that any rational modern society must eliminate. But, at the very same time, it must be reiterated that these old quarters offer incomparably better prototypes for response to the desert climate than do the current public housing models being imported from East London and the Bronx. To ignore this central fact is to caricature modern scientific method, not to employ it. Young architects, whether Egyptian or American, would profit greatly from studying the *principles* embodied in this folk-cultural patrimony; and Cairo, Egypt, and Tucson, Arizona, would profit equally from the light such study would cast on contemporary practice.

Peasant agriculture offers as many suggestions for modern landscaping as does its house- and village-building practice. In many parts of the world, the peasant finds himself in a marginal zone for a given crop. Success or failure hangs upon the closest observations of microclimatic phenomena. Thus, in areas where wind is a problem, as around Arles in the south of France or in western Japan, he will plant windbreaks around either the farm-house complex or the entire field. In another situation, like the loess lands of China, he will build underground to escape bitter winter winds. The thermal advantages here are twofold: not only does his house escape the wind-chill effect on all above-ground structures, but it also takes full advantage of the completely stable and relatively high subsurface temperatures of the soil.

In another marginal situation, the north Italian lemon grower will have only just enough winter sunlight to mature the fruit, providing the

terraces are oriented to the south, protected from winter winds, and high enough to guarantee frost "drainage." Along the northern coasts of Portugal, exposure rather than elevation above sea level is critical. The peasants have learned that, because of microclimatic variations, they can have two distinctly different agricultures on different faces of the same hill: oranges, lemons, and olives on the south slope; apples, cabbages, and potatoes on the north—two kinds of crops that are normally separated by hundreds of miles rather than hundreds of feet!

Sheer necessity has forced the peasant on occasion to evolve structures that are as elegant and refined, in purely formal terms, as any of his town or city contemporaries. For example, grain storage raises some delicately balanced problems. All grains must be dried by sun and air and then stored in such a way as to protect them from falling rain, atmospheric moisture, and—above all—rats. Small grains could be stored in baskets or jars. But American corn is usually stored on the ear, which means it must be continuously ventilated by passing air through the storage bin. This requirement gives the corncrib an identical physiognomy the world over: long and narrow, with slotted sides and overhanging gabled roof, it is preferably built on an east-west axis and always stilted off the ground on piers topped by rat guards. The American farmer, with ample wood at his disposal, at first built log cribs and then louvered ones of milled lumber. But Spanish and Portuguese peasants, with no wood on hand, built "log" cribs out of hewn granite. And in districts where the growing and storage of corn were always close to disaster, as in the cool and rainy mountains of northeast Portugal, the corncrib was given the sunniest spot available. In the villages of Lindoso this happened to be the very center of town (3.6).

The Lindoso craftsmen have developed an astonishing expertise, in

3.6

Corncribs in Lindoso, northeast Portugal. Although the stilted grain storage bin, with rat guards and slotted sides, dates from earliest antiquity, these are unusual in several respects. Built entirely of granite—with hewn floorslabs, perforated wall panels and roof slabs, and the ubiquitous rat guards atop each pier—these cribs are carefully oriented to sun and breeze and occupy the center of the town. The earliest dates from mid-seventeenth century, latest from 1957.

which the most obdurate materials are carved into slabs, grilles, and latticework with as much apparent ease as a cabinetmaker with his woods. The resulting forms are as grave and noble as any monumental urban architecture. And, indeed, there are many historical instances in which urbane ruling-class institutions have expropriated such folk idioms and raised them to the level of high-style monumental architecture. Such are the tombs in the great necropolis at Hierapolis in Asiatic Turkey, where craftsmen of the Hellenistic age handled the local light tough stone (siliceous sinter) as effortlessly as though it were cedar or pine. And across the world, in medieval Japan, we can observe the same sort of transmutation of folk into palace idiom. At Ise, the timber-and-thatch granary of primitive farmers has been refined into temple architecture; while, at Nara, the great imperial treasure house is a log cabin elevated to the scale and majesty of the marble Parthenon (which, incidentally, was also the product of a slow process of transmutation from primitive wooden prototypes).

I have cited only a few examples of the sensitivity of folk and primitive architects to their physical environment and the sagacious economy of their response. One could cite hundreds of others, all of which deal successfully with problems that modern technology has not "repealed," whatever its pretensions to the contrary. Merely from a utilitarian point of view (and not counting the fact that, for modern urbane taste, they are uniformly handsome) they represent a cultural resource of immense value.[21] This resource must be made available to the architects and urbanists of tomorrow, who have no comparably effective theoretical apparatus. It is for such reasons that we should establish an international program of rescue and preservation of characteristic primitive and folk settlements. These should be selected to afford the students of the world an opportunity to visit and study the full spectrum of architectural response—of different peoples in different times and climates—to experiential circumstance. Viable communities should be subsidized in such a way as to preserve the autochthonous life models of their populations. Extinct communities should be excavated and preserved according to the best archaeological and art-historical standards. Museums and facilities for living and study should be provided near each big project but designed in such a way as to minimize the intrusion both culturally and aesthetically.

In many advanced countries, preservation programs already exist.[22] They would of course become an integral part of any international program—would in fact be the source of its expertise, at least initially. But many (perhaps most) of the significant examples of primitive or folk architecture would be found in the underdeveloped and less wealthy countries of Africa, Southeast Asia, and Latin America. And it is in precisely such countries, where the future of traditional art forms is in the gravest jeopardy, that funds and trained personnel are most desperately short.[23] Hence, any program like that just outlined could only be effectuated by an international organization with adequate funding and personnel. The first function is already implicit in UNESCO's successful effort to save the monuments at Aswan; the second is suggested by the recently formed International Council on Monuments and Sites, with headquarters in Paris. Such an organization, operating under the general protection of the United Nations, could attract the support of member nations necessary for a long-term project.

When we come to the preservation of historic architecture in the Western world itself, we confront a somewhat different problem. The ultimate aim of all such activity is also didactic—that is, to show the layman "how it really was" when Washington slept in this house or Franklin set type in that one. This is a perfectly valid activity, but it is, by definition, nationalist in its approach to history, reflecting each society's special perspective of its own past. Currently, we find a whole spectrum of preservationist activities, above and beyond the traditional art and ethnographic museums. (The distinction between these two is rapidly vanishing because of the new aesthetic values attached to artifacts that hitherto would have been regarded as of only anthropological significance.) We see the preservation of entire historic towns, as in Williamsburg or at Telĉ in Bohemia; historic districts in big cities, such as the Vieux Carré in New Orleans or the Stare Miasto in Warsaw; isolated mansions or castles, as at Monticello or Versailles; outdoor architectural museums like Skansen in Sweden or Shelburne and Cooperstown in the United States; and indoor architectural and decorative arts museums like Winterthur. We even begin to witness the first promising results of industrial archaeology in such national monuments as the Edison Laboratories at East Orange, New Jersey, and the prerevolutionary iron smelters at Hopewell Furnace, Pennsylvania.

All these projects aim at the presentation of some special aspect of the past through the media of its material remains. They represent different philosophical attitudes and employ different levels of expertise. Yet each acts to organize the general facts of history around a particular axis—a hazardous but essential cultural task. For each aims at teaching modern man the central fact he seems most in danger of losing: *that nothing is to be taken for granted*—not the electric light bulb or the Bill of Rights, or the results of Harpers Ferry or those of Walden Pond, not central heating or the cure for typhoid and tuberculosis. Each advance has been appallingly hard to win and, as is now frighteningly clear, would be all too easy to lose. And it is quite as important for the contemporary architect to absorb this lesson as for laymen in general.

In architectural and planning circles, one often hears current restoration and preservation projects criticized for their "superficiality" or "artificiality." There is some basis for both criticisms. American activity in this field stands at about the same level, conceptually, as did archaeology under Sir Arthur Evans at Knossos at the turn of the century. Our technical expertise is, in general, quite highly developed, but our theoretical (one might properly say, philosophical) approach to the preservation of the artistic patrimony is still inadequate. This is due in part to the fact that the field is relatively new and has always been dominated by private institutions and individuals. Remarkable collectors like Du Pont at Winterthur, Rockefeller at Williamsburg, and Webb at Shelburne have left the imprints of their powerful but necessarily private tastes upon it. Until very recently, government at every level has ignored historic preservation. But all this is now rapidly changing.[24]

In a certain mechanical sense, any conscious effort to preserve the past may be called "artificial." But so, too, could museums, art galleries, libraries—indeed, the whole process of formal education—be criticized. In each case, the artifact or theory has been removed from its life context in order to study it, in contrast to the apprenticeship methods of instruction of primitive cultures. One consequence of this approach, in the field of preservation, is a tendency to "prettify" the past. To the extent that any museological or curatorial role involves editing and selection, this tendency is endemic to the activity. The whole past could never be displayed, if only for reasons of space and budget. But there are many aspects that cannot be replicated and exhibited for reasons of convention and taste: the smell of the burned flesh of the branded slave, the blood on the headsman's axe, the mud and ordure of eighteenth-century streets, the flies and stench (not to mention the truculent bull) of the barnyard. Health and safety regulations would prevent the re-creation of such phenomena in any case. On the other hand, the more attractive aspects of life in earlier times can easily be magnified, and too often are: hoop skirts and knee breeches, candle light and mulled wine, chamber music and coaching horns.

Because of such limitations, many historic monuments have been bowdlerized. Mount Vernon has only recently been able to bring itself to re-create the living quarters of a few of the slaves (and those of the most fortunate "house" servants, at that). At Monticello and elsewhere in the American South, the whole ugly fact of slavery is coyly sidestepped. The brutal and squalid system that supported these old mansions has been expunged. The result is that the visitor is given a quite inaccurate and prettified idea of what life was like when Washington and Jefferson were in residence there. This particular tendency is international. It is impossible to get any idea of how Versailles was actually staffed and run from even many visits there. Service areas, stables, pantries, kitchens, privies, fuel and water storage—all the vast apparatus necessary to support palace life (and necessary to any true understanding of the historic role of the monarchy) is invisible to the visitor. Ironically, the Communist countries handle their aristocratic past in much the same way. The immaculately restored royal palace of Walanov, near Warsaw, has been shorn of the village serfs that once made it possible. And the great agglomeration of serfs and animals and the quarters required to house them have vanished from around Catherine of Russia's blue-and-white summer palace outside Leningrad. Thus, for visitors to these monuments, absolute monarch, Polish king, and czarina could all appear as genial amateurs whose only enthusiasms were gardening and interior decoration.

But such errors as these by no means invalidate preservational activities; they merely indicate how much work remains to be done in our methods of interpreting the past. Artificiality and bowdlerization can be held to a minimum by the rigorous application of scholarly standards—scientific, historiographic, archaeological. Where the significant fact or event cannot be replicated in multidimensional reality, audiovisual presentations, documentary films, and literature can be employed. Artifact and document must be employed in tandem to supplement each other's inadequacies, correct each other's possibility of error.

Our past is too important to our future to contemplate its being lost through inattention or lack of imagination.

NOTES

1.   Winckelmann's *Geschichte der Kunst des Alter-thums* was published in Dresden in 1764.

2.   *The Antiquities of Athens* was published in five volumes at London between 1762 and 1787.

3.   Theodor deBry, a Flemish engraver, bought LeMoyne's water colors from his widow and published them in Frankfurt in 1591 under the title *Breuis narratio eorum quae in Florida Americae prouicia Gallis acciderunt, secunda in illam nauigatione, duce Renato de Laudōniere.*

4.   Some of these drawings were published by deBry in 1590; so great was the success of the venture that it went through some seventeen printings in four languages by 1620.

5.   Oswald Siren cites two French works as especially influential: *Lettres édifiantes et curieuses, écrites des missions étrangères, par quelques missionnaires de la Compagnie de Jésus* and *Mémoires concernant l'histoire, les sciences, les arts, les moeurs, les usages, etc., des Chinois; par les missionnaires de Pékin.*

6.   *Description de l'Egypte* was published by the Commission des Monuments de l'Egypte between 1808 and 1828 in some thirty-eight volumes of text and illustrations.

7.   Sir Banister Fletcher's *History of Architecture on the Comparative Method* quite accurately reflected the British Empire's view of the world. First published in 1896, its sixteenth edition (1954) still found it possible to devote 860 of its pages to the "historical styles" —i.e., Egyptian to American—and the remaining 76 pages to the "non-historical styles"—i.e., Chinese, Indian, Japanese, Middle American, and Saracenic! Prehistoric architecture is allotted 3 pages in this edition, primitive and folk building none at all.

8.   This bias in favor of upper-class, urban, and permanent artifacts has persisted in art history and archaeology until the very recent past. Even epigraphy consolidated this bias: the illiterate peasant could leave no written record of his contribution to culture. Only recently have archaeologists begun to pay as much attention to rural or pastoral sites as to the great urban centers of wealth and power.

9.   "If we compare the form of the newly invented machine with the perfected type of the same instrument, we observe, as we trace it through the phases of improvement, how weight is shaken off where strength is less needed, how functions are made to approach without impeding each other, how straight becomes curved, and the curve is straightened, till the straggling and cumbersome becomes the compact, effective and beautiful engine" (Horatio Greenough, *Form and Function*, p. 59). For a more extended treatment of the evolution of Greenough's remarkably prescient theories on functionalist design in the era of modern industrialism, see James Marston Fitch, *Architecture and the Esthetics of Plenty*, pp. 46–64.

10.   Lewis Henry Morgan, *Houses and House-Life of the American Aborigines*.

11.   Eugène Emmanuel Viollet-le-Duc, *Histoire de l'habitation humaine depuis les temps préhistoriques jusqu'à nos jours*, published in Paris in 1875, was reissued in English the following year in Boston.

12.   Even the avant-garde discovery of African Negro art, which shook Paris around 1907 and influenced such painters as Pablo Picasso, was prepared for by the arts and crafts and folkloristic movements. So, too, at a later date would have been the immense success of "Art of the South Seas," an exhibition of preponderantly ethnographic material presented by the Museum of Modern Art in New York, January–May 1946, and the foundation of the Museum of Primitive Art in 1957.

13.   See James Marston Fitch, *American Building*, vol. I: *The Historical Forces That Shaped It*, pp. 60–73.

14.   Pausanias, probably a native of Lydia, apparently completed his great travelogue of the Greek world before A.D. 180.

15.   A few definitions may be in order. As used here, the term *folk architecture* describes the product of craftsmen of civilized societies, working for themselves. Some of them, becoming skilled specialists, may also work on the high-style architecture of ruling-class clients. Such craftsmen may or may not be literate, but they would be continuously influenced by a literate ruling class whose high-style concepts would percolate down (just as the high-style idiom would be influenced by folk art beneath it—e.g., Mozart and folk melodies, classic ballet and folk dance). *Primitive architecture* is the product of craftsmen in a preliterate, classless society, whether extant or vanished. In such societies tradition is transmitted orally, technical competence is generalized, training is by apprenticeship, production is handicraft, all energy sources are animal, building tools are pre–Iron Age, and modular mensuration has not yet appeared.

16.   For a more extensive treatment of the subject matter of the following paragraphs, see James Marston Fitch and Daniel P. Branch, "Primitive Architecture and Climate," *Scientific American* 203, no. 6 (December 1960): 134–144.

17.   Such qualities increasingly attract the attention of contemporary architects. See Bernard Rudofsky, *Architecture without Architects*; also Ernest G. Schwiebert, Jr., "The Primitive Roots of Architecture," Ph.D. dissertation.

18.   Charles Abrams, *Housing the Alaska Native*.

19.   It is obvious that even primitive structural concepts have an evolutionary history of change and development in response to environmental pressures and sociocultural change. But the rate of change would have been so slow that, at any given time, the individual craftsman would have been unaware of it.

20.   They did not understand that the vector of malaria was the mosquito, not the "bad air" they blamed. Yet they located the new towns in safety, just above the reach of the marsh-based mosquitoes.

21.   For cool rainy climates, the arcaded sidewalks of Bohemia and Poland; for heavy snows, the gabled roofs of Scandinavia, neatly calibrated between snow-holding and snow-shedding characteristics; for hot dry climates, the centripetal patios of Middle America; for cold dry climates, the south-facing terrace housing of the American Pueblos; and for hot wet climates, the stilted parasol-roofed house form of the Caribbean with its perimetral galleries and jalousies.

22.   See James Marston Fitch, "The Phoenix Cities of Poland," *Horizon* 6, no. 2 (Spring 1964): 52–59; see also idem, "Historic Preservation in Czechoslovakia," *Journal of the Society of Architectural Historians* 25, no. 2 (May 1966): 119–135. For a general summary of French and English experience, see Stephen W. Jacobs, "Architectural Preservation in Europe," *Curator* 10, no. 3 (1966): 119–135. The best account of American experience (up to 1927) will be found in Charles B. Hosmer, *Presence of the Past*.

23.   For an account of the critical status of the artistic patrimony in Africa, see James Marston Fitch, "An African Notebook," *Horizon* 6, no. 4 (Autumn 1964): 49–59.

24.   The professionalization of the field is forecast by many developments, including the passage by the U.S. Congress of the first legislation permitting federal intervention in preservation (1966); the creation in the U.S. Park Service of the new Office of Archaeology and Historic Preservation under the direction of Dr. Eugene Connally (1967); and the inauguration by me of the first course of graduate studies in restoration and preservation of historic architecture at Columbia University (1964).

BIBLIOGRAPHY

Abrams, Charles. *Housing the Alaska Native.* Anchorage: Alaska State Housing Authority, 1967.

———. *Man's Struggle for Shelter in an Urbanizing World.* Cambridge, Mass.: M.I.T. Press, 1964.

Art of the South Seas. New York: Museum of Modern Art, 1946.

deBry, Theodor. *Breuis narratio eorum quae in Florida Americae prouīcia Gallis acciderunt, secunda in illam nauigatione, duce Renato de Laudōniere* . . . Frankfurt: J. Wechel, 1591.

Description de l'Egypte; ou, Recueil des observations et des recherches qui ont été faites en Egypte pendant l'expédition de l'armée française, publié par les ordres de sa majesté l'empereur Napoléon le Grand. 21 vols. Paris: L'imprimerie impériale, 1809–1828.

Fitch, James Marston. "An African Notebook." *Horizon* 6, no. 4 (Autumn 1964): 49–59.

———. *American Building.* Vol. I: *The Historical Forces That Shaped It.* Vol. II: *The Environmental Forces That Shaped It.* 2d ed. rev. and enl. Boston: Houghton Mifflin Co., 1972.

———. *Architecture and the Esthetics of Plenty.* New York: Columbia University Press, 1961.

———. "Historic Preservation in Czechoslovakia." *Journal of the Society of Architectural Historians* 25, no. 2 (May 1966): 119–135.

———. "The Phoenix Cities of Poland." *Horizon* 6, no. 2 (Spring 1964): 52–59.

———, and Daniel P. Branch. "Primitive Architecture and Climate." *Scientific American* 203, no. 6 (December 1960): 134–144.

Fletcher, Banister F. *A History of Architecture on the Comparative Method, for Students, Craftsmen & Amateurs.* 16th rev. ed. London: B. T. Batsford, 1954.

Greenough, Horatio. *Form and Function: Remarks on Art, Design, and Architecture.* Edited by Harold A. Small, with an introduction by Erle Loran. Berkeley: University of California Press, 1947, 1958.

Hosmer, Charles B. *Presence of the Past: A History of the Preservation Movement in the United States before Williamsburg.* New York: Putnam, 1966.

Jacobs, Stephen W. "Architectural Preservation in Europe." *Curator* 10, no. 3 (1966): 119–135.

Lettres édifiantes et curieuses, écrites des missions étrangères, par quelques missionnaires de la Compagnie de Jésus. 34 vols. Paris: LeClerc, 1717–1776.

Mémoires concernant l'histoire, les sciences, les arts, les moeurs, les usages, etc., des Chinois; par les missionnaires de Pékin. 16 vols. Paris: Nyon, 1776–1791.

Morgan, Lewis Henry. *Houses and House-Life of the American Aborigines*. Contributions to North American Ethnology, no. 5. Washington, D.C.: Bureau of American Ethnology, 1881.

Pausanias's Description of Greece. Translated with a commentary by J. G. Frazer. 6 vols. London: Macmillan & Co., 1898.

Rudofsky, Bernard. *Architecture without Architects: A Short Introduction to Non-Pedigreed Architecture*. Garden City, N.Y.: Doubleday, 1964.

Schwiebert, Ernest George, Jr. "The Primitive Roots of Architecture." Ph.D. Dissertation, School of Architecture, Princeton University, 1966.

Stuart, James, and Nicholas Revett. *The Antiquities of Athens Measured and Delineated*. 5 vols. London: J. Haberkorn, 1762–1787.

Viollet-le-Duc, Eugène Emmanuel. *Histoire de l'habitation humaine depuis les temps préhistoriques jusqu'à nos jours*. Paris: J. Hetzel, 1875. Translated by Benjamin Bucknall as *The Habitations of Man in All Ages*. Boston: J. R. Osgood and Co., 1876; reprint, New York: B. Blom, 1971.

Winckelmann, Johann Joachim. *Geschichte der Kunst des Alterthums*. 2 vols. Dresden, 1764. Translated as *History of Ancient Art*. 2 vols. New York: F. Ungar Publishing Co., 1968.

4. American Cultural Geography and Folklife

Fred B. Kniffen

If students of American folklife find acceptable Sigurd Erixon's statement appearing in the first issue of *Folkliv*, and if they further find illuminating the graphics of Erixon's presentation, it appears that American geography has something worthwhile to offer them in concept, method, and content. Erixon stated: "For the cultural science now under consideration, life itself is the main thing. The material, sociological, and psychological factors are studied with due regard thereto, in as universal a manner as possible. The social structure and cellular system provide the framework, the functions of life provide the contents, that are to be studied as regards type, historical development, and origin."[1]

Geography and folklore show partial concurrence of the phenomena with which they deal. They share broad ultimate aims to understand cultural processes. Beyond these marginal contacts, the interests of the two fields diverge widely. It would therefore be presumptuous for a geographer gratuitously to instruct a folklorist in specific procedures. It is deemed more fitting to outline geographic methodology and techniques from which the folklorist may borrow if he so chooses.

Geography is the formal expression of man's universal interest in the earth about him and his curiosity concerning unfamiliar places. Physical geography seeks to understand the natural processes that mold the earth's surface; human, or cultural, geography seeks to understand the human, or cultural, processes that mold the earth's surface out of the natural base. Cultural geography is a more limited term than human geography. It implies explicit recognition of the concepts of culture in the organization of its data. It is with cultural geography that we are here concerned.

Cultural geography deals with cultures of all levels of sophistication. Folk practices and cultures are therefore of neither greater nor less importance than others. Depending on the area or people selected for study, geography may be entirely concerned with folk cultures. Since cultural geography's concepts and methods are distinctive, at least in combination, it appears that they may produce results not otherwise attainable.

Cultural geography's field is the last chapter in earth history, that is, the alteration of the earth by man. Man places his imprint on the earth in two quite different ways. One is largely inadvertent, as man is an unwitting modifier of natural processes and conditions: induced erosion, alteration of native vegetation, pollution of air and water, for example. Man also changes the face of the earth as a positive agent of culture, in the building of houses and villages, the establishment of lines of communication, the laying out of fields and pastures, the damming of streams—in short, in constructing the whole fabric of his occupance of the earth.

If cultural geography's objectives are not those of the student of folk-life per se, neither are they those of culturologists or anthropologists. The latter are charged with understanding the whole culture. The geographers' ultimate purpose is to understand cultural landscapes, that is, the whole of man's imprint on the natural earth. They employ the concepts of culture to attain that end. It may be said that geographers deal with cultures, culture types, and culture areas, rather than with culture. By the very nature of their subject, geographers are concerned with material traits as their primary data. Nevertheless, as students of culture, they are quite aware that material objects cannot be severed from the ideas and values that lie behind them and therefore play a necessary explanatory role.

Fundamental Concepts

Three fundamental factors underlie man's group behavior respecting the positive modification of the earth's surface: the fundamental character of animal man, culture, and nature. If we can imagine man stripped of all cultural attainments, we find an animal guided in his activities by inherent biopsychological needs and urges. He would of necessity be restricted to the warmer sections of the earth, where absence of fire and clothing would be no great handicap. He would need ready at hand a supply of potable water and a constant source of food available by simple collecting techniques.

The visible animal-stage occupance pattern would likely consist of no more than a crude shelter—cave, rock shelter, or brush pulled together —a stream for water, and paths to a ready and steady source of food, say a reef of edible shellfish accessible at low tide. This simple pattern of living, representing satisfaction of man's basic needs, would vary little from place to place and would not be unlike that of other primates in its lineaments. Man's animal needs have not changed in time nor do they vary from one group to another. We may therefore say that animal man as a factor in man's occupance of the earth is a constant in both time and space.

Elaboration and differentiation of the basic animal occupance pattern are in large part cultural in origin. In the long history of mankind's culture growth, a first stage of development above the animal occupance pattern might include constructed houses instead of crude shelters, wood and basketry containers to give greater range of activity, hunting and fishing added to collecting, perhaps rafts or simple boats, and fire to make available new foods and to enable spread to cooler climates. All these things would permit elaboration of the basic animal occupance pattern consisting of shelter, water and food sources, and paths or trails. A completely new cultural concept would add an element to the occupance pattern when a belief in life after death resulted in the appearance of burial grounds.

The concept of an occupance pattern or complex consisting of a number of interrelated, functioning parts constituting a whole is the heart of geographic methodology in dealing with man's imprint on the earth. It attempts to be all-inclusive, not only of the economic aspects of man's existence, but also of such noneconomic expressions as those representing aesthetic or religious values. The occupance pattern is the basis for analysis of a particular culture; it serves as the basis for comparison in cross-cultural studies. The concept of occupance pattern should demonstrate that the items discussed by the cultural geographer are not random selections, that his is not a "science of leftovers,"[2] nor is geography "a field without a subject." Rather, the pattern is established by man's very animal and cultural nature. We may construct a series of model occupance patterns representative of historical points in man's cultural development.

Sequence Occupance Patterns

	Precultural	Early Cultural	Middle Cultural	Late Cultural
Shelter	Natural or crudely made "nests," caves, rock shelters, downed trees, etc.	Constructed houses of turf, stone, skin, bark, wattle-daub; special-purpose shelter for storage	Wooden shaped structures; vertical-post construction; specialized structures for headmen, priests, domesticated animals; temporary structures with herding	
Water	Natural pool, stream, spring	Wood and basketry containers for transport and storage	Dug wells; containers for catchment added	
Food	Gathering, collecting sources; tidal flats, marsh, etc.	Hunting and fishing added to collecting; used traps, nets, deadfalls, blinds, drying racks; containers for carrying and storage	Agriculture and herding added to older economy; slash-and-burn; manure piles; hay stacks; fields	

	Precultural	Early Cultural	Middle Cultural	Late Cultural
Communication	Trails to and from sources of food and water or for seasonal movements; little or no transport of food and water	Longer trails for seeking game; rafts or boats; temporary camps at distance	Trails to roads; boats; simple vehicles (sledges)	
Play	Opening for throwing, running, jumping, dancing, and other animal play	Plaza or field	Specialized game fields	
Settlement	Agglomerated	More widespread than previously; village and remote camps	Large agricultural villages; temporary herding camps; wider range of movement and territorial control	
Other		New or elaboration: fuel collection; fires for roasting, stone boiling, heat; burning and burned areas as adjuncts to hunting-gathering; burial sites and "sacred" places	New or elaboration: fences, corrals; markets for exchange; specialized structures for storage, government, religion	Highly specialized structures for government, religion, industry, commerce, sport; growth of cities; advance in transport; tendency to dispersed rural settlement; new materials: natural and synthetic (steel, concrete, etc.)

Continued elaboration of the occupance pattern by man is culturally possible because of increased technological capacity, of both tools and knowledge (4.1). Differences in the material expression of analogous elements of the occupance pattern may be due to differences in value system, that is, different group notions as to the right and wrong way to do things—what might be termed group rationale. Cultural expression in the occupance pattern has certainly varied with time and just as truly is a variable among different culture groups. We may therefore

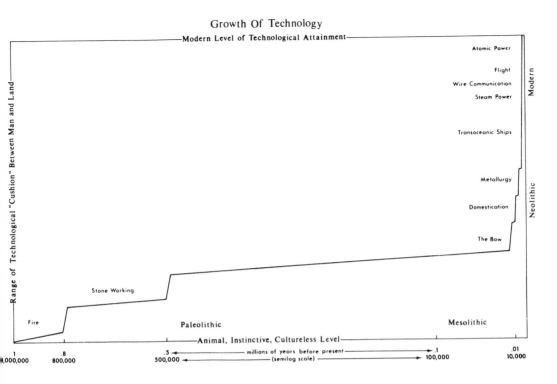

Growth Of Technology

4.1

Growth of technology.

state that the second factor, culture, is a variable in both time and space.

The third factor in determining the occupance pattern is nature. Nature must provide the raw materials with which culture works: space, location, resources, climate, relief. The simpler the culture the greater the proportion of needs that must be satisfied locally. Nature is a limiting factor in some instances; in others it supplies extraordinary opportunities. In no instance does it dictate human activity; nature has no plan for man. Decisions respecting nature are made by man acting through his culture.

The investigation of man-land or culture-land relations is a unique responsibility of geography. The very fact of inequality of population distribution over the earth is proof of the variable quality of nature as the home of man. In the main course of world cultural development, nature has been a necessary and constant component. Specific cultures have found a variable nature cause for adaptation and invention. Witness, for example, the development of proper clothing for Arctic living, an invention that had to be made before and in order that man might live under rigorous climatic conditions. Identical cultures occupying non-restrictive natural areas create similar occupance landscapes, as illustrated by British settlement in New Zealand and New England settlement in Ohio.

In any given instance the geographer must look at nature through the eyes of the cultural group he is studying, habitat measured by habit.[3] The group evaluation of the land, if expressed, would be couched in terms of technological ability and values. The student, for instance, must know the tools available for cultivation, must be cognizant of the soils and the rainfall regime, and must understand that there exists a preference for Irish over sweet potatoes.

Quite clearly, normal natural processes act much more slowly than do cultural processes, so much so that we may say that, for our purposes, nature is a constant in time. Just as clearly, nature is a variable in space. No place, no region is exactly like any other, if only in location. Practically, it should be pointed out that nature has been so widely and so greatly altered by man as to be actually a variable in time as well as in space.

Another relation between man and the land is territoriality, likely more biologically than culturally conditioned. Territoriality covers the attachment that man feels for his particular section of the earth and the vigorous defense of it that he makes against aggressors. The concept is important geographically because it supports the idea that man is not a free wanderer and that he will struggle to work out adaptations even where natural conditions are not especially favorable.

The cultural geographer is at least initially more concerned with the spatial expression of cultures than with the internal workings of the culture itself. As part of his geographical mode of organization he attempts to set up a comparative system of culture areas, these based on comparative occupance patterns. To the geographer, the culture area is the geographic expression of cultural processes and not the cultural expression of a geographic process.[4] The culture area is the expression of a culture type in a specific section of the earth's surface. The geographer's culture area as the cultural-economic expression of man-land relations is not precisely the culturologist's culture area.

Simpler cultures are as important as more complex ones for understanding culture processes as they act on the land. Simple and complex cultures differ in magnitude rather than in kind. Furthermore, simple cultures are easier to deal with and far more expressive of direct man-land relations. Likewise, the past is as valuable for the geographer's purposes as is the present. However, the necessity for reconstruction from fragmentary documentary and field evidence makes the study of the past obviously more difficult than the study of the observable and well-documented present. Fortunately, there are other benefits from studying the past. Since we can hardly conduct controlled experiments in occupance of the land, what has happened in the past is evidence as to the processes involved. Also, it is important to the understanding of the present to know past occupance sequences.[5] The cultural identity of the initial occupance of any area is largely a historical accident, an accident as to what culture got there first. It is nevertheless important in identifying characteristics that are rarely completely obliterated by subsequent cultural changes. Persistence of initial traits is especially marked in such matters as field and road patterns.

To summarize, the ultimate objective of cultural geography is to understand the processes leading to the development and evolution of the cultural landscape. Animal man, culture, and nature are recognized as the factors determining man's imprint on the land. The concept of occupance pattern provides the guidelines for research procedures. The study is historical, generic, and genetic. The recognition of the nature of initial occupance is possible where the historical depth is not too great. Initial occupance is important because it sets up characteristics, some of which fade very slowly or not at all. Initial occupance is the base from which change may be measured.

Research Procedures

The very first task faced by the research geographer, one on which he can easily expend his whole career, is what might be called cultural taxonomy. What are the types into which are grouped those things we propose to deal with? Clearly, little can be done without an initial classi-fication. Unfortunately, lack of taxonomic knowledge is not always a deterrent to investigation beyond this first task. The results might be compared with those of a biological ecologist, were he to proceed before identifying the plants and animals with which he deals.

Most of the observational items of concern to the geographer are of interest to other fields. Therefore, cultural taxonomy should be shared among geographers, folklorists, anthropologists, and, sometimes, others. Their identifications should match and be useful to all. A divi-sion of labor would lighten the burden on any one group. Even so, there are traits or qualities of little interest to other than geographers, for example, field and road patterns. More especially, however, the use made of certain data is distinctive to each field. The geographer's data must be in the form of place facts or distributions, often not provided by other disciplines. So, after a common task, taxonomy, the several dis-ciplines go their separate ways.

The cultural geographer selects for special study those traits that constitute the occupance pattern. He first divides them into the broad categories provided by the functional constituents of the pattern: shel-ter, roads, fences, field form, and the like. The individual forms in a given category may vary widely, but they are analogous since they per-form the same function. For example, a smokehouse is functionally a smokehouse, whether it is a barrel or a two-story brick building.

The geographer's observations extend from fixed and comparatively permanent landscape forms to quite transient traits: How is hay stored? How far apart are the corn rows and how deep the headlands? How is grain harvested? The first three traits can be readily justified as worthy of note because they constitute parts of the occupance complex, at least periodically. But what of the mode of harvesting, a technique rather than a form? To repeat, it and similar observations of techniques are justified as they provide a measure of man's group competence and attitude with respect to living on and from the land. Without an intimate understanding of this culture-land relationship, an ultimate aim of geography to discover the processes governing man's alteration of the earth cannot be served.

But not all the data that the geographer would like to have can be observed in the field. Especially is this true in attempting to reconstruct past landscapes, say initial occupance, where much has been lost. It is then necessary to resort to such sources as travelers' accounts, folk art that preceded the age of photography, county histories of the nineteenth century, and even archaeologic excavations.

The task of establishing a typology should not vary greatly from discipline to discipline. It normally begins with the recognition of like forms. Here the student must be able to recognize the essence of the form, devoid of all extraneous additions or ornamental flourishes. In nature an elephant never has a lion's tail; this is not necessarily true of cultural elephants. The injunction is particularly applicable to folk architecture, where appendages, porches, and other extrinsic features tend to obscure the basic structure (4.2). Geography's special contribu-

A

B

C

D

4.2

Variants of basic central-passage dogtrot
house: *A*. Two-pen, end chimneys, log
dogtrot house in New Salem Park, Illinois.
B. Sided log "I" in Arkansas. Change in the
mode of corner timbering about halfway up
suggests that the house was built in two
stages. The earlier structure was likely a
plain dogtrot house. *C*. Sided log dogtrot, in
Black Belt, Alabama, lacks the second story
of the true "I" house. *D*. Bluffland Houses,
near Baton Rouge, Louisiana, in a dogtrot
format. (Photographs *A*, *B*, and *C* from Fred
Kniffen, "Folk Housing: Key to Diffusion,"
reproduced by permission from the *Annals
of the Association of American Geographers*
58 [1965]: 562, 557, 574.)

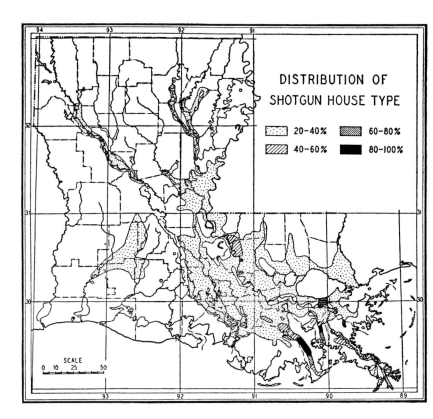

DISTRIBUTION OF SHOTGUN HOUSE TYPE

tion to typological resolution is application of the so-called geographic method, the plotting of areal distributions of supposed types. For example, if assumed type A shows a compact and continuous distribution, this is good evidence of its validity (4.3).

In the difficult task of preliminary classification, a great difference in competence exists between the experienced and the inexperienced observer. Much of the expertise of the former is hard to explain to the novice. It rests on long application and a developed ability to pick out diagnostic traits. The experienced observer can study a culture with which he is unfamiliar and very quickly establish typologically diagnostic qualities and identities.

However successful the student may be in establishing preliminary generic types, the proof of their validity must rest on evidence of genetic relationship. This is a difficult matter of seeking historic connections, of such evidence as persistent unit sizes and proportions over long periods of time. Again, the geographic method can aid by plotting temporal-areal distributions, thus establishing the course of diffusion from a possible point of origin (4.4).

One might well suggest, why not simply ask the folk themselves to distinguish types? Rarely does this work, for even where answers are readily given, they may prove to be invalid rationalizations. It may take a long time and much indirection to discover just what constitutes a type in the folk mind. Consider the case of the "I" house. It is abundantly and continuously represented from the old middle colonies throughout

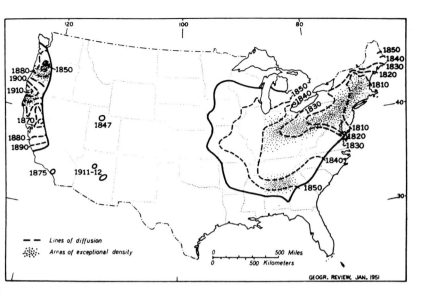

the Upland South and adjacent borders. It exhibits a number of variations in interior plan (4.5), position of chimneys, porches, wings, and
construction material. But there are several qualities invariably present
that define the type: two stories, one room deep, and two or more rooms
long. The variables at most distinguish subtypes.

Assume that the geographer has now completed the systematic coverage of his area of operations. The next step involves combining types
into complexes. The complexes are combinations of elements of the
occupance pattern, farmsteads, villages, and so on in order of increasing
magnitude. Each complex is identified by its types of housing, forms of
production (such as fields and fences), means and patterns of communication, and the like.

At a still higher order of magnitude, characteristic combinations of

4·3

Compact distribution of shotgun house in
Louisiana. (From Fred Kniffen, "Louisiana
House Types"; reproduced by permission
from the *Annals of the Association of
American Geographers* 26 [1936]: 191.)

4·4

Origin and diffusion of covered bridge.
(From Fred Kniffen, "The American
Covered Bridge"; reproduced by permission
from the *Geographical Review* 41 [1951]:
119, copyrighted by the American
Geographical Society of New York.)

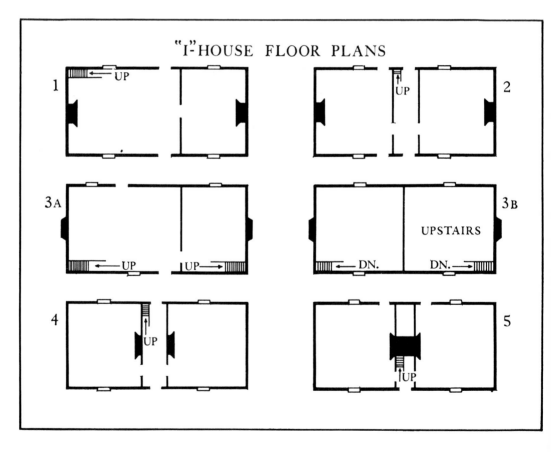

4·5

"I" house with interior plans. (From
Kniffen, "Folk Housing," p. 556.)

complexes constitute culture types. Here is the complete geographical representation of culture—a functioning whole consisting of integral, mutually dependent parts and occupying a given segment of the earth. But there is something inert about the culture type. It is an idealized combination of systematically arrived at traits and complexes grouped in a series of stereotype models. Even though the observer can scarcely be unaware of them, the unique and rare have little or no place in the assemblage. Nor is the culture type specifically and intimately matched against the natural qualities of the area in which it is situated. Nor is there meaningful concern with temporal differences of constituent elements. There is one more step in harvesting to the fullest the fruits of geographical research.

This final step is the consideration of the culture area, or what the geographer commonly refers to as the region. Now the interest is in the intimate and specific relationships between culture and nature. With the generalized culture type fully in mind—here the departures from type—the unique, the culturally pathologic, are considered as possibly revealing of culture processes. A subtle departure from type may portend change and the development of a new type. Culture trends are established by balancing fading relics against innovations (4.6). Rela-

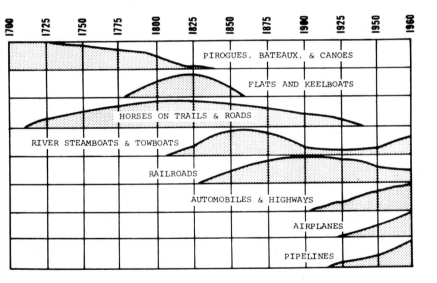

4.6

Transportation succession, Lower Mississippi Valley. (From Fred B. Kniffen, *Louisiana: Its Land and People* [Baton Rouge: Louisiana State University Press, 1968], p. 146; courtesy Louisiana State University Press.)

tions between culture and nature, so important to geographers, are of more than passing interest to folklorists when they effect cultural adaptations creative of new folkways.

Quantification as a research technique is strongly in vogue among modern American geographers. Of course it should be employed where advantageous, but its potential application should be no criterion for the acceptance or rejection of a particular research problem. Space relations lend themselves particularly well to quantitative treatment, and systematic studies almost as well. But, equally important, historical and regional research, with all its vagaries and incomplete data, offers limited opportunity for the application of quantitative methods.

The Results

Now, finally, when geographic research is completed, from systematic taxonomy through culture area or region, what are the tangible results? Aside from useful compilations of information, there should be contributions to the understanding of culture processes as they relate to man's occupance of the earth. There should be revelations regarding the significance of location and space and, perhaps, their changing values to keep pace with a revolutionary technology of transportation. There should be new understanding of special geographical processes, such as cultural diffusion and environmental adaptation. The geographer should detect in terms of his own phenomena—the details of the regional occupance pattern—evidence portending change, stability, or even retrogression. On the basis of the evidence he may venture prediction, the ultimate proof of the efficacy of his method.

With the restraint promised in the introduction, it is left to the student of folklife to evaluate for his own ends the geographic methodology and techniques outlined above. Perhaps the examples cited in the concluding section may suggest specific applications.

Geographic Studies of Folklife

As should be expected, a very small percentage of geographic studies deals exclusively with folklife. Those that do are largely systematic in nature, that is, the geographical treatment of a single, usually material, aspect of folklife. A few are regional, such as instances in which the area studied is occupied by a folk-level culture.

Systematic studies cover a great variety of subjects, but in common they employ the geographic method, at least to the extent of mapping distributions. Outstanding among them is Erhard Rostlund's monograph, *Freshwater Fish and Fishing in Native North America*,[6] in which are shown distributions of fishing techniques, species and abundance of fish, and utilization. From comparative distributions inferences are drawn regarding origins and diffusions.

Other examples of systematic studies include several by Mather and Hart, on fences and tobacco barns, and by the former on the Finnish sauna in the Lake States.[7] A wealth of material exists in theses and dissertations available on microfilm: for example, Knipmeyer on Louisiana boat types, Johnson on presteamboat navigation on the Mississippi, and Wright on log culture in Louisiana.[8]

Place names lend themselves readily to geographic treatment. Two excellent examples are Zelinsky's "Some Problems in the Distribution of Generic Terms in the Place-Names of the Northeastern United States" and his "Classical Town Names in the United States."[9] Another geographer, Meredith Burrill, is the discipline's most systematic student of place-name generics.[10] Place-name studies inherently carry implications of origin and diffusion.

Among the relatively few American regional geographical studies dealing exclusively with a folk-level people is Ekblaw's "The Material Response of the Polar Eskimo to Their Far Arctic Environment."[11] Here, with the restricted and isolated location of the Polar Eskimo, the horizontal geographic measure of areal extent is hardly a pertinent matter. Instead, another geographic measure that might in contrast be considered a vertical relationship, the adaptation of culture to environment, is the thesis of this study.

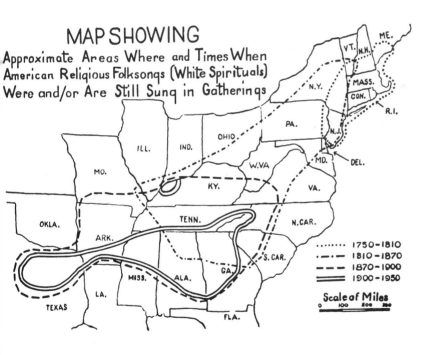

4·7

Diffusion of religious folksongs. (From George Pullen Jackson, "Some Factors in the Diffusion of American Religious Folksongs," *Journal of American Folklore* 65 [1952]: 367; courtesy American Folklore Society.)

Another regional-type study dealing with a folk culture is Homer Aschmann's monograph, given in large part to the ecology of the Central Desert Indians of Baja California.[12] By balancing documentary cultural evidence against observed natural conditions, he reconstructs the man-land ecological relations as they must have been. To be grouped with Aschmann's study is Robert West's *The Pacific Lowlands of Colombia*.[13] A thorough treatment of natural conditions is matched by an equally detailed account of the material culture of the several ethnic groups occupying the area.

The geographic method of plotting areal distributions has been effectively employed by many nongeographer students of folklife. Well-known examples are Hans Kurath's *Word Geography of the Eastern United States* and Driver and Massey's "Comparative Studies of North American Indians."[14] Unfortunately little known is George Pullen Jackson's "Some Factors in the Diffusion of American Religious Folksongs."[15] Jackson's map (4.7) employs isochrones to mark the time-place diffusion of the songs from New England to the Upland South and their progressive extinction in the older areas.

Utilization of the data and method of geographical observation to answer specific questions regarding the processes involved in man-land relations is exemplified in a number of studies. Wilbur Zelinsky's "Where the South Begins: The Northern Limit of the Cis-Appalachian South in Terms of Settlement Landscape" is an attempt to set off a cultural boundary by means of observed data.[16] Against a carefully derived delimitation of culture areas in terms of settlement landscapes, the boundary of the Cis-Appalachian South is matched against Kurath's lexical regions, Negro population, Democratic vote, and the mule-horse ratio. The last of these, with a preference for mules as draft animals in the Southern settlement region, shows the closest correlation.

Kniffen and Wright's "Disaster and Reconstruction in Cameron Parish" examines the hurricane-prone coast of southwestern Louisiana to seek the motivations governing the selection of house architecture to replace destroyed homes.[17] It was found that throughout discernible history the type currently popular on the populous upland, little subject to storm damage, has been invariably selected, regardless of its suitability to withstand hurricanes. Literally, the coast dwellers would rather be dead than out of style.

Dominance of contemporary fashion is further demonstrated by the historical succession of house types diffused westward from New England (4.8).[18] What was currently the popular type in New England was carried westward by the contemporary migrants. The younger types were numerically the more dominant with greater distance from New England and the older types correspondingly less represented.

Progressive adaptation to spatial change in natural conditions has been demonstrated by means of geographic data and method. An example is provided by change in function of the same basic barn type diffused southward from Pennsylvania.[19] To match moderating winters, longer summers, and increasing humidity, the barn is progressively less used for animal shelter and correspondingly more for crop storage, with changes in size and form to match change in function.

It is possible to demonstrate by means of a time-place consideration of

MICHIGAN 1830	OHIO 1810	UPSTATE NEW YORK 1790	PERIPHERAL NEW ENGLAND 1770	NUCLEAR NEW ENGLAND
				1850
				1800
				1750
				1700

4.8

Diffusion of house types from nuclear New England. (From Kniffen, "Folk Housing," p. 559.)

geographic data that innate cultural conservatism yields to change, not gradually, but abruptly through unusual events or circumstances (4.9).

These are but few of many possible illustrations of geographic treatment of folk subjects. The sharply awakening interest of geographers in the material aspects of folk cultures will hopefully produce greater understanding of fundamental cultural processes involved in man-land relations. May these findings not be of primary interest to others than geographers?

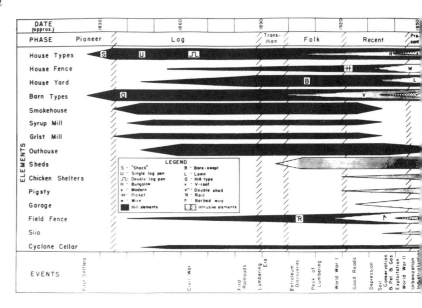

4·9

Evolution of log culture in hill Louisiana. (From Martin Wright, "Log Culture in Hill Louisiana," Ph.D. dissertation, Louisiana State University, 1956, p. 156; courtesy School of Geoscience.)

NOTES

Note: The somewhat parochial limitation implied by the title of this article is adopted because of Ronald H. Buchanan's more general "Geography and Folk Life," which appeared in *Folk Life* 1 (1963): 5–15. Since Dr. Buchanan most ably presents the European point of view and Old World data, it seemed proper here to emphasize American developments.

1.   Sigurd Erixon, *Folkliv* 1 (1937): 10.

2.   So suggested in a review of Wagner and Mikesell's *Readings in Cultural Geography*, in *Science*, May 11, 1962, p. 511.

3.   Expression used by Carl O. Sauer in "Foreword to Historical Geography," *Annals of the Association of American Geographers* 31 (1941): 15.

4.   So stated by John Leighly in "Some Comments on Contemporary Geographic Method," *Annals of the Association of American Geographers* 27 (1937): 136.

5.   Fred Kniffen, "Geography and the Past," *Journal of Geography* 50 (1951): 126–129.

6.   Erhard Rostlund, *Freshwater Fish and Fishing in Native North America*.

7.   Eugene C. Mather and John F. Hart, "Fences and Farms," *The Geographical Review* 44 (1954): 201–223; John F. Hart and Eugene C. Mather, "The Character of Tobacco Barns and Their Role in the Tobacco Economy of the United States," *Annals of the Association of American Geographers* 51 (1961): 274–293; Eugene C. Mather and Matti Kaups, "The Finnish Sauna: A Cultural Index to Settlement," *Annals of the Association of American Geographers* 53 (1963): 494–504.

8.   W. B. Knipmeyer, "Settlement Succession in Eastern French Louisiana," Ph.D. dissertation; John A. Johnson, "Pre-Steamboat Navigation on the Lower Mississippi," Ph.D. dissertation; Martin Wright, "Log Culture in Hill Louisiana," Ph.D. dissertation.

9.   Wilbur Zelinsky, "Some Problems in the Distribution of Generic Terms in the Place-Names of the Northeastern United States," *Annals of the Association of American Geographers* 45 (1955): 319–349; idem, "Classical Town Names in the United States: The Historical Geography of an American Idea," *Geographical Review* 57 (1967): 463–495.

10. Meredith F. Burrill, "Toponymic Generics," *Names* 4 (1956): 129–137, 226–240.

11. W. Elmer Ekblaw, "The Material Response of the Polar Eskimo to Their Far Arctic Environment," *Annals of the Association of American Geographers* 17 (1927): 147–198; 18 (1928): 1–24.

12. Homer Aschmann, "The Central Desert of Baja California: Demography and Ecology," *Ibero-Americana* 42 (1959).

13. Robert West, *The Pacific Lowlands of Colombia*.

14. Hans Kurath, *Word Geography of the Eastern United States*; Harold E. Driver and W. C. Massey, "Comparative Studies of North American Indians," *Transactions of the American Philosophical Society* 47, part 2 (1957): 165–456.

15. George Pullen Jackson, "Some Factors in the Diffusion of American Religious Folksongs," *Journal of American Folklore* 65 (1952): 365–369.

16. Wilbur Zelinsky, "Where the South Begins: The Northern Limit of the Cis-Appalachian South in Terms of Settlement Landscape," *Social Forces* 30 (1951): 172–178.

17. Fred Kniffen and Martin Wright, "Disaster and Reconstruction in Cameron Parish," *Louisiana Studies* 2 (1963): 74–83.

18. Fred Kniffen, "Folk Housing: Key to Diffusion," *Annals of the Association of American Geographers* 58 (1965): 549–577.

19. Ibid., p. 23.

BIBLIOGRAPHY

Aschmann, Homer. "The Central Desert of Baja California: Demography and Ecology." *Ibero-Americana* 42 (1959).

Buchanan, Ronald H. "Geography and Folk Life." *Folk Life* 1 (1963): 5–15.

Burrill, Meredith F. "Toponymic Generics." *Names* 4 (1956): 129–137, 226–240.

Driver, Harold E., and W. C. Massey. "Comparative Studies of North American Indians." *Transactions of the American Philosophical Society* 47, part 2 (1957): 165–456.

Ekblaw, W. Elmer. "The Material Response of the Polar Eskimo to Their Far Arctic Environment." *Annals of the Association of American Geographers* 17 (1927): 147–198; 18 (1928): 1–24.

Erixon, Sigurd. Introduction. *Folkliv* 1 (1937): 5–12.

Hart, John F., and Eugene C. Mather. "The Character of Tobacco Barns and Their Role in the Tobacco Economy of the United States." *Annals of the Association of American Geographers* 51 (1961): 274–293.

Jackson, George Pullen. "Some Factors in the Diffusion of American Religious Folksongs." *Journal of American Folklore* 65 (1952): 365–369.

Johnson, John A. "Pre-Steamboat Navigation on the Lower Mississippi." Ph.D. Dissertation, Louisiana State University, 1963.

Kniffen, Fred. "Folk Housing: Key to Diffusion." *Annals of the Association of American Geographers* 58 (1965): 549–577.

————. "Geography and the Past." *Journal of Geography* 50 (1951): 126–129.

————, and Martin Wright. "Disaster and Reconstruction in Cameron Parish." *Louisiana Studies* 2 (1963): 74–83.

Knipmeyer, W. B. "Settlement Succession in Eastern French Louisiana." Ph.D. Dissertation, Louisiana State University, 1956.

Kurath, Hans. *Word Geography of the Eastern United States*. Ann Arbor: University of Michigan Press, 1949.

Leighly, John. "Some Comments on Contemporary Geographic Method." *Annals of the Association of American Geographers* 27 (1937): 125–141.

Mather, Eugene C., and John F. Hart. "Fences and Farms." *The Geographical Review* 44 (1954): 201–223.

Mather, Eugene C., and Matti Kaups. "The Finnish Sauna: A Cultural Index to Settlement." *Annals of the Association of American Geographers* 53 (1963): 494–504.

Rostlund, Erhard. *Freshwater Fish and Fishing in Native North America*. Berkeley: University of California Press, 1952.

Sauer, Carl O. "Foreword to Historical Geography." *Annals of the Association of American Geographers* 31 (1941): 1–24.

Trindell, Roger T. "American Folklore Studies and Geography." *Southern Folklore Quarterly* 34 (1970): 1–11.

Wagner, Philip L., and Marvin W. Mikesell, eds. *Readings in Cultural Geography*. Chicago: University of Chicago Press, 1962.

West, Robert. *The Pacific Lowlands of Colombia*. Louisiana State University Studies, Social Science Series, no. 8. Baton Rouge: Louisiana State University Press, 1957.

Wright, Martin. "Log Culture in Hill Louisiana." Ph.D. Dissertation, Louisiana State University, 1956.

Zelinsky, Wilbur. "Classical Town Names in the United States: The Historical Geography of an American Idea." *Geographical Review* 57 (1967): 463–495.

——. "Some Problems in the Distribution of Generic Terms in the Place-Names of the Northeastern United States." *Annals of the Association of American Geographers* 45 (1955): 319–349.

——. "Where the South Begins: The Northern Limit of the Cis-Appalachian South in Terms of Settlement Landscape." *Social Forces* 30 (1951): 172–178.

5. Film Documentation of Folklife

Leslie P. Greenhill

Many aspects of folklife in the United States are undergoing rapid change, while others are disappearing from the culture or have already disappeared. This unfortunate fact applies to customs, folk dances and songs, and religious rituals as well as many aspects of the material culture, for example early ways of making pottery or basketware, methods of preparing foods, or ways of farming. It seems to be true that most serious students of ethnology are more interested in the cultures of other countries than those of their own; and changes in their own country's culture frequently go unnoticed and unnoted until it is too late to record them accurately. Fortunately, there seems to be a rising interest in the United States among students of folklife in the study of our own changing culture. This interest is being manifested in efforts to preserve old customs, in programs to educate the public and students about our national folklife heritage and in scientific studies of folklife.

The Roles of Film in Folklife Studies

Films for Popularization of Folklife

The film can play several important roles in the field of folklife. First, it can do much to inform the public about various aspects of our cultural heritage and to help develop an appreciation of it. This can be accomplished through films designed for general showing, for use in schools, or for release over commercial or educational television stations. To be of genuine value such films should give accurate, authentic portrayals that are not exaggerated or overly dramatic. In many instances such films may portray ways of life from earlier periods, using authentic settings, costumes, and objects from the period but involving actors or recently trained persons instead of the individuals who actually practiced the old customs or skills.

There are a number of good films of this type, such as those on colonial Williamsburg and the National Educational Television series "Lyrics and Legends" and "The Glory Trail." The first of these series deals mainly with folk music and related aspects of our culture; the latter with the opening up of the West. The need is great for more films of this type.

The Scientific Documentation Film

There is also a growing need for the scientific documentation of changing aspects of our culture. In the United States this documentation has most commonly been in written form, sometimes supplemented with drawings or photographs. While this method of documentation is satisfactory for some aspects of folklife, those aspects that involve movement, or sound, or manufacturing processes call for the use of motion pictures as a medium for documentation.

Unfortunately, little use has been made of film for the scientific documentation of folklife in the United States, and those films that have been prepared are sometimes not very satisfactory. There are several ways in which such films are produced. A folklorist, in conducting research on some aspect of folklife, may attempt to produce his own film documentation, with results that are scientifically accurate but more often than not technically poor. On the other hand, there are competent cinematographers with an amateur interest in folklife who have produced technically excellent films, which are not quite scientifically accurate or which overemphasize some "quaint" or "interesting" aspect of a subject. There are of course notable exceptions in which excellent scientific film recordings have been produced by a professional folklorist who is also a highly competent cinematographer, and vice versa.

In the United States few serious efforts have been made to document folklife research on film by combining the scientific approach of the folklorist with the technical skill of a competent cinematographer in order to produce film documents that are both scientifically accurate and technically adequate. Furthermore, granting agencies that support such research have apparently not realized the value of scientific film documentation. Consequently, it has not been easy to obtain the necessary financial support to include such films as an integral part of a research project or as basic materials for use in college courses. Notable exceptions to this general practice include the support given by the National Science Foundation to the University of California at Berkeley to produce a series of film documents on the American Indian and to the Education Development Center of Newton, Massachusetts, to produce a series of films on the Netsilik Eskimos of northern Canada. Both of these projects combined the efforts of social anthropologists with those of cinematographers who had competence in scientific film documentation.

Characteristics of Scientific Film Documents of Folklife

We have much to learn from our European colleagues, especially those in Germany, Austria, Scandinavia, Switzerland, France, and the Netherlands, where the documentation of various aspects of folklife on film has a long tradition and has become highly developed.

Such film documents are invaluable as a means of preserving records of changing culture, especially those aspects that are rapidly disappearing and that cannot be adequately documented in written form or with still pictures. They are useful for cross-cultural research and for teaching purposes, especially at the university level. Sections of such film documents may also be included in films designed for more popular use or in television programs, both educational and commercial.

Accuracy and Authenticity

Authenticity and accuracy are unquestionably the prime requirements in the film documentation of folklife. It is essential that the customs, rituals, or processes being filmed should be performed by the individuals who actually do them. They should not be reconstructions performed by actors. However, even under these circumstances, such individuals will often want to make a good impression and will wear their "Sunday best" clothes instead of their usual working clothes. They may also introduce variations into the procedure that they think will make it more interesting for the photographer. Indeed, the photographer may even encourage such variations if he thinks they will make for a more "interesting" film.

It is for these reasons that such films should be made under the direct supervision of a folklorist who is expert in the particular subject being filmed and who can take steps to ensure that an accurate, authentic record is obtained.

Naturalness

Naturalness is another essential requirement for scientific film documents of folklife. This is best achieved when the folklorist develops a close rapport with the individuals who are being filmed, puts them at ease, and assists them in giving an accurate, unself-conscious portrayal of the activity to be documented.

The cinematographer can play an important part here by using a minimum of camera equipment and simple lighting and by doing everything he can to ensure that the subjects behave as naturally as possible.

Limited Scope

The tradition with film production in the United States is to make one film on a subject that gives a rather general, interesting, though often somewhat superficial treatment. For example, a film on the Indians of the Southwest might show their physical environment, their methods of agriculture, living conditions, games or ceremonial dances, and so forth. While such films may be useful for giving the public a general impression of such a group, no single aspect of the subject is treated with sufficient detail that it could stand on its own as a scientific film document.

To be maximally useful each film document should give a thorough and complete treatment of a single cohesive topic or aspect of behavior. This could be a single ceremonial dance, a religious ritual, the making of pottery, the preparation of a particular kind of food, a method of agriculture, and so forth. These units, or "single-concept" films, can be put together to give a complete picture of the activities of a specific group of people; or the single units can be compared with similar film units showing the same type of behavior in a different group of people.

Completeness

Related to the scope of a film is its completeness. A given film unit

5.1

Harvest custom, southern Germany. (Film
E 976 T; courtesy IWF.)

5.2

Shrovetide, southern Germany. (Film E
1168; courtesy IWF.) [*On following pages*]

5·3

Folk dance, Rumania. (Film E 1667;
courtesy IWF.)

5.4

Folk dance, Rumania. (Film E 1668;
courtesy IWF.)

should include all the essential elements of a specific activity. For some kinds of activity, such as a traditional dance or a folk song, this may necessitate complete and continuous coverage of the entire event. For other activities, such as the making of a material object, it will be necessary to record only the crucial elements. However, in both instances, it will be essential to obtain general orientation views as well as adequate close-ups. Also, if rapid movement is involved, it may be highly desirable to include some slow-motion scenes. Most human movements can be slowed down adequately by filming them at sixty-four pictures per second.

When a selection of crucial elements is to be the basis of a film document, it is essential that a folklorist oversee the filming in order to decide what needs to be covered and to avoid omission of any important aspects of the subject.

Authentic Sound

Typical expository films have sound tracks with a commentary, sometimes with musical background. The commentary will give the author's views and opinions about the subject. The music is selected and included because it is thought to lend "atmosphere" to the film or because such films generally have music, even if it is completely nonfunctional.

The scientific film document will include sound only if it is an important integral aspect of the subject, and, if it is, it will be recorded in exact synchronism with the picture. Accordingly, a film recording of a traditional dance or folk song should obviously have synchronized sound along with the picture. The same is true for other activities in which the speech of the individuals or other natural sounds are important elements of the subject.

Scientific film documents will not ordinarily have a commentary recorded for them, except when they are released in a form suitable for classroom use by individuals who are not completely conversant with the subject or where they are part of a program for the general public.

Color or Black-and-White Film?

The requirement of accuracy may appear to dictate the use of color film, and certainly in many cases this is desirable. However, unless color is a crucial aspect of the subject matter, it is more economical to use black-and-white film; prints are less costly, and there are fewer technical problems, especially if much interior filming is involved. If color film is used, considerable care needs to be taken with interior lighting if the color is to be an accurate representation of the original subject. Many aspects of folklife involve colorful costumes or the mak-

5·5

Flute carver, Rumania. (Film E 1748; courtesy IWF.)

5.6

Potter's workshop, southern Germany.
(Film in preparation; courtesy IWF.)

ing and decoration of articles in which color is important, and in these instances the use of color film is highly desirable.

Accompanying Written Documentation

In the recording of folklife, film and written documentation complement one another. Written documentation can provide background information and other details that cannot or need not be included in the film.

Thus, it is highly desirable that a written document be prepared to accompany the film document. This written text might have the format of a typical article for a professional journal. It could include details of location and dates of filming, names of subjects, background of the types of behavior documented, significance of the behavior, and references to other studies of the same subject, either in the literature or on film. Such written documents are extremely useful if the film is to be used for teaching or if parts are to be included in a popular version for general showing.

High Technical Quality

While scientific accuracy and validity must of necessity come first in the production of film documents of folklife, good film quality is also an essential requirement.

Far too common are films that have out-of-focus scenes, wide variations in exposure, inadequate close-ups, unsteadiness because of failure to use a tripod, short jumpy sequences, scratches, or partially light-fogged edges. If the film is to be fully suitable for distribution to and use by other scientists, it should avoid these shortcomings. In addition, it should have the intent of accurate, thorough documentation of natural behavior, not the intent of being "a show."

It is therefore urged that a team approach be made to the filmed documentation of folklife. The essential members of the team are a folklorist who is competent in the subject area to be filmed and a cinematographer who is technically competent and who has an interest in scientific film documentation.

The Production of Film Documents of Folklife

Since the primary objective is to obtain an accurate, authentic portrayal of specific aspects of folklife, it is essential that the camera work, lighting, and sound recording, if needed, be as unobtrusive as possible so as not to change the behavior of those whose activities are being documented. Furthermore, as was mentioned in the previous section, the

5·7

Decorating pottery, southern Germany.
(Film in preparation; courtesy IWF.)

5.8

Potter's workshop, Rumania. (Film in
preparation; courtesy IWF.)

portrayal should be as natural as possible, not dressed up or with undue emphasis on those aspects of the behavior that are quaint or picturesque. With these thoughts in mind, some suggestions will be made on several technical aspects of production.

Camera Crew

The camera crew might consist of one person, a competent cinematographer, with experience in and an orientation toward accurate documentation of human behavior and an ability to work with people who are apt to be self-conscious. When the filming is to be done out of doors or when little if any artificial lighting is needed, a folklorist and a cinematographer can make an effective team.

However, if lighting equipment is necessary or if two cameras are required, two cinematographers will probably be needed, and, if sound is to be recorded, someone experienced in the recording of sound on location will also be needed. Thus, the filming crew could consist of three people in addition to the folklorist. This number should be the absolute maximum, and, if possible, fewer people should be involved so as not to overwhelm those being filmed or to give the impression that the film is to be a show. Under some circumstances, the folklorist may be his own cinematographer if he has the necessary competence.

Camera Equipment

The camera equipment should be of high quality, light in weight and compact so as not to be too conspicuous, and with the ability to take good close-up views in sharp focus. These requirements suggest the need for a camera that has through-the-lens focusing and viewing. Furthermore, if relatively long film runs are needed, as in filming many human activities, a camera driven by an electric motor rather than a spring motor will be required. Under some circumstances 100-ft. film capacity of 16-mm film (2¾ minutes) will be sufficient, but 400-ft. film capacity (11 minutes) is highly desirable.

If synchronous sound recording will be involved, the camera should be driven by a synchronous electric motor and should be capable of operating synchronously with an appropriate sound recorder. In addition, the camera should be very quiet in operation so that its operating noise will not be picked up by the sound recorder, or it should be capable of operation in a light-weight "blimp" (a soundproof casing) or with a "barney" (a sound-absorbent cover).

Since a variety of shots will be needed, including good close-ups, several high-quality lenses will be required. For a 16-mm camera these would normally include a 15-mm wide-angle lens, a 25-mm normal lens, and a 75-mm long-focus lens. For the 25-mm lens a maximum

5.9

Basketweaving, southern Germany. (Film E 1163; courtesy IWF.)

aperture of f 1.4 is desirable for photography at low light levels. For the other two lenses a maximum aperture of f 2.8 is usually adequate. A high-quality zoom lens can be substituted for three separate lenses. Its focal length should be capable of varying between 15 mm and 75 mm or between 20 mm and 100 mm. However, fast "zooms" should be avoided.

The camera selected should be capable of operating at the normal speed of twenty-four frames per second, at which speed most subjects should be filmed even if they do not have synchronous sound. It is also advisable to have slow-motion speeds of thirty-two and sixty-four frames per second so that movements can be slowed down for closer study when necessary.

The 16-mm cameras that are used most widely for scientific ethnographic filming and that have the above characteristics are the Bolex, the Arriflex, and the Eclair. All are capable of producing excellent results. It is desirable to use the camera on a sturdy tripod with pan and tilt head in order to ensure steady pictures. A suitable shoulder mount is an acceptable alternative if carefully used.

Film

It is recommended that, in general, 16-mm film be used for the production of scientific film documents. If 8-mm prints are desired for some special use, they can be reproduced from the 16-mm originals in either regular-8 or super-8 format.

If color film is used in the camera, it should normally be the professional type of reversal film, which is designed to produce high-quality color prints. If only a few copies are needed, they may be printed directly from the edited original. If many prints are needed or if the film is to be used in a variety of ways so that several different versions will be made from the original, one or more color internegatives can be made from the original reversal film and used to produce prints.

The speed of the film should be selected according to the nature of the subject to be photographed. For outdoor filming, or when good light is available indoors, regular-speed color film is appropriate; for interior filming at low light levels, high-speed color film will be necessary.

For many folklife subjects color film will not be essential. For these subjects black-and-white reversal film is recommended for use in the camera. This can be of medium speed for outdoor filming or for well-lit interiors. High-speed black-and-white reversal film will be needed for interior filming with natural light. Some cinematographers prefer, however, to use 16-mm black-and-white negative film because of its wider exposure latitude or if good reversal processing is not available.

"Normal-speed" film ranges from 25 to 80 ASA (e.g., Kodak Ektachrome ECO or Plus X); "high-speed" film ranges from 160 to 400 ASA (e.g., Kodak Ektachrome EF or 4X). While normal-speed film generally yields superior quality images, modern high-speed films are remarkably good and produce acceptable results when properly exposed and processed. A good light meter, properly used, is essential for ensuring correct exposures.

Considerable care should be taken in handling the original film to

5.10

Laying wooden water pipes, south Tyrol.
(Film E 1163; courtesy IWF.)

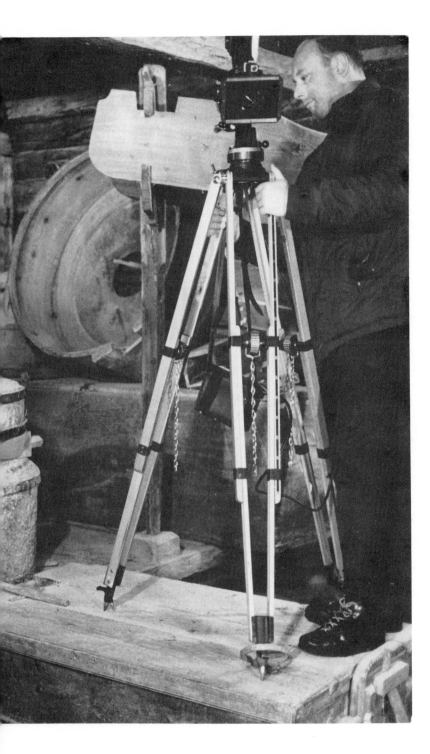

Water-powered mill, south Tyrol. (Film E
1221; courtesy IWF.)

5.12

Halloween customs, central Pennsylvania. (Film E 1647.)

5.13

Halloween customs, central Pennsylvania.
(Film E 1647.)

avoid fogging of the edges by direct sunlight if used out of doors and to avoid scratches. The film channel in the camera must be kept scrupulously clean.

Lighting

Lighting for ethnographic filming should be as simple as possible, consistent with the need to obtain a clear picture of the subject matter. For most outdoor subjects natural lighting can be used, but a white reflector may help if the lighting is excessively contrasty. For most subjects filmed indoors, some artificial lighting will be needed, but this should be kept to a minimum in order not to inhibit the individuals who are being filmed. Also, under some conditions, the heat generated by too many lights may affect the process being recorded on film, as, for example, in the preparation of certain foods. Today's fast films minimize the need for artificial lighting. Also, available power may impose a further restriction.

To light the activities of one or two people working in the average room, four or five portable lighting units of the quartz-iodide type are usually sufficient. One or two of these can be focused directly on the subject, and the remainder can be bounced off the ceiling or walls to give a lighting effect that reinforces the natural light in the room.

Sound Recording

If natural sound is an important part of the subject to be documented, it should be recorded in synchronism with the picture. Good-quality sound recording on location requires considerable skill and experience in placing the microphone or microphones and in adjusting the sound levels. Poor room acoustics may present further problems.

The sound-recording equipment should be portable, of high quality, and capable of operation in synchronism with the camera out in the field. A magnetic tape recorder that is widely used for such work is the Nagra.

Filming

In order to ensure adequate coverage of a subject, it is important that an outline be made by the folklorist and the cinematographer indicating the activities to be filmed, what orientation shots and what close-ups will be needed, and so forth. The subject may be covered from several different viewpoints, and, when there is some doubt as to the adequacy of the coverage, additional footage should be exposed. All film should be exposed at the standard speed of twenty-four frames per second even if there is no immediate plan to use sound with it. The exception will

5.14

Baking flat bread, south Tyrol. (Film E 676; courtesy IWF.)

be for those aspects of the subject for which slow motion is needed. For these, speeds of sixty-four frames per second may be necessary.

Many activities that do not require continuous coverage can be successfully filmed with one camera. Other processes or activities may need to be recorded in their entirety and this will necessitate continuously running cameras. Such a requirement is generally considered essential in the documentation of dances or folk music. To accomplish this will usually require at least two cameras operated alternately, perhaps with a third camera for close-up scenes. Or, if 400-ft. film magazines are available, two cameras may be used simultaneously: one for general scenes, one for close-ups. The editing of three camera films, together with a synchronous sound track, requires a good deal of skill and experience.

Editing

The original camera film should be carefully processed and a "work print" obtained for editing purposes. This work print is usually a direct reversal print from the original reversal camera film. A black-and-white work print is usually satisfactory, even if the original film is in color. This work print and the original film should be edge-numbered by the laboratory to facilitate matching the original film to the edited work print.

The original film should be carefully protected from scratches, excessive heat and humidity, dust, and finger marks. It should never be projected and the film editor should always wear clean cotton gloves when handling the original film.

After the work print has been edited to the satisfaction of the ethnographer, the original film is cut to match it. If the original is a black-and-white reversal film, it is the usual practice to obtain a duplicate negative from this edited original, and projection prints are then made from this negative. The original can be stored in the vault of the processing laboratory or some other appropriate place. As was mentioned previously, direct color prints can be obtained from the color original or through the medium of a color internegative.

It is impossible to overemphasize the need for careful handling of the original film. Many good films have been ruined by careless handling of the original.

If synchronous sound was recorded on magnetic tape, an optical sound track on 16-mm film will be needed. This is edited in synchronism with the picture and is combined with it to produce the final projection prints.

In all of the above technical operations the folklorist and the cinematographer should work closely together in order to obtain the desired result, a high-quality film document that is accurate, authentic, and complete.

5.15

Bake oven, central Pennsylvania.
(Film E 1021; courtesy Pennsylvania State University.)

Funding of Film Documentation of Folklife

Scientific films documenting folklife activities are not likely to have a large market. Therefore the production of them is not likely to be of interest to commercial or educational film producers as a profitable venture, even though such films are not highly expensive to produce in terms of the usual commercial cost standards. Such films, however, are of inestimable value for the future, for both research and teaching, and segments of them may be quite useful for inclusion in more popular versions and for educational television programs. These latter uses, however, are not likely to yield sufficient income to defray the costs of production.

Since the value of the films is largely scientific, their production costs could be included as part of research-project budgets, which are funded by state or federal agencies or by private foundations interested in the accurate documentation of changing aspects of the nation's culture. When funded in this way, the additional cost of film production may constitute a modest addition to the research budget since the basic costs associated with the folklorist's work are already covered in the budget.

Such films may also be funded as important aspects of curriculum-development projects, especially at the college level, and found worthy of support by various agencies that fund these types of projects. Costs may be minimized by working through academic departments of universities, which frequently have access to university film-production services. These film units usually have the necessary equipment and personnel for this specialized type of work.

Distribution of Folklife Films

It is necessary but not sufficient simply to produce accurate film documents of American folklife. Unfortunately, far too much research film footage that has been produced in the past is reposing in a film laboratory vault or, even worse, in the researcher's files, where it is exposed to heat, humidity, dust, and the like. Since most such films have a limited market, they have little appeal to commercial educational film distributors. Special distribution channels are needed that parallel professional journals in their operation and the clientele they reach.

One example of such a means of distribution is the Psychological Cinema Register, a growing collection of films in the behavioral sciences that has been developed over the past twenty-five years at Pennsylvania State University. This is a nonprofit activity that serves those in the behavioral sciences with specialized films that are useful for teaching and research.

A second example is the Encyclopaedia Cinematographica. This is an international collection of scientific film documents made to the standards described in the earlier sections of this article. At the present time the Encyclopaedia Cinematographica comprises some 2,000 films, principally in the biological sciences and ethnology. It includes nearly 200 films on various aspects of European folklife that are excellent models to emulate in the documentation of American folklife. The

Encyclopaedia Cinematographica is a nonprofit organization, founded by Professor Gotthard Wolf, with headquarters at the Institut für den Wissenschaftlichen Film (IWF) in Göttingen, West Germany. It contains 16-mm films contributed by scientists from many countries, and new films are being added at the rate of approximately 150 per year. Each film is expected to be accompanied by a written document.

The American Archive, which loans prints, has been established at Pennsylvania State University with the aid of a grant from the National Science Foundation.

A National Film Center for Folklife Films

One approach to the problems of meeting the urgent need to collect information about films on folklife, to develop a reference film collection, to stimulate the production of such films, and to disseminate information about them would be to establish a national center for folklife films. Such a national agency could also identify needs, locate possible subjects for photography, fund film projects, and perhaps undertake the production of such films itself. It is important in producing these materials that the door be kept open to permit multiple uses of such films, perhaps in different versions, for research, for teaching, for public information, and for television use. This would ensure the widest possible use of the material. Such an organization could make a most important contribution to the preservation of our national heritage and to the dissemination of information about it.

BIBLIOGRAPHY

Baddeley, Walter H. *The Technique of Documentary Film Production*. New York: Hastings House, 1963.

Balikci, Asen, and Quentin Brown. "Ethnographic Filming and the Netsilik Eskimos." *Education Development Center, Quarterly Report* (Newton, Mass.) (Spring–Summer 1966): 19–33.

Collier, John, Jr. *Visual Anthropology: Photography as a Research Method*. Studies in Anthropological Method, edited by George and Louise Spindler. New York: Holt, Rinehart, and Winston, 1967.

Dauer, Alfons M. "Afrikanische Musik und völkerkundlicher Tonfilm: Ein Beitrag zur Methodik der Transkription." *Research Film* (Göttingen) 5, no. 5 (1966): 439–456.

Fuchs, Peter. "Völkerkundliche Tonfilm-Dokumentation." *Research Film* (Göttingen) 5, no. 5 (1966): 457–461.

Greenhill, Leslie P. *Encyclopaedia Cinematographica: English Translation of Film Titles*. University Park: Pennsylvania State University, 1971.

————. "The Encyclopaedia Cinematographica and Folklife Studies." *Pennsylvania Folklife* 19, no. 3 (Spring 1970): 24–26.

————. "A Film on Halloween in Pennsylvania." *Keystone Folklore Quarterly* 14, no. 3 (Fall 1969): 122–123.

————, ed. *The Psychological Cinema Register*. University Park: Pennsylvania State University, 1975.

Heider, Karl G. *Films for Anthropological Teaching*. 5th ed. Washington, D.C.: American Anthropological Association, 1973.

Kennedy, Peter, ed. *Films on Traditional Music and Dance: A First International Catalogue*. Compiled by the International Folk Music Council. Paris: UNESCO, 1970.

Mook, Maurice A. "Bread Baking in Mifflin County, Pennsylvania: Commentary for the Documentary Film in the 'Encyclopaedia Cinematographica.'" *Pennsylvania Folklife* 21, no. 1 (Autumn 1971): 42–45.

Leslie P. Greenhill

Research Film. Göttingen: Institut für den Wissenschaftlichen Film. [Issued twice a year.]

Simon, Franz. "Volkskundliche Filmdokumentation." *Research Film* (Göttingen) 5, no. 6 (1966): 604–611.

Studies in the Anthropology of Visual Communication. Washington, D.C.: Society for the Anthropology of Visual Communication. [Issued three times a year.]

Wieser, Marianne. "Bemerkungen zur filmischen Dokumentation von Volkstanzen." *Research Film* (Göttingen) 6, no. 3 (1968): 250–256.

Wolf, Gotthard, ed. *Encyclopaedia Cinematographica, Index 1974*. Göttingen: Institut für den Wissenschaftlichen Film. [Available from American Archive, Audio Visual Services, Pennsylvania State University, University Park, Pennsylvania.]

———. *Der wissenschaftliche Dokumentationsfilm und die Encyclopaedia Cinematographica*. Munich: Barth, 1967.

6. Folk Boats of Eastern French Louisiana

William B. Knipmeyer

Introduced and edited by Henry Glassie

Introduction

Work boats are ideal artifacts for folkloristic study. They exist within complicated traditional systems devised for dealing with the resources —fish, shellfish, and waterfowl—and hardships—sudden seas and swampy land—presented by the thousands of miles of coastal and inland water in the United States. The systems involving small craft include not only fishing gear and boat-building tools, but also elaborate means of trade (the retention, for example, of unnecessary middlemen), matters of status (the difference between a waterman with a farm and a farmer with a boat, between captain and crew on even a two-man clam-digging boat), and the cultural wisdom essential to success in an occupation where man interacts directly with nature (turn the hatch cover on a skipjack upside down and you might become tangled in the oyster dredge and drown; fail to note the pattern of wind on the water and you might find yourself too far from shore when a storm comes up). The boat, like the rest of the waterman's culture, is at once conservatively retained and readily changed; the situation is precarious, at least economically; what has worked before will work again, perhaps.

Though American folklorists have not as yet rendered attention to boats as folk things, boats, unlike most other material manifestations of American folk culture, have received good historical taxonomic scrutiny of the kind that folklorists normally accord their interests. Studies by scholars like Howard I. Chapelle[1]—and the consciousness of type, terminology, and change on the part of the watermen themselves, a kind of awareness that will be both surprising and refreshing to the fieldworker used to interviewing carriers of the culture of agriculture— will save the folklorist much time in research and classification and allow him to get on, if he will, to more dynamic considerations. Still, in the study of boats as objects in the grand schemes of space and time, there are things that need doing. The boat scholars have limited their studies largely to the era of sail in a way reminiscent of the ballad scholar's rejection of instrumental accompaniment: of the rigged canoe on the Chesapeake, M. V. Brewington writes nostalgically, "Where once the waters of the Bay were alive with hundreds of trim canoes, all busy sailing to and from their work, one now finds only oily, grimy motorboats on the oyster beds."[2]

Oily and grimy, but practical and traditional, boats that can be classed as folk outlasted the days of sail and are still being built regularly in many parts of America. William B. Knipmeyer, a cultural geographer rather than a sailboat enthusiast, told the full story of the folk boats of a single area in the dissertation he submitted for his Ph.D. degree from the Department of Geography and Anthropology at Louisiana State

University in 1956. Like many of the dissertations prepared under the direction of Professor Fred Kniffen, it is an original work of prime importance for students of American folk culture. The dissertation, entitled "Settlement Succession in Eastern French Louisiana," begins with the physical and historical settings for settlement and then examines in detail aspects of the cultural landscape: the form of settlement, the morphology of economic landscapes, and house, outbuilding, fence, and enclosure types. The last chapter before the conclusions is on folk boats. It is in this chapter that his work is most pioneering. Dr. Knipmeyer, now professor of geography at Northwestern State College of Louisiana in Natchitoches, was approached by Professor Kniffen about publishing his chapter on boats. He had no interest in reworking it for publication but gladly gave permission for me to do so.

The text of Chapter 7 from Professor Knipmeyer's dissertation, unchanged except for minor matters of style, follows without abridgement.

Folk Boats

One of the most outstanding characteristics of the settlements in eastern French Louisiana is their location near some body of water; most settlements are on or near bayous, rivers, lakes, swamps, or marshes. Water bodies are important in the daily living of the people, serving as both resources and communications—without them many settlements would never have come into existence. Each body of water has its own particular use and resources; each is the center of different kinds of activity and has different requirements of trafficability. The marsh, for example, is essential to the trapper, who must use special boats and methods in his work. There are many settlements of people along the margins of the large swamps who make a part or all of their living from the swamp in diverse ways. These swampers spend much of their time on the water and have developed several kinds of boats.

The bayou is generally important to all people as a means of local communication. Although this function has greatly decreased in importance since the advent of good roads, at the time of settlement and throughout the pioneer period, the bayou was vital to internal communications. Locally, all water had the same importance, whether it was the Mississippi or a small bayou; only the scale of use was different: the Mississippi carried greater cargoes on larger boats than did the bayous. Today many bayous are no longer important drainage features, because the Mississippi floods are well controlled. Where bayous have become relict, few boats are in evidence; but the boat tradition is strong, as is the memory of the time when boats were in use daily.

Bayous that are important for drainage and transportation are kept open by dredging. Under these conditions the use of boats is more extensive than the situation requires; that is, boats survive where they can, though their use may not be quite what it was originally. With the advent of the automobile, the bayou became a disadvantage in one respect: it had to be crossed. When people moved up and down the bayou by boat, it was as easy to stop on one side as on the other. Before autos were common possessions, short trips or visits within walking distance along the bayou were often made by boat. In many places boats are retained for ferrying purposes; movement of a short distance on one side of a bayou is accomplished by automobile. Few bayous have roads on both sides and those that do can be bridged only at certain critical points separated by a distance of miles. The use of boats has declined to the extent that some people in urbanized sections of a bayou settlement, in order to reach a point almost directly across the bayou, will travel miles by auto to a bridge and return on the opposite side.

The small boat is a typical feature of the cultural landscape of eastern French Louisiana. It is present in large numbers on all water bodies where there are settlements. The tradition is no longer what it used to be, but boats are still essential in the trapping, fishing, and swamp economies. On many bayous boats are in demand daily as a means of transportation. Even where there is no longer any real need for boats, they are still widely used.

The boat is as much a medium for cultural expression as is any other trait. Where the boat is important and the tradition is strong, a complex is developed involving several kinds or types of boats and a large number of related phenomena, such as the devices and methods of propelling the boats and the many traits associated with their use. There is always a critical recognition of the different types of boats and their proper uses and a careful adherence to a precise terminology. Such is the case in the bayou settlements of French Louisiana.

The boat tradition survives even beyond the bayous throughout French Louisiana. In the northern part of the state there is a distinct absence of a boat tradition except in the Mississippi River flood-plain region and on the larger streams where there are small numbers of commercial fishermen.[3] In the hill areas of the north, there is no such thing as a boat type; boats are constructed along individualistic lines and generally with a quality of workmanship not acceptable in the south. A relationship exists between the abundance of water bodies and development of a boat tradition, but it does not have a direct bearing on the fundamental facts of type distribution and cultural associations.

Two general characteristics of the small folk boats in Louisiana are significant and should be considered when extraregional comparisons are made. First, all boats are carvel-built: the planks of the hull are placed edge to edge so as to give the hull a smooth surface. This is also true in Mediterranean Europe. In contrast to this, the boats of north-western Europe are generally clinker-built; that is, the edge of one plank overlaps the edge of the next.[4] Second, all Louisiana boats are flat-bottomed, a general characteristic of small boats on inland waters. If a keel is used, it is always external. It is generally true that all littoral water craft of Europe and America have internal or structural keels, and those of the inland waters are flat-bottomed.

The many boats of French Louisiana can be recognized as belonging to different categories or types for which there are, or were, special uses and names and with which certain specific secondary traits usually are associated. The boat complex readily distinguishes the cultural pattern of the bayou settlements and, in general, the French Louisiana pattern from the surrounding Anglo-American pattern. The complex is intricate, and for some boat types it is possible to distinguish subregional associations based on minor differences in form or construction. The six major types are pirogue, plank pirogue, *chaland*, *esquif*, bateau, and flatboat.

The Pirogues

The oldest type of small boat in French Louisiana is the dugout canoe, or pirogue (pronounced "pēro"). The modern boat is the direct descendant of an aboriginal boat made by the Indians in approximately the area that is now the southeastern United States. It was the chief means of water transportation in that region. Bark canoes were used to the north, bull boats in the west, and dugouts on the west coast. The dugout canoe was the principal native boat of the West Indies. The French there and in Louisiana called these boats *pirogues*.[5]

LePage DuPratz describes a raft of canes, termed a *cajeu*, which was used by the Indians of Louisiana.[6] However, the raft must have been of greater importance on the upper Mississippi and Missouri than in the lower valley. In the area that is now Louisiana, the dugout canoe was by far the most important boat. John Swanton mentions canoes of elm bark for the Chitimacha Indians,[7] but most early narratives mention only dugouts. These boats were fashioned from the trunks of large trees, usually cypress, sometimes poplar, and rarely other species. The tree had to be felled by burning, and the excavation of the canoe had to be done with fire before the Indians acquired steel axes. The best description of their manufacture is given by DuPratz in his 1774 *History of Louisiana*:

For this reason they always cut a tree close to the ground so that the fire they build at the foot of the tree would more easily consume the filaments and fibers of the wood which the axe had mashed. Finally, with much trouble and patience, they managed to bring the tree down. This was a long piece of work, so that in those times they were much busier than at present, when they have the axes we sell them. From this it happens that they no longer cut a tree down at the base, but at the height which is most convenient.

This occasions them an infinite amount of labor, since they have no other utensils in this work than wood for making fire and wood for scraping, and only small wood is required to burn. In order to set fire to this tree destined for making a pirogue, a pad of clay, which is found everywhere, has to be made for the two sides and each end. These pads prevent the fire from passing beyond and burning the sides of the boat. A great fire is made above, and when the wood is consumed it is scraped so that the insides may catch fire better and may be hollowed out more easily, and they continue thus until the fire has consumed all the wood in the inside of the tree. And, if the fire burns into the sides they put mud there which prevents it from working farther than is demanded. This precaution is taken until the pirogue is deep enough. The outside is made in the same manner and with the same attention.

The bow of this pirogue is made sloping, like those of the boats which one sees on the French rivers. This bow is as broad as the body of the pirogue. I have seen some 40 feet long by 3 feet broad. They are about 3 inches thick which makes them very heavy. These pirogues can carry 12 persons and are all of buoyant wood.[8]

The Indians used only paddles, which were "about six feet long, with broad points, which are not fastened to the vessel, but managed by the rowers like shovels."[9] The pole must have been unknown to the Indians, for it is never mentioned. DuPratz observed that, with a difficult job of navigation on the Red River, "if the waterman's pole was used, as on the Loire and other rivers of France, this obstacle would be easily surmounted."[10]

When the French entered the region, they adopted the Indian dugout, which proved to be well suited to frontier conditions. There was little choice, for tools and materials were scarce and boats of European manufacture were not available. In 1700, at Biloxi, the need for boats and the lack of materials caused the governor of the colony to have "12 pirogues 30 to 35 feet long" constructed.[11] The frontiersman was largely self-sufficient, with the exception of a few tools of European manufacture, and the dugout was ideally suited to his situation. If a boat could not be obtained from the Indians, he could make his own. The material was found in any backswamp; for tools he needed only an ax and an adz. The Indian provided the idea; the methods were changed to suit the new tools. The time-consuming and less-accurate method of burning was superseded by the chopping method.

The pirogue must have had some advantages over the boats the French had, though that would be difficult to determine. DuPratz learned that he could make better speed in the pirogues than in the boats he had with him.[12] The dugout was very durable. There was little damage that it could suffer, and, if cared for, it would last a lifetime. The weight, however, must have reduced maneuverability and certainly made portages difficult. The early pirogues, which were large and weighed several thousand pounds when empty, were dragged across portages. This was an unimportant matter where regular traffic was concerned, for the river routes were not uninterrupted. Within the region, almost all of the settlements could be reached on water by some route, however circuitous.

Bark canoes were introduced into Louisiana by the Canadians. They were used by the French before there was any settlement, and a voyageur coming from Canada would have had a bark canoe. The canoes used by the explorers also were often bark canoes. They were used at times by Tonti, Iberville, and Bienville.[13] The Mobile River was explored in 1701 by Sauvolle and four Canadians in a birch-bark canoe.[14] The early narratives often refer simply to canoes, which could have been either dugout or birch bark.[15] Although the word *pirogue* was used for the dugout canoe from the very first, it was not used to the exclusion of the term *canoe*. Thus, it is somewhat questionable as to when the use of bark canoes was discontinued, but it could not have been long after the period of exploration. They were quite foreign to the Indians and to all but the Canadian French; nothing was known of their construction and there was no suitable bark in the region from which to build them.

The form of the native dugouts changed in the hands of the French. They built them on less angular lines with pointed bow and stern, the shallow ends were made more hollow, and the thickness of the shell was reduced. The latter was controlled by putting auger holes in the shell at certain places where the carpenter needed to see how thin he was cutting. These holes were usually placed at the curvature between the bottom and sides and were spaced about two feet apart. Thus, there were two parallel rows of holes that ran from bow to stern. When the boat was finished, the holes were plugged and sometimes caulked with pitch. The bottom of the dugout was not left entirely in the round but was slightly flattened near the widest part in the center. The bottom ran to a slight ridge at both ends. The sides were curved and very slightly flaring. Pirogues built by either Indians or French were without sheer; that is, the gunwales were horizontal from bow to stern. These general features have marked pirogue construction from frontier times to the present.

Within the limitations of form, there was plenty of room for individual variation. The proportional difference between beam and length, which created the greatest differences, was governed by the size of the trees from which the pirogues were made. Individual boats may have had narrow beams and relatively great length with a linear appearance; others might have had the bulging appearance created by a wide beam. The ordinary pirogues of the region, up to modern times, were generally over fifteen feet in length, but seldom more than thirty.[16]

During the frontier period, pirogues were the only cargo carriers in the Mississippi Valley, and special long-distance cargo pirogues were improvised for this need.[17] These were used in Louisiana on the Mississippi and important bayous, but they were not the commonplace boats of the Creoles. The period of the great cargo pirogues ended about 1775, though in Louisiana some cargo was still being carried to New Orleans in 1830, during the steamboat era.[18]

The decline of the pirogue on the Mississippi preceded that event on the smaller streams in more remote areas throughout the southeastern United States. In 1900 the dugout was still being used for ferrying and fishing purposes on nearly all of the large streams in Louisiana. After that time the decline in its use was rapid everywhere, except in the bayou country. Within two decades the distribution diminished to about the present limits. Southwestern Louisiana retained the pirogue a few years longer than did the northern part of the state. Pirogues predating the decline are easily distinguished from the modern boat. They are larger and more varied in form. Many of these boats, most of them between fifty and one hundred years old, are still to be found throughout French Louisiana and the Mississippi and Red River valleys. A few of the old boats are in good condition, having been stored in basements or barns or under houses, but these are not used today. Some were put into service during the 1927 flood, never to be used again. Many more have been used for feed troughs or have just been left rotting in ponds and sloughs.[19]

Following the disappearance of the pirogue in the rest of the state, the pirogue of the bayou country attained its modern form. The modern pirogues are remarkable for their similarity (6.1 & 6.2). All are almost identical with a nodal type, as if they were cut from the same pattern, and differ only slightly in size. They are made to be used by only one person, though they might hold more. None is over fourteen feet in length—twelve feet is about average—and some are as small as ten feet. A fourteen-foot boat might be considered two-place, though it would not be normally used for two riders.

The beam measurement for the typical pirogue is between twenty and twenty-four inches, or just about wide enough for a person to sit in. The depth is about ten to twelve inches. The run to the stern is a little longer than that to the bow, so that the boat is slightly wider toward the bow. Both bow and stern taper rather sharply to a point. The bow is more deeply hollowed than the stern. The sides are straight above the waterline and curved below. The bottom is flat for the widest part and abruptly runs to a ridge at the bow and stern, which become almost vertical above the waterline. The sides curve up slightly toward both bow and stern. The bottom is about one inch thick and the sides a little less. Usually there are two thwarts, each about a third of the boat length from the end. The front thwart may be a little higher than the one in the stern, which often serves as a seat. These may be wedged in, nailed, or held by wooden stops. The bow and stern are reinforced with fillets three or four inches in length, level with or below the gunwales. A small strip of molding, about one inch wide and half an inch thick, is added all around the outside about one inch below the gunwales to protect them against any damage that might be caused by the boat striking anything.

This boat is regularly called a "pirogue" and sometimes a "dougout." It is never called a "canoe" in the area where it occurs.[20] The modern pirogue has been built since about 1910, which was just after the time that the distribution of pirogues was rather sharply reduced to about the present limits. The explanation for this decline cannot be found in a single factor. The usual explanation given is that from that time no large cypress trees were left. Although that is partially true, the cypress lumbering period was then not yet ended and undoubtedly some of the big trees were left. The cost of a prime log might have been a different matter. At that time roads were being improved and automobiles were coming into use. These developments would have reduced the necessity for the large freight pirogues, and at the same time they would not have affected the importance of the work pirogue. This early-twentieth-century period marked the beginning or advance of a number of economic activities that enhanced the value of the small pirogue. In the earliest days of cypress lumbering, trees were often felled from small pirogues. Probably the trappers were the first to use smaller boats.

The modern pirogue is constructed from a cypress log sawed in half lengthwise. The traditional tools are a hatchet, *arminette* (foot adz), "tisch" or "tee" (hand adz), drawknife, plane, and *couteau de manche* (templates) (6.3-6.5). These are the only tools used, and the drawknife and plane are not absolutely necessary. The *arminette* is the regular long-handled adz with a straight blade. The hand adz has a deeply curved blade and is used for more careful work on interior curves. The

6.1

Modern dugout pirogues: *left*, Kraemer;
right, Bayou Du Large.

templates are flat strips of wood curved to mark the form of the pirogue.

The bark is removed from the log as the first step, and a center line is marked off on the flat side, which is to be the top of the dugout. A template is placed so that the ends of the curve are against the center line, and a line is drawn on the top of the log to outline one side of the bow. Then the template is turned over and the other side of the bow is marked out. Another template is used in the same way to outline the shape of the stern. Two more templates are used to mark the sheer, or downward curvature, from bow to stern toward the middle. This is very slight, seldom more than two or three inches. A series of transverse notches, as deep as the sheer line, are chopped into the log. Then the wood between the notches is split off. The inside is hewn out with a hatchet or *arminette* about two inches inside the lines that mark the outline of the dugout. When the inside has been roughed out, the log is turned over and the outside is shaped with the same tools. A smooth finish is achieved on the inside by means of the hand adz. This tool is used like a plane or scraper rather than as a chopping tool. Small pieces are shaved off until the inside has the proper curvature. The drawknife and plane are used to smooth the outside. The entire process takes only a few days for a good pirogue maker. The dugout is then fitted with battens and fillets. It must be allowed to dry for several months before being painted. The color is always green.

The pirogue, a very versatile boat and suited to many conditions, is used almost exclusively by men, especially for work in marsh and swamp. Other boats have taken its place for ferrying and travel in most cases. It is essentially a single-place craft, and there is room in the bow for a small cargo. In the marsh, the pirogue has an advantage in its single-piece construction with rounded or smoothly curved lines: there are no sharp angles to offer resistance to the marsh grasses or mud, through which it must frequently be dragged. Travel in the marsh for a trapper typically requires movement from one "pond" or "lagoon" to the next over various kinds of marsh surfaces. The one disadvantage of the pirogue is its weight. In the swamp, where the chance is great that a boat will collide with a tree or run upon a cypress knee, the durable construction of the pirogue is its most valuable asset. The dugout is immune to knocks that soon ruin a boat of planks. Running upon a cypress knee is especially destructive to other boats, but a dugout will slide or glance off, or overturn, and a swamper would much rather suffer an overturn than the loss of his boat.

A pirogue will last almost indefinitely if cared for properly. The most important thing is to not allow it to dry out, for if it is not kept moist, the wood splits and cracks. Many owners who do not intend to use their boats any more store them beneath their houses. They could be better preserved, but generally the underside of the house is damper and cooler than are other places, and it is always out of the direct sunlight.

6.2

Modern dugout pirogues: *above*, Barataria; *below*, Bayou Du Large.

6.3

Pirogue-making tools, Kraemer.

6.4

Pirogue construction, Kraemer.

6.5

Pirogue construction, Kraemer.

6.6

Methods of paddling a pirogue: *above left*, Bayou St. Jean Charles; *above right*, Bayou Du Large; *below right*, Bayou Boeuf near Kraemer.

Some men now use their pirogues only during the trapping season; they store them in the same way but fill the inside of the boat with moss or palmetto leaves. Just before it is used, the boat is submerged in the bayou and soaked for a few days. Boats that are used more frequently are allowed to stand half submerged in the bayou. Some owners pull them up on the bank in the shade of shrubbery and fill them with wet moss and cover them with palmetto leaves. Cypress wood does not rot easily when water-soaked.

Paddles and poles are used to drive the dugout under different conditions, but paddles are normally used. Paddles for all boats are hand-made and the best ones are those made for pirogues. A cypress picket from a fence is the most desirable wood for making a paddle. It has been well seasoned, is light and easy to carve, and will last long. The average length for a paddle is five feet, but the exact length depends upon the reach of the individual when the paddle is held in position. The proportional length of shaft and blade is about three to two. Handles are usually T-shaped and the blades have blunt or slightly rounded ends.

The paddler sits on the stern thwart, which is about two feet from the middle of the boat. In the usual posture one leg is folded in front of the paddler or under the seat and the other is extended and braced on the bottom of the boat. A double kneeling position, in which the paddler sits upon his heels, is sometimes used without a seat. The standard position might be used with the paddler sitting on his folded leg. The boat is always paddled on one side, usually the right. The handle of the paddle is held in the left hand and the right hand holds the shaft about four inches above the blade. In a full stroke the hand almost touches the water. All maneuvers are made from one position; sides are seldom changed. For straight distances a modified J-stroke is used. Occasionally, a person may stand to paddle, but no paddles are made for this purpose, since considerable distances could not be covered in this fashion and speed is impossible. The standing position is used mostly by women, who either cannot fit in the pirogue or who do not want to get their dresses wet when they cross a bayou (6.6).

Push poles, or *fourches*, are used mainly in the marsh and are especially designed for very shallow water. They vary in length from six to twelve feet, but most are between eight and ten feet long. A small tree limb with a natural fork at one end may be used, with or without the bark being removed, but generally the *fourches* are made with greater care. Bamboo poles are considered good by some because of their light weight, but they do not last long. Most good push poles are made of a heavy wood about two inches in diameter. Forks are added to one end by nailing two small pieces of wood, about one inch round or square and less than one foot long, opposite each other, or by inserting a forked piece of wood in a slot in the end of the pole. The purpose of the fork is to prevent the pole from sinking too deeply in the soft muck at the bottom of ponds and ditches when it is being used to propel the boat. If it were not for the fork, all energy would be exerted in sinking the pole and no thrust would be imparted to the boat. A push pole is used while the boatman stands in the stern.

Sometimes the ends of the push poles opposite the forks are used for special purposes. In an old method of crab fishing, small circular nets are suspended on several feet of cord from cork or wooden floats. These are picked up by hooks on the end of a push pole, which are made by binding two pieces of wire opposite each other. The wires extend about eight to ten inches beyond the end of the pole and are bent in a curve. This is hooked around the cord beneath the float and the crab net is removed from the water. Bamboo poles for this purpose alone are also made. A push pole may be made into a moss-picking pole by adding a hook of wire about one foot long to the end opposite the fork.

The pirogue is common only on the lower bayous in the southeastern part of the state or, roughly, the Mississippi delta (6.7). The proportional representation of the pirogue is given in percentage figures, which are not a measure of the importance of the boat or an indication of the actual number. The pirogue is very important in the marsh east of the Atchafalaya River, but is not mapped there, because of the peculiar circumstances under which it occurs. It is significant in the areas where it attains 6 percent and above.

The decline of the pirogue is imminent; rarely is one built today.

6.7

Distribution of the dugout pirogue.

There are a number of expert pirogue makers living, but adequate logs are lacking. If a suitable log is found, it is generally saved for a pirogue. They are still to be had but are obtained at a great cost. The last stronghold of the pirogue is among the trappers. Some think that there are many advantages to the plank boat, which is taking the place of the dugout, but many still prefer the dugout. The matter of preference is undoubtedly in the realm of individual choice. It cannot be said whether this is due to the actual superiority of the dugout or whether the trappers are just reluctant to abandon a tradition.

The boat that is replacing the dugout pirogue is almost identical with it in form but is made of planks and does not have the smooth lines of the dugout (6.8). It is known by several names. Within the area of the dugout, it is often called a pirogue, especially by the younger generation. When it is necessary to distinguish it from the dugout, it is called "plank pirogue" or *pirogue en planche*. Most older people call it a "plank boat" or sometimes *peniche*. Outside the area of dugouts, it is rarely called a pirogue, for that word means dugout. In southwestern Louisiana the plank pirogue is called either "skiff" or "canoe." On the lower Bayou Teche and toward Terrebonne Parish, "Cajun skiff" is sometimes used. Where fishermen and sportsmen have recently introduced the boat in northern Louisiana, it is generally called a pirogue. Such introductions do not always preserve their identity, and names like "gar" and "sharpshooter" have been improvised.

Most informants remember the plank pirogue as becoming important about 1910. It is not certain whether it was created at that time, or whether it was in existence previously but not yet able to compete with the dugout in popularity. The remarkable similarity between the dugout and the plank pirogues in form, size, use, and associated equipment makes it clear that the former was the inspiration for the latter. The time of the plank pirogue's arrival coincides with the expansion of cypress lumbering activities, which created new uses and a greater need for pirogues. It seems certain that these new interests did not invent the plank boat, but they were undoubtedly responsible for making it more popular and spreading its use.

The form and construction of plank pirogues vary a great deal locally. There are distinct subregional differences, and the conformity to subregional patterns is so marked that in many cases it is possible to identify the source area of a plank boat by its appearance. The quality of construction varies in a like manner. In general, it is desirable to have as few planks as possible in the bottom because then the construction is sturdier, fewer braces are required, and there are fewer seams. The

6.8

Plank pirogues: *left*, Barataria; *right*,
near Bayou Bonfuca.

value of a plank pirogue may be judged in part by the number of planks in the bottom. In such cases they are designated as either "two-plank pirogues" or "three-plank pirogues." The number of planks can also be an indication of beam. A single plank is always used for each side. These two planks are formed around the bottom and are joined at the bow and stern, either by simply nailing them together or by nailing them to triangular stem and stern posts. There is actually no frame. Elbow braces are added on each side opposite one another and may be connected by horizontal braces on the bottom. The smaller details of construction vary with the quality of the boat and the district in which it is built. The seams of a well-built boat are covered with tar and sometimes battens. If a boat is painted, the color is green.

These boats serve many purposes and have generally filled the functions of the dugout, being used for trapping, fishing, hunting, swamp work, and ferrying in all kinds of situations. The equipment and meth-

6.9

Distribution of the plank pirogue.

ods of use are the same as for the dugouts. The plank pirogue occurs in a much larger area than does the dugout, but it is not uniformly important throughout. The distribution roughly corresponds to the region of French Louisiana, approximately the area in which the dugout was being used about 1910 (6.9 & 6.10).

The plank boats of the southeastern bayou country resemble the modern dugout more than do those of any other district. They are the best constructed and have smooth lines, flaring sides, and usually some sheer. Twelve feet is about the average length; braces are few and small; and thwarts, molding, and paint are generally used in the southeast, but not elsewhere. The plank pirogues of the southwestern district north of the marshes are larger and less well formed. The sides may be slightly flaring or vertical, braces are large and angular, and sheer is slight or absent. Often bow and stern fillets are nailed to the top of the gunwales. The largest boats are made in the marshes of southwest

6.10

Distribution of the plank and dugout pirogues.

Louisiana: fourteen feet is about the average length. In the typical boat, the sides run straight at the waist for a few feet before curving toward the ends. Beams are wider and braces most numerous in these boats. In the Atchafalaya Basin, plank pirogues are smallest and have the most sheer. Generally they have a coaming about two inches wide at the waist, which diminishes to nothing toward the bow and stern. Often they are equipped with fish wells, which are made by placing two boards about two feet apart across the waist of the boat. Holes are bored in the bottom of the boat and closed with plugs.

Recently pirogues have been made of marine plywood. They are most common in the center of the dugout-pirogue country and are primarily used by trappers. The best examples are in the Delacroix Island area. Plywood is superior in some ways: it weighs much less, is easily shaped, and makes for sturdy construction with fewer pieces—a single piece is used for the bottom. A plywood boat is finished with the same details as are found in a well-built southeastern plank pirogue, with the addition of a removable plankwalk to protect the bottom.

6.11

Chalands: left, Bayou Pointe au Chien; *right*, Bayou Terre aux Boeufs.

The Chaland

Several kinds of small rectangular flat-bottomed boats occur almost
everywhere throughout the state. The *chaland* is one type that is restricted to the lower bayou country. Its form and construction seem
crude by comparison with other boats of the region, but it is usually
well built of inexpensive planking and is never painted. The typical
chaland is perfectly rectangular (6.11). The nonflaring sides run
straight to a square bow and stern, and the end boards are vertical.
There is no sheer; instead the bottoms of the ends have an abrupt,
angular, upward slant, which serves the purpose. There may be several
seats or none. The extreme ends are often covered with boards about
one foot wide, which are nailed to the top of the gunwales. The *chaland*
is from ten to fourteen feet long, two and a half to three feet wide, and
eight to twelve inches deep. A few are a little larger, and some have a
small triangular external keel.

Other kinds of boats similar to the *chaland* might be collectively
termed "paddle boats," although there are a number of local names.
There is a considerable variation of form and quality of construction in
the paddle-boat class that has no regional associations. The most important differences between these boats and the *chaland* are that the
paddle boats characteristically have flaring and curving sides and a

certain amount of sheer. In the most common subtype, the width of the bow is less than that of the stern. Another boat that has a bow and a stern of the same width and a beam wider than the ends is called a "double ender" in some places. The dimensions of these boats are similar to those of the *chaland*. The paddle boat has a very wide distribution throughout the state (6.12).

"Paddle boat" is a north Louisiana name, and among boatmen it is used with some consistency. Otherwise, the paddle boat in north Louisiana might be called a "skiff," which is a general name for any small boat. Some kinds of boats are made that closely resemble the *chaland* in that they are perfectly rectangular, but there is no relationship. The construction of the *chaland* is the measure of boat knowledge and need in the region.

Chaland has a broad meaning that includes rectangular flat-bottomed boats of almost any size.[21] Although it might be used specifically to

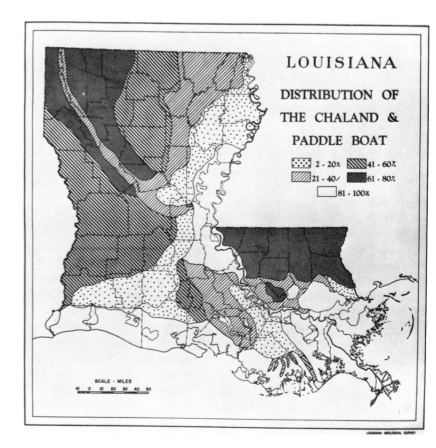

6.12

Distribution of the *chaland* and paddle boat.

refer to the small boat previously described, it could also mean a camp boat. The term would not exclude the paddle boats, but they are rare where the typical *chaland* occurs. The area of the *chaland* is almost limited to Terrebonne, Lafourche, and Assumption parishes. The name is known throughout French Louisiana, but it is used mainly in the lower bayou country. Thus, where the paddle boat occurs in French Louisiana, it might be called *chaland* or, beyond the flatboat area along the Mississippi, "flatboat." It may be significant that in the lower Atchafalaya area the *chaland* is sometimes called a "plank boat." Special kinds of "plank boats" were occasionally used for logging in the Atchafalaya swamps. They were perfectly rectangular and very narrow, about ten to twelve feet long and less than two feet wide. It is possible that the term *plank boat* was transferred from this boat to the plank pirogue.

In the lower bayou country the typical *chaland* is used only for crossing a bayou, never for going even a short distance up or down the bayou. For that reason there is no need to distinguish between bow and stern. Stability, rather than speed, is the most important quality. The boat is always operated by hand—characteristically, paddling in a standing position, for it is not worth sitting down to go a short distance. Any kind of paddle may be used, but there is a special *chaland* paddle, which has a shaft about four feet long without an end grip and a blade roughly squared at the end. A special *chaland*, a little larger than average and sometimes propelled by oars, is used for moss gathering.

The Esquif

Of all the folk boats in French Louisiana, none is more carefully distinguished than the *esquif*, or "skiff." The essential features of this boat type are its flat bottom, pointed bow, and blunt stern; these characteristics do not identify the boat, however, for they are quite general. A "rowboat," for example, has these characteristics, but it is not the same thing; the distinguishing features are intangible. The differences are a matter of degree rather than kind. The type is valid, for it is recognized as such throughout the bayou country by those who are aware of boat lore.

The Louisiana French *esquif* is the same as the standard French.[22] In standard French the word is equivalent to the English "skiff." Both terms have a very broad meaning and may be locally used to designate any small open boat, with the exception of any kind of canoe. In Louisiana the English "skiff" is used in the same sense, except in the lower bayou country and along the Mississippi, where it refers to a specific type. The French *esquif* has come to have a restricted meaning, and, in the region where the boat is used, *esquif* and "skiff" are synonymous and are not used in the general sense. Elsewhere, a skiff might be so called with no particular meaning intended. In north Louisiana the rowboat is also a skiff, and in French Louisiana "rowboat" is not used.

The general design of the skiff is ancient, and boats of that form are common on the inland waters in many parts of the world.[23] There are many examples in America with European antecedents. The form is very susceptible to change, and the slightest difference in the lines of the boat may cause it to be given a more specific name. Boats resembling the modern skiff could have been present in the Louisiana colony from the earliest times, though not recognized specifically as such. In the coastal waters and on the Mississippi and large streams, several kinds of small vessels resembling the skiff were propelled by sail and oar. Some of these were the *peniche, chaloupe,* and *galere.*[24] The name and type appeared early in the Mississippi Valley. Some of the large flat-bottomed boats that were used on the river in the latter part of the eighteenth century were called skiffs if the bow or the bow and stern were pointed; later they were called barges. Small skiffs were generally carried on the big flat-bottomed boats of all kinds. In lower Louisiana, the function of the skiff during the pioneer period was largely filled by the dugout, that is, travel for a considerable distance with or without a small cargo. As the pirogue declined in popularity, the skiff became more important. Many bayou dwellers remember having to travel for several days by skiff to get ordinary household supplies. Now that transportation need no longer exists.

The skiff in Louisiana today is used along the Mississippi, in large coastal and interior lakes and bays, and in the bayous that lead to such water bodies (6.13). The main concentrations are around Lakes Pontchartrain, Maurepas, and Borgne; Lakes Salvador and Des Allemands; the lower Atchafalaya Basin; and the Mississippi below New Orleans. In those areas it is used constantly; elsewhere it is used only occasionally. Where it is important, it is used primarily for some fishing activity and, because it is handy, it may also be used for ferrying. One specialized use is required in commercial crab fishing. On the Mississippi below New Orleans, the skiff is used to tend fish lines and traps. Above New Orleans those tasks are generally performed in a flatboat. Large numbers of skiffs are kept for hire on the bayous frequented by sportsmen.

Three kinds of skiffs can be distinguished, but the differences are not always clear—ordinarily not clear enough to justify a special name. However, any boatman in the region will point out the merits of the different kinds, though not referring to them by a particular name. The largest of these varieties might be termed the "lake skiff" (6.14). It is best suited to open water and is dominant on the big coastal lakes and bays. Thick and heavy planks are used in its construction. The length is about fourteen feet, but this is not constant. The beam is the greatest in proportion to length of all the skiffs, and the stern is wide and rectangular.

Intermediate between the lake skiff and the smallest is the "Mississippi skiff." It is generally no shorter than the lake skiff but has a smaller beam in proportion to the length. The stern board is less rectangular and more V-shaped. The lake skiff has a broad, bulging appearance, and the Mississippi skiff is slender.

The smallest and lightest is called the "Creole skiff" wherever it is in a minority relation to the other types. The name occurs from Bayou Bonfuca near Slidell to Bayou Boeuf near Morgan City. The Creole skiff characteristically occurs on small interior water bodies and attains its most typical development in the Atchafalaya Basin, where it is specifically *esquif.* The distinguishing features are a narrow beam, considerable sheer, and a high, slightly overhanging V-shaped stern (6.15).

The *canotte* is a special kind of large skiff (6.16). The length is usually over fifteen feet, but size alone is not the determining characteristic. The *canotte* always has an inboard engine. It may be open, partially decked fore and aft, or fitted with a cabin and decked around. Small open skiffs with an inboard engine are usually called "gas boats" but, if decked, *canotte*. The difference between a large *canotte* and a small lugger is not always clear.[25]

The skiff is always rowed if a motor is not used. Even if the boat has a motor, it is generally equipped with oars. Most boatmen make their own oars and oarlocks, although manufactured oars and modern metal swivel oarlocks are occasionally used. The ordinary handmade oars resemble the manufactured oars. Special oars, which are very thick near the handle end, are made for the "standing skiff." The standard oarlock is the tholepin and strap (*tolet* and *estrope*).

The "standing skiff" is one that is operated in a standing position. It could be any type but is most commonly the Creole skiff. In the standing

6.13

Distribution of the skiff.

William B. Knipmeyer

6.14
Lake skiffs: *above*, Bayou Bonfuca; *below*,
Bayou Gauche.

6.15

Creole skiffs: *above left*, Grand Bayou; *above right*, Bayou St. Jean Charles; *below right*, Attakapas Landing.

method of rowing, the oarsman faces the bow and imparts a thrust to the boat by pushing on the oars. This is an old Mediterranean method; immigrant Dalmatians and Italians remember having used the method in their homeland. In the Lake Pontchartrain area, it is known as the "Dago" method. Elsewhere in the United States, it is used by the Greek fishermen around Tarpon Springs, Florida.

Although ordinary oarlocks can be used with the standing method, the operation is awkward and tiresome, and a special device is needed. In Louisiana this rowing device is called a *joug*.[26] The function of the *joug* is to elevate the oars and extend the fulcrum beyond the sides of the boat. Several types are used (6.17, see also 6.15). All types have the oars secured by means of a tholepin and strap. The simplest *joug* con-

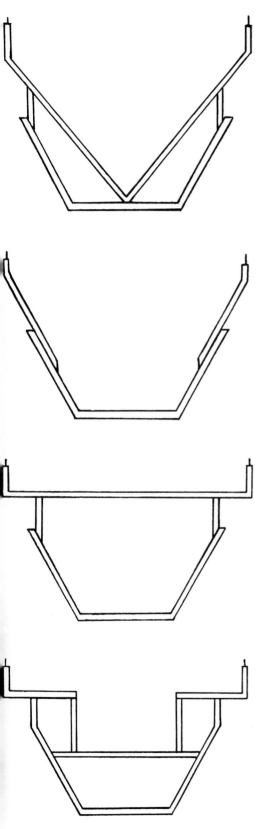

6.16

Canottes: *above*, Bayou Boeuf near Kraemer; *below*, Bayou Pointe au Chien.

6.17

Diagrams of types of *jougs*.

sists of a pair of separate removable pieces. Each piece is a small board about two inches wide and two feet long with a block of wood on one end to hold the tholepin. These are inserted in a slot on the inside of the gunwales. Other types are a single piece fixed for holding both oars, which may be removable or permanently attached to the boat.

At present, the *joug* is used in only two locations—on the lower Mississippi around Venice and in the lower Atchafalaya Basin from Lake Verrett southward. It, or the standing skiff, is remembered throughout the bayou country from Bayou Teche to Bayou Bonfuca. About 1900, it was commonly used throughout French Louisiana. It is distinctly associated with the skiff, but it is occasionally used on other types of boats. In the Lake Verrett area, *chalands* used for moss gathering are sometimes equipped with *jougs*. There are a few plank pirogues in Terrebonne Parish with *jougs*, but these are oddities. The big premodern dugouts commonly had *jougs*; some had two and three pairs. The very largest used a man on each oar. It is possible that the *joug* was first used on skiffs and then transferred to the pirogue in the early days, as the pirogue was the common boat.

Small water-cooled motors have taken the place of the *joug* almost everywhere, and it is surprising that it is still used at all. Generally, if a skiff has a motor, it is called a "gas boat." These are steered with a rudder, which is connected by means of a line and pulleys to a vertical control stick in the center of the boat. The gas boats are used for long trips, especially those connected with fishing. They are necessary to the crab fisherman, who, with one hand, controls the boat and, with the other, scoops the crabs off his line with a net.

The Bateau

Bateau as now used in Louisiana has a very restricted meaning that applies to only one kind of boat (6.18).[27] The bateau is a large flat-bottomed boat with a blunt bow and stern. The length is usually over fifteen feet, and the width is between four and five feet. A large amount of forward sheer is typical, causing the bow to rise out of the water. The bow is narrower than the stern and the run forward longer than the run aft. It is partially decked fore and aft and sometimes on the sides, which leaves an open well in the waist. The well is surrounded by a coaming of several inches. Most bateaux are so large that they must have an inboard motor. The largest have cabins over the well but still belong to the type. On the other end of the scale, they become indistinguishable from flatboats. If they have an inboard motor or a small amount of decking, they are bateaux, even though they might be smaller than some flatboats. A motor is not essential, and a few of the smaller ones are equipped with *jougs*.

The term *bateau* is old in the Mississippi Valley and was adopted into English during the period of the big flatboats. Beginning about 1790, the great pirogues were replaced as the main cargo vessels by several kinds of large keelless flat-bottomed boats. Many names were used for these boats, some of which were not specific. *Bateau* was used by English- as well as French-speaking boatmen for a flatboat that had a pointed bow

5.18

Bateaux; both boats were photographed at
Attakapas Landing.

and stern. From almost the beginning of settlement, the French in Louisiana built a similar boat, which they called *bateau plat*.[28] It is possible that *bateau* was an abbreviation of the full French word and thus acquired its specific meaning. Once the term was adopted into English, it became established throughout the valley. The modern bateau is very likely not a descendant of the old boats; rather, it is probably a development from the modern flatboat.

The only place where the bateau is important today is the Atchafalaya Basin (6.19). There it takes the place of the *canotte*, a boat for long-distance travel and fishing on the large lakes. The bateau was used in cypress lumbering, which may account for its becoming the motor-powered boat of the locality; elsewhere in French Louisiana the skiff serves the same purpose. A few bateaux on the lower Nepique and Queue de Tortue are used in small-scale logging activities. The bateau was once used on the large streams in the northeastern quarter of the

6.19

Distribution of the bateau.

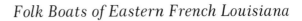

6.20

Flatboats: *above*, Grand Ecore; *below*,
Simmesport.

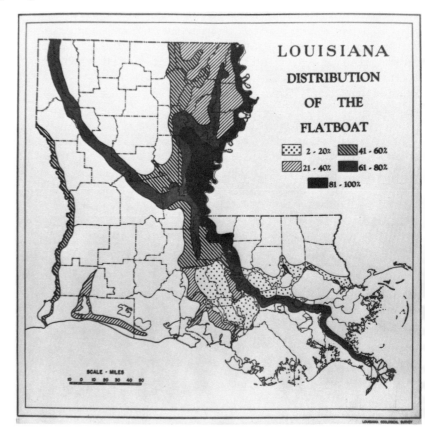

state to pull ferry barges, where it was called a "joe-boat" or sometimes "john-boat."

The Flatboat

All of the inland boats of Louisiana have flat bottoms, but only one kind is called a "flatboat" (6.20). More commonly it is simply called a "flat." Both ends of the boat are blunt, and the stern is always wider than the bow. The maximum beam is always a little aft of the waist, and the typical flat has enough forward sheer so that the bow rises above the water. The average boat is between twelve and fourteen feet long and has a beam of about three feet. A good flat must have flaring sides. Horizontal and elbow braces are used on the inside. A fish well is standard. The boatman's seat is in the extreme stern, for generally the boat is driven with an outboard motor; if not, oars are used.

Boats bearing the name *bateau plat* were used from the very earliest

6.21

Distribution of the flatboat.

days of French settlement in Louisiana. In 1720 colonists were transported on flatboats from Biloxi to New Orleans.[29] These were large
boats and may have had a pointed bow and stern, for the rectangular
boat was called a *radeau*.[30] Although flatboats are best known for their
importance on the Mississippi, they were also used on the smaller
streams and bayous.[31] These were very likely smaller versions of the
Mississippi flats. The present flat probably did not exist as long as the
dugout and skiff were important.

The distribution of the flatboat shows it to be distinctly a Mississippi
River boat (6.21). It is important only on the large streams, and it is of
little consequence on the large lakes. In scattered localities outside
French Louisiana, it is sometimes called "bateau," where that boat has
not been used for three or four decades.

NOTES

1.   See especially Howard I. Chapelle, *American Small Sailing Craft*.

2.   M. V. Brewington, *Chesapeake Bay Log Canoes and Bugeyes*, p. 30.

3.   [An excellent study of traditional fishing from outside the French sections of Louisiana is Hiram F. Gregory, Jr., "The Black River Commercial Fisheries: A Study in Cultural Geography," *Louisiana Studies* 5, no. 1 (Spring 1966): 3–36.—H.G.]

4.   [The conventional distinction between the clinker-built boats of northwestern Europe, including the British Isles, and the carvel-built boats of the Mediterranean is a true one (for example, T. C. Lethbridge, "Shipbuilding," in *A History of Technology*, ed. Charles Singer, E. J. Holmyard, A. R. Hall, and Trevor I. Williams, II, 563–588), but the Louisiana practice cannot be seen as a definite link with France, as boats are now carvel-built in parts of Britain, and that mode of construction has become most usual throughout America.—H.G.]

5.   The word *pirogue* is the standard French form of a word derived from the Spanish *piragua*, which ultimately comes from a Carib Indian word for the dugout canoe (William A. Read, *Louisiana-French*, p. 146; Auguste Jal, *Glossaire nautique*, p. 1177). Many different spellings and pronunciations of this word were used by the English, such as pirog, periogue, perigua, pirogue, perrogue, pirogua, and pettiaugar Leland D. Baldwin, *The Keelboat Age on Western Waters*, p. 41).

6.   Le Page du Pratz, *History of Louisiana*, pp. 123, 343.

7.   John R. Swanton, *Indian Tribes of the Lower Mississippi Valley and Adjacent Coast of the Gulf of Mexico*, p. 347.

8.   Le Page du Pratz, *History of Louisiana*, pp. 66–67.

9.   Ibid., p. 343.

10.   Ibid., p. 148.

11.   Roland Dunbar and Albert G. Sanders, *Mississippi Provincial Archives*, II, 11.

12.   Le Page du Pratz, *History of Louisiana*, p. 22.

13.   Bénard de La Harpe, *Journal historique de l'établissement des Français à la Louisiane*, pp. 17–18; Pierre Margry, *Mémoires et documents pour servir à l'histoire des origines françaises des pays d'outre-mer*, IV, 412–417.

14.   Marc de Villers, "Documents concerning the History of the Indians of the Eastern Region of Louisiana," [*Journal de la Société des Américanistes de Paris* 14 (1922)] tr. George C. H. Kernion, *Louisiana Historical Quarterly* 8 (1925): 30.

15.   Tonti in Margry, *Mémoires*, I, 600–602, 566–568; Penicault in Margry, *Mémoires*, V, 457, 512, 554–557; Gravier in John Dawson Gilmary Shea, *Early Voyages Up and Down the Mississippi*, pp. 132–136.

16.   For a few descriptions of pirogues at different times, see Edith Dart Price, "Inventory of the Estate of Sieur Jean Baptiste Prevost, Deceased Agent of the Company of the Indies, July 13, 1769," *Louisiana Historical Quarterly* 9 (1926): 448; Henry E. Chambers, "Early Commercial Prestige of New Orleans," *Louisiana Historical Quarterly* 5 (1922): 451; Caroline S. Pfaff, "Henry Miller Shreve in Biography," *Louisiana Historical Quarterly* 10 (1927): 235; Walter Prichard, Fred B. Kniffen, and A. Clair Brown, "Southern Louisiana and Southern Alabama in 1819: The Journal of James Leander Cathcart," *Louisiana Historical Quarterly* 28 (1945): 804; Alcée Fortier, *Louisiana Studies*, p. 343. The Louisiana State Museum in New Orleans has a number of dugouts; two are believed to date from about 1840, and one is believed to date from about 1750. The Anthropology Museum of Louisiana State University, Baton Rouge, has one that dates from about 1870. [Since the preparation of Knipmeyer's dissertation, an additional description of the pirogue has appeared: Hiram F. Gregory, Jr., "The Pirogue-Builder: A Vanishing Craftsman," *Louisiana Studies* 3, no. 3 (Fall 1964): 316–318.—H.G.]

17.   Baldwin, *Keelboat Age*, p. 41, describes the great cargo pirogues.

18.   Fortier, *Louisiana Studies*, p. 343.

19.   An example of an early pirogue is in the U.S. National Museum. Its dimensions are length, 17 feet, 8 inches; beam, 30 inches; depth, 11½ inches. C. W. Mitman, in *Catalogue of the Watercraft Collection in the United States National Museum*, p. 205, describes it as "an open, flat-bottomed, keel-less dugout canoe; with round and flaring sides; sharp hollow bow, straight and nearly vertical above the waterline, curved below; long easy run; V-shaped non-overhanging stern; two wooden rowlocks on each side with two thole pins in each; a seat at each end; battens for thwarts along the sides."

20.   The word *canotte* is used for a flat-bottomed cabin boat with an inboard engine in Terrebonne and parts of adjacent parishes.

21.   This usage is Louisiana French; cf. Read, *Louisiana-French*, p. 135. In standard French, *chaland* is a barge or scow, and *chalan* a rectangular flat-bottomed river boat (Jal, *Glossaire nautique*, p. 452).

22.   Read, *Louisiana-French*, p. 135.

23.   *Encyclopaedia Britannica*, 14th ed. III, 761–764.

24.   Dunbar and Sanders, *Mississippi Provincial Archives*, II, 248; Fortier, *Louisiana Studies*, p. 351; John Sibley, "The Journal of Dr. John Sibley, July–October, 1802," *Louisiana Historical Quarterly* 10 (1927): 474–497; Stanley Faye, "Types of Privateer Vessels, Their Armament and Flags, in the Gulf of Mexico," *Louisiana Historical Quarterly* 23 (1940): 118–130.

25.   [In Louisiana the name *lugger* is applied to a large motor-powered workboat (see Harnett T. Kane, *The Bayous of Louisiana*, pp. 81–101). Boats rigged with a dipping lugsail, popular in many parts of Europe, were found in America, in the late nineteenth century, only around New Orleans, and it is likely that the name of the powerboat was appropriated from the older lug-rigged boat (see Chapelle, *American Small Sailing Craft*, pp. 282–285). The term *lugger* drifted from sailboat to motorboat in Ireland, too (see E. Estyn Evans, *Mourne Country*, pp. 155–156).—H. G.]

26.   Other pronunciations are "jouc" and "joup." In both Louisiana and standard French, the word means "yoke," and it can be used in other ways. In nautical terminology, the *joug* (English, yoke; Italian, *giogo*) secured the oars of a galley (Jal, *Glossaire nautique*, pp. 866, 748). The European device is called a "fork" (French, *fourche*; Italian, *forca*). It is different in that it does not cross the waist of the boat; there is a single piece for each oar—the oars are not yoked together. The rowlock itself is a hook, rather than a tholepin and strap. A special example is the *forcola* of the Venetian gondola; it is a single piece and the gondolier uses the oar with both hands (Jal, *Glossaire nautique*, pp. 710–711). A small boat, resembling the plank pirogue of Louisiana, is used on the Po River. It is equipped with a "fork" on each gunwale. It would seem that the particular details of the *joug* were worked out in Louisiana; however, the European connections are clear.

27.   [Boat names have a way of attaching themselves to unrelated types. The dory of the New England coast and the "dory boat" of the Potomac are totally dissimilar. The name *bateau*, here applied to a kind of scow, has been given to the flat-bottomed, fore- and aft-planked, double-ended dorylike boats of the northern lumbermen, which were generally propelled by paddles (Chapelle, *American Small Sailing Craft*, pp. 80–84) and to the V-bottom, sloop-rigged, centerboard, oyster-dredging boats of the Chesapeake (Charles H. Coe, "Adventuring along the 'Eastern Shore,'" *Motor Boat*, November 25, 1922, p. 8).—H. G.]

28.   Chambers, "Early Commercial Prestige," pp. 451–461; Pfaff, "Henry Miller Shreve," pp. 192–240.

29.   Warrington Dawson, "A History of the Foundation of New Orleans (1717–1722)," *Louisiana Historical Quarterly* 3 (1920): 151–251.

30.   Jal, *Glossaire nautique*, p. 1252; Pfaff, "Henry Miller Shreve," p. 236.

31.   In 1819, James Leander Cathcart mentioned them for Bayou Teche and Bayou Plaquemine. These boats must have been smaller than those on the Mississippi, for, according to Cathcart, the Teche was wide enough for only "flats" and "canoes" (Prichard, Kniffen, and Brown, "Southern Louisiana and Southern Alabama in 1819," pp. 826, 835, 842).

BIBLIOGRAPHY

Baldwin, Leland D. *The Keelboat Age on Western Waters*. Pittsburgh: University of Pittsburgh Press, 1941.

Bénard de La Harpe, Jean Baptiste. *Journal historique de l'établissement des Français à la Louisiane*. New Orleans: A.-L. Boimare, 1831.

Brewington, M. V. *Chesapeake Bay Log Canoes and Bugeyes*. Cambridge, Md.; Tidewater Publishers, 1963.

Chambers, Henry E. "Early Commercial Prestige of New Orleans." *Louisiana Historical Quarterly* 5 (1922): 451–461.

Chapelle, Howard I. *American Small Sailing Craft: Their Design, Development, and Construction*. New York: W. W. North, 1951.

Coe, Charles H. "Adventuring along the 'Eastern Shore.'" *Motor Boat*, November 25, 1922, p. 8.

Dawson, Warrington. "A History of the Foundation of New Orleans (1717–1722)." *Louisiana Historical Quarterly* 3 (1920): 151–251.

de Villers, Marc. "Documents concerning the History of the Indians of the Eastern Region of Louisiana." [*Journal de la Société des Americanistes de Paris* 14 (1922)]. Translated by George C. H. Kernion. *Louisiana Historical Quarterly* 8 (1925): 28–40.

Dunbar, Roland, and Albert G. Sanders. *Mississippi Provincial Archives: 1701–1729: French Dominion*. Jackson, Miss., 1929.

Evans, E. Estyn. *Mourne Country*. Dundalk: Dundalgan Press (W. Tempest), 1967.

Faye, Stanley. "Types of Privateer Vessels, Their Armament and Flags, in the Gulf of Mexico." *Louisiana Historical Quarterly* 23 (1940): 118–130.

Fortier, Alcée. *Louisiana Studies: Literature, Customs and Dialects, History and Education*. New Orleans: F. F. Hansell and Brothers, 1894.

Gregory, Hiram F., Jr. "The Black River Commercial Fisheries: A Study in Cultural Geography." *Louisiana Studies* 5, no. 1 (Spring 1966): 3–36.

———. "The Pirogue-Builder: A Vanishing Craftsman." *Louisiana Studies* 3, no. 3 (Fall 1964): 316–318.

Jal, Auguste. *Glossaire nautique*. Paris: Firmin Didot frères, 1848.

Kane, Harnett T. *The Bayous of Louisiana*. New York: W. Morrow, 1943.

Le Page du Pratz. *History of Louisiana*. Reprint of London edition of 1774. New Orleans: Pelican Press, 1947.

Lethbridge, T. C. "Shipbuilding." In *A History of Technology*, edited by Charles Singer, E. J. Holmyard, A. R. Hall, and Trevor I. Williams, II, 563–588. London: Clarendon Press, 1956.

Margry, Pierre, ed. *Mémoires et documents pour servir à l'histoire des origines françaises des pays d'outre-mer*. 6 vols. Paris: Maisonneuve, 1879–1888.

Mitman, C. W. *Catalogue of the Watercraft Collection in the United States National Museum*. United States National Museum, Bulletin no. 127. Washington, D.C.: Smithsonian Institution, 1924.

Pfaff, Caroline S. "Henry Miller Shreve in Biography." *Louisiana Historical Quarterly* 10 (1927): 192–240.

Price, Edith Dart. "Inventory of the Estate of Sieur Jean Baptiste Prevost, Deceased Agent of the Company of the Indies, July 13, 1769." *Louisiana Historical Quarterly* 9 (1926): 411–498.

Prichard, Walter, Fred B. Kniffen, and A. Clair Brown. "Southern Louisiana and Southern Alabama in 1819: The Journal of James Leander Cathcart." *Louisiana Historical Quarterly* 28 (1945): 735–921.

Read, William A. *Louisiana-French*. Louisiana State University Studies, no. 5. Baton Rouge, 1931.

Shea, John Dawson Gilmary. *Early Voyages Up and Down the Mississippi*. Albany, N.Y., 1861.

Sibley, John. "The Journal of Dr. John Sibley, July–October, 1802." *Louisiana Historical Quarterly* 10 (1927): 474–497.

"Skiffs." *Encyclopaedia Britannica*. 14th ed. III, 761–764. 1932.

Swanton, John R. *Indian Tribes of the Lower Mississippi Valley and Adjacent Coast of the Gulf of Mexico*. Bureau of American Ethnology, Bulletin no. 43, pp. 1–387. Washington, D.C., 1911.

7. Afro-American Coil Basketry in Charleston County, South Carolina

Affective Characteristics of an Artistic Craft in a Social Context

Gerald L. Davis

In a note to his 1942 article on Afro-American art, James Porter comments, "Whereas, studies of the Negro spiritual and the Negro folksong are plentiful, research has done very little to provide the student of culture with materials for criticism of folk and craft arts of the early Negro American."[1] While few can argue with the specifics of Porter's note, particularly in light of the current activity in Afro-American studies, a wider application of the note to the fields of folkloristics and folklife studies should not be overlooked. Certainly, American folklorists have been slow to define a place in the scholarship for the phenomenon popularly known as "arts and crafts," and folklife scholars who recognize folk arts and crafts as being well within their scholarly purview are perhaps a bit too preoccupied with the classification of cultural materials under a popular or traditional culture rubric to see the value of research in "expressive" material culture.

Yet, folklorists, folklife scholars, and other students of cultural research are fully aware that a considerable portion of the metafolkloric and creative nonverbal and philosophic systems of a culture may be heavily invested in that culture's expressive systems, of which craft processes are certainly part. For folklorists, the reluctance to move more solidly into these areas stems from the dominance of oral materials in the scholarship. There is little recognition that such a major emphasis is prohibitive of the investigation of nonverbal forms of "artistic expression"[2] in culture and encourages the needless fragmentation of the study of cultural interlock and generic complementarity, so obviously important in Afro-American cultural systems.

Ruth Boyer, however, does attempt to broaden the parameters of folk arts-and-crafts evaluation by introducing into her definition of folk art the aesthetics of the community from which an item or a creative system comes.[3]

The Folk Arts are arts made by and enjoyed esthetically by members of a society as a whole or by a recognized smaller group within that society. Based on shared philosophical concepts of life and bounded by collective ethos, they represent the tastes and points of view of the group. The Folk Arts are not commercial or industrially produced arts, nor are they the products of commercial artists. But such arts can be combined and utilized so as to form part of a folk arts complex.

At times, the Folk Arts are traditional in the sense that the means of production and usages are transmitted from one generation to the next, but definitions of generations must conform to the specific group involved. At other times, the Folk Arts may be the creative output of a single generation, but to be classified as Folk Arts in this instance, they must be recognizable as a representative manifestation, in a sense, a community symbol shared by the majority of its members. The sharing may involve production or usage or both. They may or may not be traditional in that they utilize designs and forms of the past. Folk Art may include products of cottage and family industries even when the families of that industry do not avail themselves of what is made, provided each object possesses some shred of individuality resulting from the means of its manufacture or the personal foibles of the producer, and provided it conforms to the larger framework of homogeneity requisite to a group's identity. Individual expression per se is active only within bounds of shared and accepted patterns. This definition does not classify 'folk' according to economic or social levels, or geographical location.

One restricting factor: an art form can be classified Folk Art only when representing a group within the matrix of a society having a complex structure or a group that has had a prolonged contact with a complex society.

Although Phil Peek does not represent his excellent survey of research on Afro-American material culture and craftsmen as being a major work,[4] it is nonetheless important because it brings to the attention of other scholars in cultural materials the inescapable occurrence of a material culture event at the nexus of a cultural complex that overlaps with similar events within the culture to produce the strong interlocking of cultural forms that characterizes, broadly, Afro-American culture. Robert Plant Armstrong comes closest to articulating at once the range of the semantic confusion surrounding the vagueness of the terms *art* and *crafts* in the humanities and social sciences, while offering a definition that argues for a created object and the cultural systems that support it being viewed solely on their own terms. Armstrong is quoted at some length here because of the excellence and appropriateness of his statement:

I would seek a word or term . . . that serves to describe what a certain class of objects and events *is* rather than one which tries to indicate the presence or absence of that state of special grace which when present makes one object "art" and another, sometimes surprisingly like it, "not art." . . . For this reason . . . I shall speak of *affecting things and events*, which are those cultural objects and happenings resulting from human actions directed toward producing *them* rather than anything else, which is to say that they are not accidental. These objects and happenings in any given culture are accepted by those native to that culture as being purposefully concerned with potency, emotion, values and states of being or experience—all, in a clear sense, *powers*. Further, irrespective of such considerations, under certain circumstances and in some cultures such things and events may be admired for the excellence of their own properties; thus, this admiration is in itself of an affecting nature. In other words, such things and events are characterized by some people in some cultures as having "beauty." These affecting things and events may be *depictions* of subjects, objects, and states of

affairs, or they may be *abstractions* from or *variations* upon such subjects, objects or conditions. In any case, they are regarded by those
co-cultural with them . . . as being in and of the real world, however
constituted, including the mythical.[5]

Specifically, this article will explore and amplify the following points:
1.
Basketweaving as engaged in by Afro-Americans in South Carolina is a
cultural system that articulates its own aesthetic principles and can
be evaluated accordingly.
2.
Skill in basketweaving symbolizes mastery over the immediate physical
environment of the artisan and, by extension, selected particulars of
the social environment.
3.
Basketweavers manifest a high degree of self-consciousness and personal power within a loosely collective community informally bound
together by esoteric knowledge and performance.
4.
Basketweaving falls well within Armstrong's conceptualization of
affecting things and events.

The data on which this article is in part based were collected during
three field trips to Charleston County, South Carolina, in December
1970 and January, May, and June 1971. With the exception of Judith
Wragg Chase, part owner of the Old Slave Mart in Charleston, all the
people who shared their knowledge with me were Afro-Americans
living in three small communities seventeen to forty-five miles north of
Charleston.

Both in type and in crafting process, the South Carolina coast coil
baskets are African derived,[6] though South Carolina basketmakers
have had to somewhat modify certain of the craft elements. Baskets
similar to those woven in Charleston County are commonly found
throughout West and Central Africa and in recent years have been reported as being woven by the Ovambo people in South Africa as well.[7]
The bias of many non-African "Africanists" favorable to West Africa
obscures East Africa as yet another location for this particular type of
coil basket. In fact, so accustomed have scholars become to presuming
the dearth of cultural materials in East Africa that Robert Perdue could
easily report, "I have not observed such coiled basketry in Tanzania,
Uganda, or Kenya . . ."[8] However, I can report from my own collection
that this basket type is commonly found in central Tanzania and in
other parts of East Africa. In any event, it can no longer be regarded as
speculative to state that this basket type was transported to the South
Carolina coast through the skills of bodily enslaved Africans during the
years of the so-called slave trade.[9]

Although reports of "local legend" support coil basketry as being introduced by Africans in Charleston County,[10] Afro-Americans who currently sew the baskets, with one exception, strongly urged me away

from African origins for the basket technique and offered instead local etiological explanations. In interviewing one basketmaker, Edna Rouse, in preparation for an Educational Television Network presentation on the coil-basket tradition during the spring of 1971, researchers were told that "one day a few decades ago, when Edna Rouse was sick and unable to go to work, she sold one of her handmade baskets to a woman from Timmonsville who had stopped to buy some vegetables. The woman must have admired the baskets, because she asked Mrs. Rouse, 'Why not hang them up,' so that others who passed could see them. Mrs. Rouse followed the suggestion, hung all her baskets so that they could be seen, and sold all of them that first day. Before long basket stands dotted Highway 17 North of Charleston, and, along with other weavers, Edna Rouse still 'hangs baskets.'"[11]

Peter Alston, with whom I spoke at length, tends to corroborate Mrs. Rouse's recollections on the beginnings of the basket stands along Highway 17 N, though Mr. Alston (7.1) provides considerably greater detail. In the following excerpt and throughout the paper, symbol *A* designates Mr. Alston, and symbol *D* the researcher.

A.   I used to make 'em [baskets] in . . . 1926. I was in teenage like.

D.   Why did you take up basketweaving?

A.   Well, in those times and days you have to try to do something mostly like Africa. You know Africans would never take up no trade, you know, but they would just try to make something out of carving or weaving to see how it would come out, you see. So these days and times them people be doing that on their own experience, see? It wasn't much education. Whatever they have in their experience to do a thing, they do it. They never get tired. They fight at it until it finished. They complete a job. Self-experience. Most of the time in back days, see, they might have some leaders, but I don't think they . . . have to have teachers now 'cause they been doing these things so long.

D.   Were the baskets first made in Africa or were they . . . ?

A.   Well, I'll tell you the first from the bygone days. They used to make the rushel, make baskets out of rushel, rushel from the salt-water coast.[12] And they used to make these fanner . . . wide fanner . . .

D.   . . . for the rice?

A.   . . . for the rice [laughter] . . . and then from that, then they come out that they could sell baskets. . . . We had to measure the basket, nobody used to come through for the baskets. You used to have to carry them to a grocery store.

D.   In downtown Charleston or right around . . . ?

A.   No, right around in the country, and they would take 'em and they would ship 'em right off, but they would pay you for the basket at the store. And they would retail them, for they would send 'em out . . .

D.   How much [an inch] would you sell 'em for?

A.   Well, they say, I pay you so much and so much for a seven-inch basket, or a seven-by-four, or a seven-by-five. We get 'round about a dollar and a half or seventy-five cents for a small one or 'round about two dollars.

D.   And how much would he sell 'em for?

A.   Oh, I reckon . . . you never get any details about what white peoples gets. Yeah, they send them off. They get big money . . .[13] In them days and times . . . them people start in 1929, 30's, they start to put stand on the road. So they travelers who come along could buy the baskets, see? They learn a little better. The road wasn't nothing but a shell road. They built them out of shell.[14] Had a man from Dillon, South Carolina, was a contractor and went to get all his shell from the factory. Oyster factory. Them days and times . . . So now the people is from them time and time runs on, since that shell road people been putting up the basket . . .[15]

7.1

Mr. Alston, basketsewer, fifty years, plus . . .

These two statements tie the roadside basket stands to the late 1920's and the early 1930's and provide an economic rationale for their purpose and development. It further appears that the stands developed as a direct attempt by the basketmakers to control the economics of the industry that had, up to this historic moment, permitted the basketmakers to be exploited by white petty tradesmen.

When asked again how the baskets came to his area, Mr. Alston responded, "Well, I don't know. I never did heard of anybody started it down here. Well, some of the old people might look after somebody, get example from . . . that might be the old foundation they get them from, 'cause seven mile ain't but a jump from ten mile."[16]

Margaret Wilson, another basketmaker living some twenty miles closer to Charleston than did Mr. Alston, was at first reluctant to answer any questions on coil basketry. However, Mrs. Wilson (7.2) finally offered a highly individualistic saga, very much in the traditional generic vein, to explain the origins of her craft and her artistic response to the social situation in which she lived. (W=Mrs. Wilson.)

D.   Do you know when the basketweaving started in this area?
W.   . . . if I know when it started?
D.   . . . when it started and how it first started.
W.   . . . um um [negative response].
D.   Did it start during slavery times?
W.   No . . .
D.   . . . after?
W.   After.
D.   Long after?
W.   Yeah, it's a good while after. I believe it started from an old man by the name of Frank Jefferson. Old man. They had his picture on a postcard a long time ago. And he used to make basket, but he used to make them out of broomstraw like that brown straw over there, growing over there? He used to make fanners, rice fanners. This is a fanner, like this. Like you do rice. Then he started . . . they make up they would get some of this grass [sweet grass] to try it out, and that's how it started.
D.   And it just passed on?
W.   . . . right on around.
D.   Is Frank Jefferson dead now?
W.   Died. Oh, that's since I was a child.
D.   He's from this area, Charleston?
W.   To the Boone Plantation; you been there . . . ?
D.   Yeah, we visited there one time.
W.   Well, that's where it started.
D.   On the Boone Plantation?
W.   Right there. That's where I learned to make it, too.
D.   From the time you used to work on there?
W.   I used to . . . no, we were little kids and playing around there.[17]

(Mrs. Wilson was my first informant in the Charleston County area, and the conversation from which the preceding information is ex-

7.2

Mrs. Wilson, basketsewer, fifty years, plus . . .

cerpted is taken from my initial interview with her.) While a good bit of
Mrs. Wilson's information was plausible and well rationalized, much of
it was not matched by either the experiences or the knowledge of her
colleagues. It was not possible to find another basketmaker who knew
of Frank Jefferson, and Boone Hall Plantation had "misplaced" its slave
records. In fact, a front-page article in the *News and Courier* (Charleston, S.C.) of May 23, 1971, questions the colonial legacy of Boone Hall,
since on authority of the architects and contractors who did the work,
the present main house was built "from the ground up" in 1935.[18]

On one point at least, all the basketsewers are agreed—there are
distinctly different forms of basketry in Charleston County. Mrs. Wilson
mentioned that Frank Jefferson made his earlier baskets from rushel, a
long tough brown grass found along the "salt-water coast" and alongside
the brooklike inland salt-water ways that meander about in the South
Carolina Low Country (7.3). It is from this grass that the type-name
"rushel basket" comes. (This is the same grass currently called "Russian" grass and held to be unsuitable for baskets because it is "too
brittle.") Concurrent with the rushel basket is the "white oak basket"
(see note 11), again taking its name from the material used in its making. White oak is a bark that was stripped and water-softened and used
in baskets that usually bore a heavy load, such as egg baskets, clothes
hampers, and wood carriers. Both the rushel and white oak baskets
have their African prototypes.

For reasons that are not entirely evident (certainly commercial sale is
only a partial answer since money raised by selling the baskets often
went to pay property taxes),[19] coil basketry was reintroduced in two
areas along the South Carolina coast between 1900 and 1920, apparently replacing the rushel and white oak basket types. The materials
for coil basketry were certainly more readily at hand than were those
required for white oak basketry, and, though the techniques differed
somewhat and the pliant-firm relationship in the materials continued in
opposition, the wefting and warping of the materials were curiously
inverted in coil basketmaking.

Though only Mrs. Wilson offered a name and "particulars" on the
reintroduction of coil basketry in Charleston County, there is well-
documented testimony from Beaufort, South Carolina, seventy miles
south of Charleston, that handsomely supports Mrs. Wilson.[20]

In 1909, a photographer did a photographic essay of Penn Center
on St. Helena Island, near Beaufort. The photographic plates were lost
but recovered a few years ago and restored at the University of North
Carolina. Edith Dabbs subsequently used the plates in a book on Penn
Center and St. Helena Island, published in 1970.[21]

Coil baskets are prominently displayed in some of the plates, and
the name of Alfred Graham is mentioned as the first teacher of basketry

7·3

Grass identified as "rushel grass" by Mr.
Alston, growing alongside an inland
salt-water waterway, near Awendaw, South
Carolina.

at Penn Center. Graham is quoted as saying that he had brought the skill with him from Africa as a young man. About the time Graham was teaching basketry at Penn Center, the first Afro-American farm demonstration agent in the United States, B. B. Barnwell, organized coil-basket displays at local county fairs, which would suggest that coil basketry was then both vigorously enjoyed and widely practiced by Afro-Americans.

Mrs. Dabbs adds: "The materials seem a little different and I have not noticed any designs [on the Charleston County coil baskets] the same as those made on St. Helena. I would imagine that time and convenience as well as public demand have influenced these factors and am sure the source of the art as well as its original expressions are the same as that on St. Helena."[22]

The materials used in South Carolina coil basketry are all naturally grown materials found in the Charleston County Low Country. The

7.4

Sweet grass growing in wooded area in Charleston County, South Carolina.

7.5

Sweet grass approximately 16" to 18" in length.

most common of the coil, or warp, materials is locally known as "sweet grass"—*Sporobulus gracilis* (Trin.) Merr. and similar species (7.4 & 7.5). The grass is found in wooded areas rather than in marsh areas where rushel grass can be found and is usually gathered green from June to August in quantities sufficient to last a year. Mr. Alston disagrees on the matter of the sweet-grass harvesting season and states instead that the grass is gathered during the winter months for the year. The following statements from Mrs. Wilson and Mr. Alston will illustrate that the matter of material gathering is as much established practice as it is personal preference.

Mrs. Wilson

W.   Yeah, I gather them, we get them in August, July, and August, June, July, and August, and we save them up for the whole year. But you can get it in winter, but it have too much old grass in it. And then it flowers out. It has a flower that comes out of the grass.

D.   You can't use them . . . ?

W.   . . . and you can't use it then.

D.   Is this for instance . . . ?

W.   No, this is Russian . . .

D.   . . . Russian? . . .

W.   Russian.

D.   I see it's very . . .

W.   It grow near the marsh. This is the marsh grass and it gets into it. You can make baskets out this too; but I don't bother, it's too tough. It's kinda' hard.

D.   It's too hard to work with?

W.   . . . to work with.[23]

Mr. Alston

A.   In the summer, they don't have no trouble with the woods, see what I mean? They don't bother with the woods in the summertime, they get enough grass in the winter.

D.   To last the whole year?

A.   Yeah, they just keep the most of the time when they got to; some is sewing grass, all the rest is hunting grass. Sometimes they buy grass, get other people to get it for them and buy it.[24]

Mr. Alston lives within a few minutes' walk of either heavily wooded or marshy areas. Having a healthy respect for snakes, as evidenced in an elaborate corpus of snake lore, and being a successful gardener, Mr.

Alston just seems to prefer to let the sweet grass dry and age naturally. The grass is then soaked for use in basketmaking. Mrs. Wilson, on the other hand, does a brisk business in basket sales and is able to buy the materials she needs. Her grasses are used green and usually dry after having been used in a basket. Mrs. Wilson's preference seems to be the most widely spread practice now. It needs to be noted, however, that both Mr. Alston and Mrs. Wilson offer balanced practical and clearly aesthetic rationales to support their preferences.

Generally, basketsewers rarely gather their own materials, trusting the task instead to younger male members of the family (who are not "paid" directly if they are in or younger than their early teens) or to a handful of older men who seem to specialize in sweet-grass harvesting. It should be noted that much of the sweet grass is now gathered on Johns Island and Edisto Island, about thirteen to seventeen miles south of Charleston.

Most of the coil baskets are made from sweet grass, sun-dried in lengths of approximately eighteen to twenty-four inches. Basketmakers claim to like the grass because of its warm tan color and its earthy smell. A basketsewer fashions a coil from a bundle of the grass one-third to one-half inch in diameter, using this as warp material.

Long-leafed pine needles (*Pinus palustris* Mill.) are the other material used in the coil warp (7.6 & 7.7). The pine needles are much shorter than the sweet grass, approximately four to eight inches in length, and considerably stouter. When used with the sweet grass, the pine needles provide decorative relief and structural support and are used in only a few of the coils in any one basket. Occasionally, however, a basketsewer will make an entire basket from the long-leafed pine needles and will raise the price per basket to two and three times the market price of a similarly styled sweet-grass basket. The raised price is justified by the increased difficulty in working with pine needles.

Pine needles are gathered dry, after they have fallen from the trees, apparently as needed from June to the beginning of winter. When dry, the pine needles are dark brown in color and have a slight sheen. Although some dried pine is used in at least one area of East Africa (Njombe District in southern Tanzania) in coil basketry, the extensive use of this particular pine seems to be a New World modification. In East Africa, warping of varying colors is used for the same purposes—strength, decorative relief, and design modification. The pine needles are prepared for use by removing the butt end of the needle.

Dried and stripped fronds from the palmetto tree—*Serenoa repens* (Bartr.) Small—are used as wefting in the sewing of the coil baskets. Although Mrs. Wilson says there are two gatherings of the fronds monthly, the more general practice seems to be to gather the fronds as needed. Apparently this is possible the year round because of the systematic yield of the trees.

The ends of the palmetto strips, about one-quarter inch wide, are arrow-shaped with scissors for easier insertion through the coiled grasses, or warping. Like the long-leafed pine needles, palmetto trees, the state symbol, are abundant in the Charleston County Low Country and are readily available to the basketsewers.

The basketsewers rue the industrialization in the areas in which

7.6

Long-leafed pine needles growing on trees near Awendaw, South Carolina.

7.7

Long-leafed pine trees, Charleston County, South Carolina.

gatherers have traditionally been most active. New residential developments, shopping centers, recreational centers, and the like are all using
areas of the land that once bountifully supplied basketry materials.
Although some of the materials are still available locally in the vicinity
of basketsewing communities, it is more common now for suppliers to
travel some distance for the needles and grasses.[25] The basketmaker
seem to be less worried than their "concerned white friends" who pur-
chase the baskets outside the city and sell them for inflated profit in
Charleston and, now, around the country. The basketsewers themselves were prohibited from selling their products on Charleston streets
by an ordinance enacted sometime between 1939 and 1941. (This
action is reminiscent of an earlier action in Charles Town in 1744 when
"some white artisans petitioned the Commons House for relief from the
ruinous competition" of Afro-American artisans.)[26]

The only tool used by basketsewers is an awllike implement (7.8) used for "punching" the tight coils before inserting the weft strip or "taking up a stitch." Today, most of the punching tools are stems of teaspoons with filed-down ends or, less commonly, nails or split ham-bones filed down on one end with broken glass. In the past it may have been the practice to use sharpened oyster shells (see note 9).

While writing, on the one hand, that "African forms of technology, economic life and political organization had but a relatively slight chance of survival . . . and such techniques as weaving . . . were al-most entirely lost,"[27] Melville Herskovits continues elsewhere in *The Myth of the Negro Past*: "The woven trays used in the Sea Islands are made with the sewing technique called coiling, which is paramount in West Africa; more interesting is the fact that, as in Africa, the coils, in all instances examined, are laid on in a clockwise direction. This is an ex-cellent example of the way in which the determinants of behavior lying beneath the conscious level may be continued where the manipulation of materials is involved."[28]

The actual "sewing of a basket is as follows:

1.
A basket is begun, often by a helper, by gathering grasses into a suitable bundle and folding over the butt ends about one-half to one inch to form a knot.

2.
After anchoring one end of the palmetto wefting in the knot, the basket-maker begins sewing in a circle, adding lengths of grass (coils) and/or pine needles as necessary by punching through the preceding coil with the punching tool and inserting the weft. A complete "stitch" involves one complete wrapping of the coil weft with the warp material and inserting the warp through the preceding coil on the second weft wrap, in an alternating pattern (7.9).

3.
To build up the sides, the basketmaker turns the last coil slightly up-ward and sews it until the desired bowl depth is reached according to the style of basket being sewn (7.10). Basketsewers do not count the coils to measure basket dimensions but measure by eye and experience.

Several styles of baskets are manufactured in Charleston County—some decorative, some functional, some both. Most of the styles were at one time used in the homes of basketmakers, though few are used much these days, except perhaps some trays and pocketbooks. Some of the styles are fruit baskets, sewing baskets, pocketbooks, elaborate tiered

7.8

Tool used in punching an opening in coils for wefting; pictured is a filed-down spoon stem.

168

7·9

"Sewing" of coils. The "stitch" alternates a
wrapping stitch (around the coil being
worked with) with a sewing stitch.

7.10

Turning coils to form basket bowl.

baskets for storage, breadbaskets, trays of varying sizes and shapes, flower vases, and wall hangings (7.11).

The handles of the baskets are of two types—the cross handle used in fruit baskets and pocketbooks and the side handles used in breadbaskets and trays.

In constructing the cross handle, when the basketsewer has reached the place where a handle is to be added, unwrapped bundles of grass are anchored in position opposite the last completed coil (7.12). The added bundles are allowed to overlap. The unwrapped bundles are then

7.11

Roadside stand with several basket styles pictured.

wrapped separately (7.13) and finally sewn together and overlapped to form a handle (7.14). The basketmaker usually uses three to five wrapped bundles to make a sturdy handle.

The side handle is constructed by increasing the distance from the basket wall on successive coils and alternately wrapping and sewing, as in the general basketsewing technique.

Many years ago, the basketmakers apparently immersed the baskets in a saline solution to help preserve the baskets and to make them water-tight (see note 9). Possibly because of the commercial appeal of the

Gerald L. Davis

7.12

Preparation for making overlap handle.

7.13

Wrapping of overlap handle.

7.14

Overlap handle nearing completion.

174

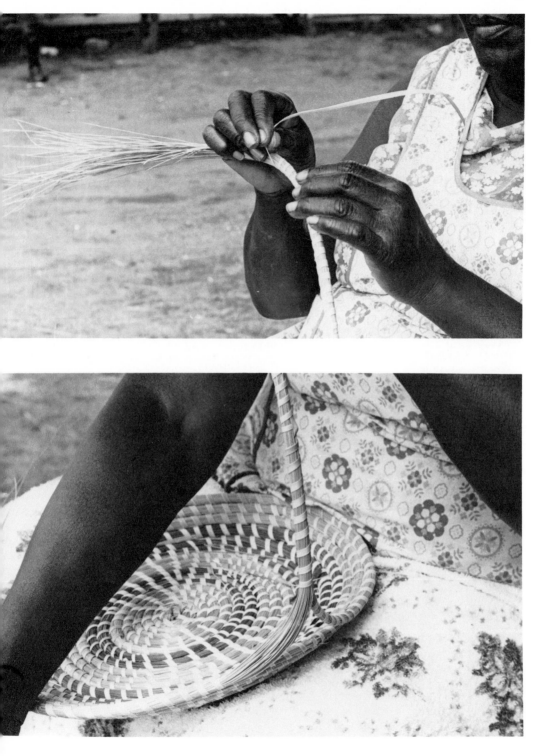

baskets or the lack of need for waterproofing, the practice has been discontinued, though most of the basketsewers generously offer the technique when asked. The one exception, again, was Mrs. Wilson, who, in answer to my question on salting the baskets for either preservation or stiffening, unequivocally responded, "Oh, no . . . we never wet ours, don't put them in water . . ."

Mr. Alston, however, did share information on the technique as it was followed some years ago.

A. . . . once upon a time when you make baskets, when we started to make baskets, we have soak 'em in salt water.

D. To soften 'em?

A. No, to stiffen it. I don't know if them do it now, but once you done make it then you let it soak in a thing of water and that salt would season the grass.

D. Would it dry it out, too?

A. Yeah. You can take cooking salt and mix it in fresh water.

D. It's like curing hams.

A. Yeah, yeah. I don't know if they doing it now; they fast making 'em, see?

D. Did it look any different?

A. Ah, it didn't look hardly different. It be much stronger, much seasoner, and it would be much tighter.

D. I'll buy some and dip 'em into salt.

A. Yeah, put it down in some season water . . .

D. How long does it stay in?

A. Oh, just let 'em soak in there for 'round fifteen minutes, then take 'em out and hang 'em up . . .

D. In the sun or the shade . . . ?

A. . . . and let 'em drip in the shade.[29]

Ethnoaesthetics is at once one of the knottier areas scholars attempt to tackle when dealing with creativity in culture, usually with little success and even less conviction. The problems are obvious enough: "beauty," or, as Armstrong writes, "that state of special grace"[30] attributed to an object or series of objects, is very rarely related to the object's creation process or even the ethnographic circumstances of the object; Western *Herrenvolk* pretensions subvert the very necessary study of ethnoaesthetics in cultures foreign to Western paradigms for reasons that seem wholly political; the mechanisms for investigating and accepting aesthetic systems and concepts foreign to Western scientific imperatives are not yet fully part of the methodological and theoretical hardware of Western investigating scholars.[31] This of course is not an exhaustive listing and probably suffers from the generous, but no less accurate, net sweep of the polemic offered here.

The word *aesthetics* is derived from the Greek verb *aisthanesthai*, meaning to feel or perceive through the senses.[32] Armstrong's humanistic approximation of aesthetics as "affecting things and events, 'those objects and happenings in any given culture . . . accepted by those native to that culture as being purposefully concerned with potency, emotion, values, and states of being or experience . . .—all, in a clear sense, powers'"[33] is remarkably close to the early Greek statement. J. G. Herder added the qualifying thought that "aesthetics must include analyses, judgments, deductions and proofs."[34]

In addition to illustrating that coil basketry in South Carolina is an affecting event as conceptualized by Armstrong, a secondary purpose of this article is to show that coil basketry is part of a larger Afro-American philosophical system that includes analysis and judgments in its normal, casual inventory of cultural hermeneutic equipment.

While the baskets and the basketsewers are important units of inquiry, there is a larger macrounit that is more suitable as a heuristic device, the notion of an aesthetic community. This concept is not as unique as it must initially appear. Folklorists have long spoken of folk groups and folk communities as voluntary and involuntary social units. Indeed, current folkloric research on the performer and his audience,[35] and to a lesser degree the uneasy distinction between active and passive tradition bearers, further implicates the performance constituency in the performance configuration, especially in African and Afro-American cultures.

"Aesthetic community" merely assumes that, in the area of the "arts and crafts" or "affecting things and events," there is a cultural base, well established in the society and articulated cross-generically via the cultural mechanisms of generic interlock and complementarity, from which the craft mode or affecting mode moves, either in opposition to or in consonance with it. This cultural base may envelop the processes and systems that support and determine the form and shape of the affecting modes native to a culture—that mystical shadow known as "tradition" that falls over cultural studies—but as well may encompass the possibility of influence by forces and factors external to the culture though not perhaps to the society. Neither the base—the principles, systems, and processes that support a society's cultural-affecting modes —nor the regulating community of participants to which it belongs is static. They are always in process, always evaluating, accepting, or discarding modal elements. A final note that must be obvious: as in Dundes's definition of folk groups, a person may belong to several aesthetic communities, though one will tend to predominate and give character to the others. Succinctly, an aesthetic community is a group of people sharing the knowledge for the development and maintenance of a particular affecting mode (or "craft") and the principles that the affecting mode must adhere to or oppose. Both conditions, articulated in and evidenced in the mode itself, must be present.

The inclusion of *community* in the definition is of primary impor-- tance. The three basketsewers I spent the most time with live in nuclear compounds. While basketsewing stretches the definition of a family and/or cottage industry somewhat, seemingly the majority of the basketsewers in Charleston County live in family units of varying sizes, most including at least three generations living on the oldest family member's land.

While the elder members of the family unit usually own the land on which the family lives, in each of the three extended families the active basketsewers are the children of the older members and parents of their own progeny. Several whole families in the county reportedly sew baskets, but the families whose members were interviewed are not among them. However, all the members of the families interviewed participate in the actual crafting process in some way, either as gatherers of materials or as "starters," the persons who assist the "master" sewer in starting the first coils on the baskets.

The mention of "master" sewers is not to suggest that there are highly organized craft unions among the basketsewers. Each family unit has at least one or, frequently, two or three "master" basketsewers, nowadays usually a female member of the family, who prepares the baskets for the commercial market. It is her obligation to pass the basketry techniques on, usually to younger women, daughters and granddaughters. Many of the basketsewers are men, but, if anything seems to be declining in the mode, it clearly seems to be the number of men who actively sew.

Unlike the women, men generally make baskets during their adolescent and teenage years, then put the basketry aside from about eighteen to roughly forty-five years of age while they work in Charleston, picking basketry up again between ages forty-seven and fifty. The exceptions are those men who are members of entire sewing families. The basketmakers interviewed could only say that young male adolescents—used here to indicate an *age* group factor, not a mental-development state—were now, when involved in basketmaking at all, concerned primarily with gathering materials. Two male high school students who were briefly interviewed acknowledged knowing how to construct coil baskets but didn't "because of school."

Mrs. Wilson reported that her apprenticeship lasted about four or five years and that her mother had been her instructor. The basketmaking technique was learned fairly quickly, but learning the several styles of baskets took a much longer period. Mrs. Wilson mentioned that her daughter learned very quickly, but no longer had time to make baskets. Mrs. Wilson's granddaughter is constantly after her to learn to sew the baskets, but Mrs. Wilson says "she isn't ready yet." Mr. Alston, on the other hand, learned to sew baskets more informally, while sitting around watching groups of older men sew and from "my own experience."

From these two testimonies, it appears that women sew either alone or with others from the family unit. When men sew, they usually do so in the company of men from other families. (A similar kind of male-female, catholic-parochial involvement in social activities is evident in many African societies in which men engage in the activities that involve wider associations than the primary living unit, while women restrict themselves to relationships within the primary and extended family unit, almost always with other women.)[36]

It is during these times that everyone involved with the affecting mode formally constitutes an aesthetic community centered around basketmaking. More informally, the entire social environment can be viewed as an aesthetic community when the life information that is shared can be utilized both in the specialized environment of esoteric basketsewing performance and knowledge and in the generalized environment of socialization.

The information that is expressed within the aesthetic community is the following:

1.
Knowledge on basketsewing:
a. The techniques of basketsewing
b. How to sew the different styles of baskets
c. How good baskets are sewed
d. How "pretty" baskets are sewed
2.
Family and regional testimonies and histories specifically related to the basketmaking context, i.e., basket lore
3.
Folkloric materials: proverbs, jokes, jests, legends, sagen, memorates, toasts, and, occasionally, tales related expressly in the basket community context
4.
Folkloristic commentaries: intersocial and extrasocial relevance of the culture's affecting modes, including folkloric materials and other affecting events

All this information is important to the development of the basketsewer and his skill in basketry. Much of the information only develops in the context of the basketmaking aesthetic community. Of the four categories of information listed, groups one and four are of major importance in this article, as illustrated below by Mrs. Wilson:

D.   When your granddaughter was small, did you ever tell her folk stories, old stories about . . .
W.   [knowing laughter and chuckles]. No, I never did tell her no story.
D.   Did she ever ask you for any?
W.   Yeah, many times, she want to hear some story, bedtime story and all like that.
D.   But you don't tell her . . . ?
W.   Yeah, sometimes I tell her bedtime story [chuckles].
D.   Which ones are your favorite ones?
W.   Hmmmm?
D.   Which ones do you like to tell the best?
W.   A prayer-story.
D.   A prayer-story?
W.   That's the only thing I ever tell her, in a prayer, you know. Say prayer and then I say: "If I should dies before I wake, I pray the Lord my soul to take. Honor thy father, honor thy mother, that thy day will be long upon the land. Bless the Lord, thy God, give it thee." That's the only one I tell her.
D.   Is it for some special reason you tell that special one?

W.   No. [pause] Then I guess there's a reason, too, 'cause I think that's a good one to tell her. [pause] O.K., then, I got to go in the store, I'll be right back.[37]

(Initially, I was convinced that Mrs. Wilson had provided me with a classic put-on. My feelings were given support by Mrs. Wilson's wry smiles and chuckles during the lead-in to the prayer-story. However, Mrs. Wilson told the prayer-story in such dead earnest and ended this section of the interview so summarily that it was obvious a good deal more must have been compacted into the material than I realized.)

The excerpt is important for two reasons. First, it clearly evidences how tightly embedded some cultural materials—in this case, folkloric minor genres—can be. This in itself is not new to folkloristic scholarship. Second, the strong clues pointing to a co-occurrence in the folkloric form of the mechanisms for aesthetic and social evaluation by culture participants are markedly different from any writing currently in the mammoth scholarship on aesthetics. For this co-occurrence strongly suggests that Afro-American performers and artisans or craftsmen consciously imbue a generic form with both an entertaining and pleasing style and the means for realizing its politicized intent.

Mrs. Wilson, for instance, clearly distinguishes a prayer from a "prayer-story" and in so doing immediately signals that a bedtime prayer,[38] traditionally held to be sacred, is in fact to be regarded as a secular narrative.[39] Since there is no audience, as such, only a grandmother and her granddaughter, it can be presumed that the intent of the narrative is directed toward personal and intimate ends. It can also be presumed that the grandmother is freeing her granddaughter to invoke liberally the rules pertaining to secular narratives and to disregard, for the duration of the narrative, the rules of behavior and evaluation that apply quite particularly to sacred narrative genres.

Perhaps it becomes apparent why there is a need to give to this bedtime narrative a special character: it is wholly political, concerned with style and instructions in the manipulation of certain units in the social environment to achieve desired personal ends. The granddaughter is strongly encouraged not to bless or ask for God's blessing for her parents, but rather to "honor"—a diminished, almost passive, form of respect—her parents, so that her days may be "long upon the land." If it can be accepted that Mrs. Wilson carefully deploys her language, it is obvious that her reference to the earth means quite specifically the land on which she and her family lives. (Ownership of the land is the hottest unspoken issue in Charleston County right now, for the land that whites are acquiring for developmental purposes is largely either owned or customarily used by Afro-Americans.)

This is a clear example of the employment of ethnoaesthetic powers in a cultural environment subsumed by Armstrong under "affecting things and events." It is also an illustration of how social elements related to a cultural-affecting mode are manipulated in some of the narratives of one basketmaking aesthetic community.

In reply to a question asking why the coil baskets were sewed on the

north side of the Charleston River and not on Johns Island where some
of the materials are gathered, Mr. Alston said:

I pay a strictly attention to that. I don't know why it takes effect this side
and it didn't start over Johns Island. I reckon that Johns Island people
have their own mind and own different category of doing things. They do
a lot of farming. They plant a lot of trucking stuff for the market, see?
And they don't have time to sit down and sew baskets, see? They do
more vegetables and things they bring into Charleston market. That's
they big minds and things, they making they money that way. But these
people [basketsewers] . . . relax from farming; more or less you travel
in various place you see lots of plantations is grown up by colored people.
Well, some people plant a piece of garden spot or something to eat. Some
of 'em plant . . . but it's nothing much they plant.[40]

The distinction Mr. Alston makes between those Afro-Americans who
farm full time and those who make baskets full time is, on the surface,
easily read "different strokes for different folks." But this reading is
just that, simplistic.

For people on Johns Island, although few in fact own large farms
anymore, the earth is unpredictable and capricious. Earth forces need to
be kept in mind; people who work the earth must be aware of the life-
yielding properties of the soil. Irreverence might produce a lighter yield,
which quickly translates into increased hunger and hardship for those
who depend on the soil for livelihood. Or, as area residents said in May
1971 when an unheard-of hailstorm ruined millions of dollars' worth
of crops on Johns Island just as they were about to be harvested, irreverence can bring disaster.

At one time Afro-Americans owned the whole of Johns Island, but,
through a combination of federal and county subterfuges, they began to
lose their land about forty years ago, so that presently about half of the
island is white owned, with much of that land being held by real estate
speculators. However, Afro-Americans are taking steps to reclaim control of their lands.

Among the basketsewers some fifty miles north of Charleston, there
is almost an arrogance about the land's products. For them the earth is
not capricious but, according to a natural rhythm of productivity, yields
predictably and generously. There is even the sense that, in bending
the materials of the land to their own use, basketsewers have mastered
parts of the land. Mr. Alston takes this one step further. An incredibly
successful gardener, he plants trees and shrubs of international varieties with a predictably high yield of fresh and exotic flowers every year,
directly attributable to his skills.

This last point is introduced to circumvent the temptation to regard
these two examples as (*a*) an active relationship with the earth demanding a certain involuntary sense of harmony with life forces (Johns Island) versus (*b*) a very passive involvement with the land requiring little
in the way of personal commitment directly to the soil. Mr. Alston's

widely regarded skills would argue instead that there is an attitudinal difference, an overt self-consciousness among basketsewers and a more subtle political consciousness among Afro-Americans on Johns Island.

Scholarship has generally not been kind to Afro-Americans in Charleston County and to the basketmaking aesthetic community in particular. Herskovits's contradictory statements cited earlier suggest that South Carolina coil basketry is only marginally African.[41] Robert Perdue writes that coil basketry is *merely* a craft in which Afro-Americans with limited creative capacities engage.[42] Patricia Greenfield and Jerome Bruner use the indices articulated in this article to opine that those who do engage in the so-called craft are powerless sycophants desperately trying to ameliorate their strong sense of powerlessness.[43]

A larger purpose of this article is to move the study of Afro-American cultural forms away from the gross ethnocentrism that has characterized research in Afro-American cultural systems for the last two or three hundred years. Rather than reciting once again the enormity of the abusive scholarship on Afro-American cultural materials, it seemed preferable to let the materials develop from context, to let the materials represent themselves, without apology, with a minimum of interference from the inherently racist bias of Western scholarship.

My deepest thanks go to the two persons whose names figure prominently in this discussion and to their families, who were generous with their time and warmth. I hope they will recognize themselves and their lives in these pages. I am also indebted to Dr. John Szwed and the Center for Urban Ethnography of the University of Pennsylvania for support during my May and June 1971 fieldtrip to Charleston County, S.C.

NOTES

1.   James A. Porter, "Four Problems in the History of Negro Art," *Journal of Negro History* 37, no. 1 (January 1942): 9–36, esp. 10 n.

2.   Dan Ben-Amos, "Toward a Definition of Folklore in Context," *Journal of American Folklore* 84 (1971): 3–15.

3.   I cite here Ruth Boyer's definition at length, from my November 26, 1968, lecture notes, because it is extremely useful and is, to my knowledge, the only serious attempt in the scholarship to define the parameters of folk art.

4.   Phil Peek, "Afroamerican Material Culture and the Afroamerican Craftsman," in *Afro-American Folk Art*, ed. William Ferris.

5.   Robert Plant Armstrong, *The Affecting Presence*, pp. 3 and 4. I found the following distinction between realism and animism helpful in looking at basketsewing in a cultural perspective against the background of anthropological research in "art and culture." (It should be mentioned that Greenfield and Bruner are psychologists on the staff of Harvard's Institute of Cognitive Studies.) "When one attributes inner psychological phenomena, such as emotion, to inanimate features of the world, we have *animism*; when one gives characteristics of the inanimate, external world to one's psychological processes, we speak of *realism* . . . Animism often has been considered the characteristic of primitive thought par excellence . . . when the culture gives no support for individualistic orientation . . . the world stays on one level of reality— the realistic." The quote is taken from "Work with the Wolof," by Patricia Greenfield and Jerome S. Bruner (*Psychology Today* 5, no. 2 [July 1971]: 42).

6.   See Robert Farris Thompson, "African In-fluence on the Art of the United States," in *Black Studies in the University*, ed. Armstead L. Robinson, Craig C. Foster, and Donald H. Ogilvie, pp. 122–170.

7.   Elizabeth McRae Scroggins ("Gullah Baskets," *ETV Guide*, April 1, 1971, p. 3) notes that Tom Waring, editor of the *Charleston News and Courier* and Col. John Doyle, of the Citadel faculty, on separate trips, both found baskets similar to the "Gullah" baskets made by the Ovambo people.

8.   Robert E. Perdue, Jr., "'African' Baskets in South Carolina," *Economic Botany* 22, no. 3 (July–September 1968): 292.

9.   This point is made in several writings. See the James Porter article already cited; also Alfred C. Prime, *The Arts and Crafts in Philadelphia, Maryland and South Carolina, 1721–1785*, I, 34, and II, 67, 79; W. E. B. DuBois, *The Negro Artisan*, pp. 17–19; Robert Perdue's article already cited; Rossa Belle Cooley, *Homes of the Freed*, p. 134; reported as far west as Kentucky in Ivan E. McDougle's *Slavery in Kentucky, 1792–1865*; Elsie Clews Parsons, *Folk-lore of the Sea Islands, South Carolina*, p. 208.

10.   Perdue, "'African' Baskets in South Carolina," p. 292.

11.   Scroggins, "Gullah Baskets," p. 3.

12.   Cooley, *Homes of the Freed*, p. 122.

13.   John Szwed, of the University of Pennsylvania, suggests that it might be useful to know what white dealers sold the baskets for, but that information is apparently not available.

14.   See Cooley, *Homes of the Freed*, p. 120, for reference to oyster-shell roads as "slave" streets. Else-where, oyster-shell roads are known as "tabby" roads.

15.   Taped interview with Peter Alston, June 5, 1971.

16.   Alston interview.

17.   Taped interview with Margaret Wilson, May 22, 1971.

18.   W. H. J. Thomas and Armistead Maupin, Jr., "Was 'Wind' Filmed at Boone Plantation?" *News and Courier* (Charleston, S.C.), May 23, 1971, p. 1-D.

19.   Cooley, *Homes of the Freed*, pp. 144–145.

20.   Personal communication with Edith M. Dabbs.

21.   Edith M. Dabbs, *Face of an Island*.

22.   Dabbs correspondence.

23.   Wilson interview.

24.   Alston interview.

25.   Scroggins, "Gullah Baskets," p. 3.

26.   See Eileen Southern, *The Music of Black Ameri-cans*, p. 57; South Carolina Writers' Program (S.C.W.P.A.), *South Carolina*, p. 119.

27.   Melville J. Herskovits, *The Myth of the Negro Past*, pp. 136–137.

28.   Ibid., p. 147.

29.   Alston interview.

30.   Armstrong, *Affecting Presence*, pp. 3–4.

31.   See Alan Dundes, "The Number Three in Ameri-can Culture," in *Every Man His Way*, ed. Alan Dundes, p. 402. See also Michael Owen Jones's article, "The Concept of 'Aesthetic' in the Traditional Arts" (*Western Folklore* 30, no. 2 [1971]: 77–104), for a lengthy but lucid discussion of folk vs. Western elite culture con-cepts of aesthetics.

32.   Joe K. Fugate, *The Psychological Basis of Herder's Aesthetics*, p. 16.

33.   Armstrong, *Affecting Presence*, p. 3.

34.   Johann Gottfried von Herder, *Sämtliche Werke*, ed. Bernhard Suphan, IV, 97, and VIII, 11.

35.   Roger D. Abrahams, "'Can You Dig It?': Aspects of the African Esthetic in Afro-America," paper pre-pared for presentation at the African Folklore Institute, Indiana University, July 16–18, 1970.

36.   Cooley, *Homes of the Freed*, p. 85. Rossa Cooley tried to "introduce" basketmaking among women on St. Helena Island in 1906. When she failed, she wrote, ". . . women do not make baskets in Africa . . . it is a man's craft and until the race changes by many more decades of contact with a new environment, it is likely to remain a man's craft."

37.   Wilson interview.

38.   The familiar form of Mrs. Wilson's prayer-story is the bedtime prayer recited in millions of American households: "Now I lay me down to sleep . . . Amen."

39.   I have written elsewhere of the polemicized tensions between sacred and secular elements, often-times used back-to-back in Afro-American folklore. See my "An Analysis of Afro-American Sermons," M.A. dissertation.

40.   Alston interview.

41.   Herskovits, *Myth of the Negro Past*, pp. 136–137.

42.   Perdue, "'African' Baskets in South Carolina," p. 291.

43.   "It may be that a collective value orientation develops when the individual lacks power over the physical world. Lacking personal power, he has no notion of personal importance. He will be less likely to set himself apart from others and from the physical world; he will be less self-conscious; and he will place less value on himself. . . . The mastery over the physical world and individualistic self-consciousness should appear together in culture" (Greenfield and Bruner, "Work with the Wolof," p. 43).

Gerald L. Davis

BIBLIOGRAPHY

Abrahams, Roger D. "'Can You Dig It?': Aspects of the African Esthetic in Afro-America." Unpublished paper prepared for presentation at the African Folklore Institute, Indiana University, July 16–18, 1970.

Armstrong, Robert Plant. *The Affecting Presence: An Essay in Humanistic Anthropology*. Urbana: University of Illinois Press, 1971.

Ben-Amos, Dan. "Toward a Definition of Folklore in Context." *Journal of American Folklore* 84 (1971): 3–15.

Boyer, Ruth. Lecture on Folk Arts, University of California, Berkeley, November 26, 1968.

Cooley, Rossa Belle. *Homes of the Freed*. With an introduction by J. H. Dillard and four woodcuts by J. J. Lankes. New York: New Republic, 1926.

Dabbs, Edith M. *Face of an Island*. Columbia, S.C.: R. L. Bryan Corp., 1970.

Davis, Gerald L. "An Analysis of Afro-American Sermons." M.A. Dissertation, University of California, Berkeley, 1970.

Dubois, W. E. B. *The Negro Artisan*. Atlanta University Publications, no. 7. Atlanta, 1902.

Dundes, Alan. "The Number Three in American Culture." In *Every Man His Way*, edited by Alan Dundes, pp. 401–424. Englewood Cliffs, N.J.: Prentice-Hall, 1968.

Fugate, Joe K. *The Psychological Basis of Herder's Aesthetics*. The Hague: Mouton, 1966.

Greenfield, Patricia, and Jerome S. Bruner. "Work with the Wolof." *Psychology Today* 5, no. 2 (July 1971): 40–43 and 74–79.

Herder, Johann Gottfried von. *Herders Sämtliche Werke*. Edited by Bernhard Suphan. 33 vols. Berlin: Weidmann, 1877–1913.

Herskovits, Melville J. *The Myth of the Negro Past*. Boston: Beacon Press, 1958.

Jones, Michael O. "The Concept of 'Aesthetic' in the Traditional Arts." *Western Folklore* 30, no. 2 (1971): 77–104.

McDougle, Ivan E. *Slavery in Kentucky, 1792–1865*. Westport, Conn.: Negro Universities Press, 1970.

Parsons, Elsie Clews. *Folk-lore of the Sea Islands, South Carolina*. Memoirs of the American Folklore Society, no. 16. New York, 1923.

Peek, Phil. "Afroamerican Material Culture and the Afroamerican Craftsman." In *Afro-American Folk Art*, edited by William Ferris. New Haven: Yale University Press, forthcoming.

Perdue, Robert E., Jr. "'African' Baskets in South Carolina." *Economic Botany* 22, no. 3 (July–September 1968): 289–292.

Porter, James A. "Four Problems in the History of Negro Art." *Journal of Negro History* 37, no. 1 (January 1942): 9–36.

Prime, Alfred C. *The Arts and Crafts in Philadelphia, Maryland and South Carolina, 1721–1785: Gleanings from Newspapers*. 2 vols. Topsfield, Mass.: Walpole Society, 1929–1932.

Robinson, Armstead L., Craig C. Foster, and Donald H. Ogilvie, eds. *Black Studies in the University: A Symposium*. New Haven: Yale University Press, 1969.

Scroggins, Elizabeth McRae. "Gullah Baskets." *ETV Guide* (South Carolina), April 1, 1971, p. 3.

South Carolina Writers' Program. *South Carolina: A Guide to the Palmetto State*. New York: Oxford University Press, 1941.

Southern, Eileen. *The Music of Black Americans: A History*. New York: W. W. Norton and Co., 1971.

Thomas, W. H. J., and Armistead Maupin, Jr. "Was 'Wind' Filmed at Boone Plantation?" *News and Courier* (Charleston, S.C.), May 23, 1971.

Thompson, Robert Farris. "African Influence on the Art of the United States." In *Black Studies in the University: A Symposium*, edited by Armstead L. Robinson, Craig C. Foster, and Donald H. Ogilvie, pp. 122–170. New Haven: Yale University Press, 1969.

8. The Whitaker-Waggoner Log House from Morgan County, Indiana

Warren E. Roberts

From early in the nineteenth century until the fall of 1966, a large six-room log house stood west of the town of Paragon in Morgan County, Indiana. While it is true that its very size alone would keep it from being termed a "typical" southern Indiana log house, still it shares a number of features with many other log houses in this area. This fact, plus the fact that it was torn down to be reassembled as one of the buildings in the projected Indiana University Outdoor Museum of Folk Life, warrants a detailed description of the house. The study of log buildings in the United States must be said to be very little developed. We have available at the present time a rather small amount of information for comparative purposes. What is needed is a series of articles and monographs describing log buildings in detail. This article may be viewed as a contribution toward this goal. It will be essentially descriptive rather than comparative; that is, it will describe the building but will not make many comparisons between it and other buildings either in Indiana or elsewhere in the United States. Comparisons are best made in the context of a broad survey, and that survey will be made at another time.

According to local tradition and a family history in the possession of a descendant,[1] the house was built in the 1820's by Grafton B. Whitaker. He was born in Kentucky in 1799 and moved to Indiana as a young man. He was a prominent person in the area, a trustee of the Samaria Baptist Church, organized in 1829, and a school trustee. He was also an officer of the Forty-fifth Regiment of the State Militia of Indiana, a captain in 1828 and a colonel in 1833. The house and land passed through a number of hands in the nineteenth and twentieth centuries. The present owner, Roscoe Waggoner, bought the farm in the 1930's. He repaired the log house, which had been vacant for some time, and lived in it until the 1950's when he built a modern frame house nearby, using some materials from the log house. The log house stood vacant for several years until it was purchased by Dr. and Mrs. James Farr of Bloomington, Indiana, who, in turn, donated it to the Indiana University Foundation. It was disassembled in the fall of 1966 and hauled to Bloomington, where it is, as of this writing, stored on a tract of land adjoining the university campus, the proposed site of the Outdoor Museum.

The house consists of two parts, which probably were constructed at different times since the logs in the two sections have corner notches of two different kinds (8.1). The main and, presumably, earliest part of the house has V-notched logs. It is thirty-six feet in width and eighteen feet six inches in depth, with two rooms of approximately equal size on the ground floor and two matching rooms above; a log partition separates the rooms (8.2). While this part of the house is not a full two stories in height, neither can it be called a one-and-a-half-story struc-

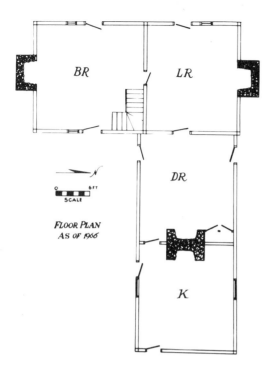

BR   LR

N

SCALE
0   6 FT

FLOOR PLAN
AS OF 1966

DR

K

8.1

Floor plan as of 1966. (I would like to thank
Thomas Kirkman for his assistance with
this and other drawn illustrations.)

186

8.2

Whitaker-Waggoner log house, front and
side views.

8.3

Rear wing, or ell, thirty-six by seventeen feet.

8.4

Sketch of foundation at southwest corner; sill, floor joist, and cross section of front wall. Note that the stones in the foundation indicate that the entire perimeter was laid at one time. The large stone in the second course at the corner is tied into the rest of the wall. The large sill projects inward beyond the log wall so that the ends of the floor joists can rest on it rather than on the foundation.

ture. The walls on the second floor are about four feet in height along the eaves; that is, above the floor level are two and a half logs plus the plate before the roof starts. There is no hallway of any kind in the house and, as is common with log, frame, and masonry houses that do not have central hallways, there are two front doors, one for each room.[2] The staircase, which is enclosed, rises directly from one room and has a storage cupboard underneath it. Each downstairs room has a fireplace so that there is a stone chimney stack at each end of the house.

The rear wing, or ell, is part frame and part log, using single dovetail corner notches. It has nearly the same dimensions as the main part of the house, thirty-six by seventeen feet, but is only one story in height (8.3). The log portion of the wing is placed farthest from the main part of the house and is connected to it by the frame portion, since it is difficult to join two separate log structures directly to each other. Large sills and plates, however, run the entire thirty-six feet. A central chimney in the wing has two fireplaces, one opening into each room.

A description of the construction features of the house can logically begin with a discussion of the foundation and the masonry work. In general it may be said that the masonry work is of very high quality. Limestone in the form of naturally occurring field stone was used throughout. I might mention that the house stood in an area where much stone was available, for the surrounding countryside is honeycombed with caves and sinkholes. Porter's Cave, for example, is a large and well-known cave not more than one-half mile from the house. The clay that was used for mortar is particularly noteworthy, for it clung with remarkable tenacity to the stones when the chimneys were taken down; indeed, it seemed that it was harder to remove from the stones than conventional modern mortar would be. The clay was probably found in the vicinity of the house. Only above the roof line, where rain had gradually washed out the clay mortar, had it been found necessary to replace or patch the clay mortar with modern mortar.

The foundations of the house and the chimney stacks went only a short distance below the level of the ground, but they had supported the great weight over the years so that the house and chimneys showed no signs of sagging or uneven settling. At the time the house was disassembled, the stone foundation went around the entire outside perimeter, and I am inclined to believe that this perimeter foundation was original in that large stones at the corners were tied in with the rest of the foundation (8.4). Much more common in southern Indiana is the corner type of foundation, wherein a building is supported only at the four corners. When this corner type of foundation is used, however, people often fill in with stones between the corners at a later date to keep out small animals from underneath the house. Hence, it is difficult to determine whether the original foundation of a log building was of the perimeter or the corner type. This question, however, is of considerable importance, for the type of foundation that is used has a decisive influence on the general structure of a log building.

Because of the lack of detailed information on log buildings in the United States, it is impossible to speak with any degree of certainty, but I would like to suggest—and this suggestion of course must be tested in the light of further evidence—that the perimeter foundation represents a general northern building type while the corner foundation represents a southern type. In the southern United States, dampness and warmth dictated a corner foundation, for a free circulation of air under the house was necessary to prevent decay, while the general mildness of the winters did not cause too much discomfort from cold floors. In the northern parts of the country, however, a perimeter foundation was necessary in order to keep the house comfortable during the cold winters. Indeed, it was customary in New England, at least, to "bank" houses in the fall by piling leaves, straw, and the like around the foundations to prevent cold air from blowing under the house. At the same time, the climate was dry enough, generally speaking, so that decay was no great problem. When a true corner foundation is used, the house must be built in such a way that the weight of the structure is transferred to the corners. Huge sills, for example, are needed to support the weight of the floor without sagging and to carry this weight to the corners. When the perimeter foundation is used, however, the sills need not be so large, for the weight of the floor is carried by the foundation, which supports the sills along their entire length. Moreover, when the corner foundation is used, huge plates are required to support the weight of the roof and transfer this weight to the corners. The majority of the nearly three hundred log houses that I have examined in southern Indiana have this combination of corner foundation, large sills, and large plates. The Whitaker-Waggoner house, however, is unusual in that it has a perimeter foundation, large sills, and large plates. This combination points once more to the fact that southern Indiana is a transitional area with both northern and southern traits.

The shape and general construction of the chimneys and fireplaces can be seen in 8.5 & 8.6. The fireplaces had been boarded up in recent years, and when the kitchen fireplace was opened the original iron crane was found to be still in place. The interstices between the logs in the house were filled with flat stones plastered over with clay, unlike most log buildings, which use pieces of wood covered with clay "chinking."

On the stone foundation are laid, first, two large sills, hewn on all four sides, ten by fourteen inches and thirty-six feet in length. These sills are about eight inches wider than the rest of the wall so that the floor joists can sit on the part that projects inside the walls (see fig. 8.4). The floor joists are small logs, roughly eight to ten inches in diameter, with the tops and two adjacent surfaces hewn flat (8.7). The ends of the joists are likewise hewn so they can rest evenly on the sills. The flooring on the ground floor of the main house is one-and-a-quarter-inch-thick tongue-and-grooved ash, while the second floor has poplar flooring of similar dimensions, also tongue and grooved.

The walls of the house are, of course, made of what are conventionally called "logs," but the inadequacy of this term is at once apparent when we examine the actual timbers. They are logs that have been hewn on two sides to a reasonably uniform thickness of about six inches. The upper and lower surfaces have, however, been left with the natural curvature of the log; indeed, in most instances the bark has not even been removed from these surfaces. As a result, there are interstices between the timbers, or logs, varying from a fraction of an inch to as

8.5

Fireplace in front section of the house.

8.6

Exterior view of chimney construction.

8.7

Cross section of a typical floor joist on the ground floors. Hewn surfaces shown at *a, b,* and *c*; bark is on the remainder of the log.

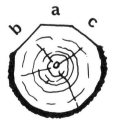

much as six inches. Larger interstices are rare because straight logs were chosen and, as previously noted, the interstices are filled with flat stones covered with clay.

The logs naturally vary in width but average about sixteen inches. The majority of them are beech, but other woods are found as well. One large log in the rear wing, for example, is of mulberry wood. The corners on the main part of the house employ so-called V-notches. Where the log partition joins the outside walls the joints are halved together (8.8). The logs in the walls are, therefore, only about eighteen feet in length; it is the thirty-six–foot–long sills and plates that tie the whole structure together. The logs rise only as high as the eaves; the gable ends between the top logs and the rafters are filled in with hewn studs. The joists that carry the second floor in the main part of the house sit in notches cut completely through the logs in the wall. These joists were sawed, probably at a water-driven sawmill that is known to have once existed in the locality. The fact that the joists are carefully planed and the bottom corners are decorated with a bead molding indicates that they were exposed to view from the ground floor when the house was built.

Where doors and windows occur, the logs have been sawed out. An oak timber approximately two by six inches in cross section, which has been rived from a log, is placed flush against the sawed ends of the logs, and oaken pins one inch in diameter have been driven through the timber and into the ends of the logs. Over these riven timbers, of course, the more finished door and window casings have been fitted.

The plates are timbers hewn on all four sides about ten by fourteen inches by thirty-six feet in length. On them the rafters rest, and they and the plates overhang the wall by about eight inches. The plate's function is, as explained previously, to carry the weight of the roof to the corners of the house where the logs in the wall rest solidly on each other. The top log on the gable end, which supports the plates, extends out to each side so that the plate can overhang the wall. A small four-square hewn timber, which crosses the gable end of the house, sits on top of the plate. An oaken pin, or trunnel (treenail), two inches in diameter and a foot in length passes through this timber, through the plate, and into the log beneath it (8.9). At the point where the log partition passes through the house, another timber spans from one plate to the other and is dovetailed into the top side of the plate and pinned. This transverse timber ensures that the outward thrust of the roof cannot bow the plate out of line.

The rafters are hewn and approximately three by five inches in cross section. There is no ridgepole; instead, the rafters are notched and pinned together at the peak. Every other pair of rafters has a tie brace passing between them, forming the shape of a squatty letter *A*. These tie

8.8

Detail of log construction, showing junction of log partition with outside walls.

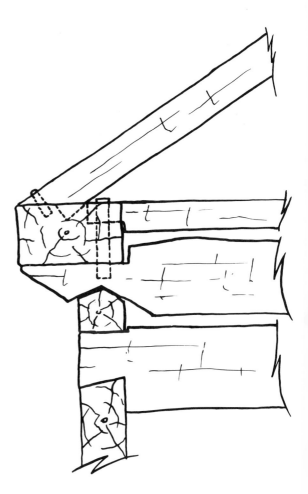

8.9

Sketch of southeast corner of rear wing showing logs in wall; log holding up plate; plate; square timber dovetailed into top of plate; trunnel driven through square timber, plate, and log beneath; rafter notched into plate; and trunnel driven through the rafter into plate.

braces are notched and pinned to the rafters. The roof decking is of wide, rough-sawed boards whose edges have not been trued in any way; they show the contour of the log from which they were sawed. Sawed red cedar shingles covered the roof in 1966. They undoubtedly replaced earlier shingles that had been rived from native lumber.

In 1966 the outside of the walls was covered with clapboards of yellow poplar (*Liriodendron tulipifera*). It seems to be taken more or less for granted in the United States that, when a log building is covered with siding of any sort, the siding is not original but a late, indeed fairly recent, addition. Hence, whenever a log building is restored, rebuilt, or moved and re-erected either by an individual, historical groups, or museums, it is stripped of its siding so that the logs and the clay "chinking" are exposed to the weather (the clay is usually replaced with modern mortar). Moreover, illustrations in books and articles usually depict hewn-log structures without any siding. The serious student of folk architecture, however, can hardly afford to take for granted notions of this sort. I feel, therefore, that I must dwell at some length on this point.

When the Whitaker-Waggoner house was disassembled, it became clear that the clapboard siding had been put on at the time the house was built because, in the first place, on the gable ends the clapboards extended across behind the chimney and could only have been put in place before the chimney was built and, in the second place, wherever the siding was still in good condition, the surfaces of the logs underneath the siding showed no signs of ever having been exposed to the weather.

The Whitaker-Waggoner house is not an isolated example. Under normal circumstances, however, only when a log house is being disassembled is it possible to investigate this point. I have been able to examine several other hewn-log houses that were being torn down; after the siding was removed, it was clear that the outer surfaces of the logs had never been exposed to the weather. I have even found one house near Trevlac, Indiana, that, underneath the siding, had no chinking in the walls—clear proof that the siding had been applied at the time the house was built. I have also seen a number of hewn-log houses standing on their original sites that had no siding. Investigation has nearly always revealed, however, that siding had been on the buildings at one time. On the basis of the evidence now at hand, I am persuaded that, in nineteenth-century southern Indiana when a substantial hewn-log house was built as a permanent home, it was customary practice to cover the outside with siding of some sort, usually clapboards. This generalization, of course, is not meant to apply to other types of log buildings, especially those built with round logs.

Why were hewn-log houses covered with siding? Was it only for the sake of appearance, to make a log house look like a frame house? Actually, studying folk architecture has led me to conclude that it is severely practical and functional and very little given to ornamentation purely for the sake of ornamentation. The fact of the matter is that the exterior surfaces of hewn-log buildings are subject to severe deterioration when exposed to the weather. As a case in point, I can cite hewn-log houses at Spring Mill State Park, Indiana. In this instance old log houses were moved into the park in the 1930's and reassembled in an artificial "pioneer village" environment. Although the houses had been covered

with siding previously and were in good condition after the passage of some one hundred years, after standing in the park without siding for about thirty years, the outside surfaces of the hewn logs have in many cases deteriorated very seriously to the point where many of the logs have been replaced (8.10).

Leaving hewn logs exposed to the weather creates at least three major problems. First of all, the logs develop cracks of various sizes as they season and water gets into these cracks and causes decay. There was in

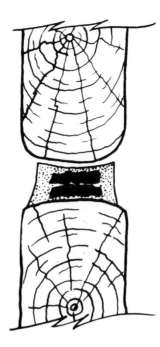

8.10

Deterioration of outside surfaces of hewn logs without siding.

8.11

Cross section through wall showing parts of two logs and chinking composed of flat stones and clay. The gap where the clay has pulled away from the upper log is here exaggerated for purposes of illustration.

the past no practical way either to prevent these cracks or to fill them. If the cracks are filled with mortar, it soon works loose as detailed below. Modern wood preservatives, of course, can be used with success, but they were not available in the past. In the second place, the "chinking" can never remain watertight for very long. No matter how well seasoned it may be, wood will continue to expand and contract with changes in humidity. When the weather is dry, wood contracts, and when it is damp, wood expands. This expansion and contraction occurs primarily

199

across the grain; in the direction of the grain it is very slight. The amount of expansion and contraction, of course, depends upon many factors: the type of wood, the amount of humidity, and so on. A log two feet in width (and logs of this size are not uncommon in southern Indiana log houses) would expand and contract at least a quarter of an inch over the course of a year with extremes of humidity. What effect this "working" of the wood has upon the joint between the log and the chinking should be apparent at once. The space between the curved surfaces of the log and the clay or mortar makes a natural channel for water to enter and cause decay, and this situation is aggravated when the bark is left on the upper and lower surfaces of the log, as is often the case (see fig. 8.11). The third problem concerns the door and window openings. It is very difficult to make a watertight seal where the casings of doors and windows meet the logs because of the uneven surfaces of the logs and the chinking. Water can get behind the trim and cause rotting. In abandoned log houses that have fallen into disrepair, one nearly always finds that the logs under windows and the sills under doors have rotted badly. It seems to me, by the way, that this is one reason why log buildings have few windows on the gable ends but usually have the doors and windows on the front and back: the overhanging eaves on the front and back of the house help to keep rain water from running down the walls and getting behind the door and window trim. When siding is used on a house and kept in good repair, on the other hand, it is possible to make a watertight seal around the doors and windows. Frame houses that are covered with clapboards, for example, have stood for centuries without any rotting of the frame under the doors and windows.

To return now to the details of the Whitaker-Waggoner house, the main structural features have been dealt with, but some remarks on other features are in order. When the house was built, two separate small porches, each six feet ten inches in width and extending six feet seven inches out from the house, covered the front doors. The outlines of these porches were still clearly visible on the siding of the house, and probing in the ground established their foundations. The plate at the front of the house was boxed in, and dentil moldings made of pieces of lath were nailed on to create an interesting neoclassic detail.

The most noteworthy features of the interior are the doors, the mantelpieces, and the built-in cupboards. It is obvious that a carpenter of unusual ability designed and built these features. The doors in the back part of the house are of simple "board-and-batten" design. They consist of vertical boards with tongue-and-groove joints and decorative bead moldings on each edge and two battens four inches wide and one inch thick with wide beveled edges nailed horizontally on the backs. The doors in the front of the house, however, are of an unusual eight-panel design (8.12). The mantelpieces, and three of the four are preserved, show clear neoclassic influences (8.5). All three are basically alike

8.12

Front door, one of two, of unusual eight-panel design.

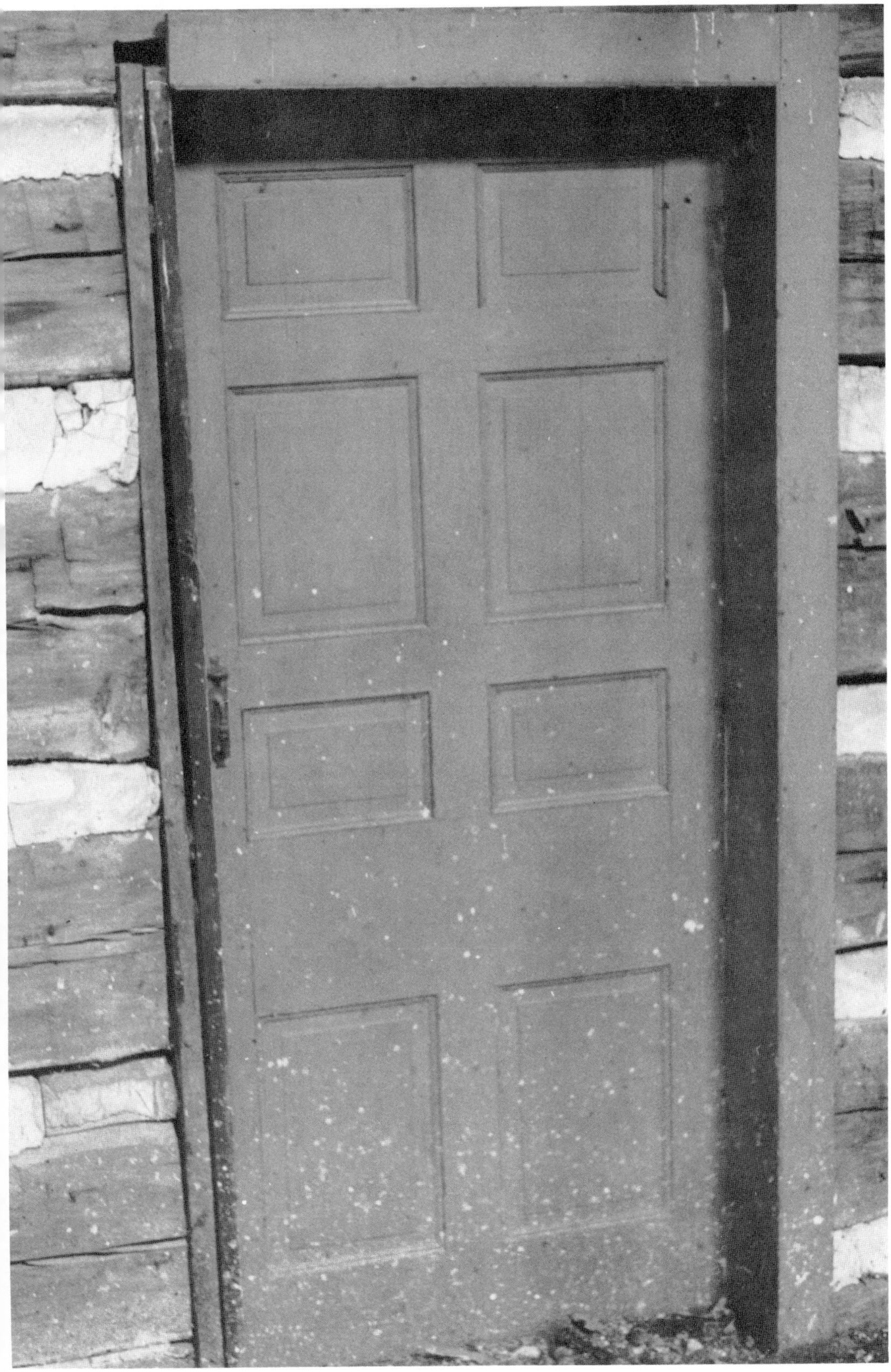

8.13

Log barn on Whitaker-Waggoner Farm.

though, of course, of different dimensions. A large built-in cupboard occupied the niche between the fireplace and the wall in the dining room (8.1).

A detailed description of the other buildings and the site is not advisable, for several of the buildings have been constructed in recent years by the present owner. While it is true that the student of folklife cannot be guided by antiquarian principles, accepting only what is old and discarding what is new even if traditional, nonetheless a detailed description of the other buildings on the site and their relative ages

would occupy too much space and deserves separate treatment. A few noteworthy features concerning the site may, however, be mentioned. About 150 yards north of the house stands a large log barn enclosed on all four sides by attached frame sheds (8.13). The barn is of the two-crib type; that is, two sets of logs are separated at the ground level by an open runway. Above the runway, however, two logs and a large plate span the entire structure and tie it together.[3] The logs in the barn are hewn on two surfaces and joined at the corners with single dovetail notches as are those in the rear wing, or ell, of the house. The logs in the main part of the house, it will be recalled, are joined at the corners with V-notches. Between the house and the barn is a small ravine with a spring. Building sites for old farmhouses in southern Indiana, I might add, seem to have been chosen because of the proximity of springs. At least, practically every old log farmhouse I have visited has been located near a spring.

It is axiomatic that written records, whenever available, should be used in attempting to date a building. Unfortunately, in this instance, as is so often the case, the written records are inadequate. Land deeds tell us when the land was entered and a family history tells us when the supposed builder or, at least, the first owner came to Indiana from Kentucky. They do not, however, establish beyond doubt that the existing house and barn were built at this time; it is always possible that other buildings that have since disappeared were the original structures and that the existing buildings are later replacements. Indeed, in this case, since the existing structures are so large and must have taken considerable time to build, there is a strong likelihood that Grafton B. Whitaker erected some smaller, less-permanent house to live in while he cleared his land and later built, or had built, these structures.

The student of folklife, of course, is always aware of oral traditions. While it would be unwise to raise here the familiar question of oral tradition as "authentic" history, it is clear that, in attempting to establish a date at which a house was built, oral traditions must be treated with caution. There seems to be a general tendency for oral tradition either to exaggerate the age of a building or to be content with the too-vague phrase "It's over a hundred years old." In this case, oral tradition reports that the rear wing of the house was added at a later date and that the logs in the rear wing came from another old building. Since the corner notches of the logs in the main part of the house and in the rear wing are of two different types, this tradition seems plausible. It is, however, also possible that the relatively small log portion of the rear wing embodies logs from the original house that was built on the site. Oral tradition also maintains that a huge stone foundation extended ten feet into the ground under each chimney stack and that all the logs in the walls were held together at the corners by hidden pins or trunnels. The fact that the chimney stacks are massive piles of stone, were in perfect condition in 1966, and had neither sagged nor settled over the years must have given rise to the tradition concerning the foundations. Excavation revealed that the foundations extended no more than a foot or two below ground level. The fact that large trunnels are visible in the attic where they penetrate the plate and hold it to the logs probably gave rise to the tradition concerning the trunnels in the corners of the logs in the wall. When the logs were taken down, no trunnels of this sort were found; indeed, the corner notches commonly employed in hewn-log buildings are designed to hold the logs tightly in place at the corners and make any other type of fastening unnecessary.

In attempting to fix dates for the construction of a building, a detailed examination of the fabric of the structure itself is essential and must be used to supplement and counterbalance the information gleaned from written records and oral sources. Unfortunately, determination of dates on the basis of such an examination is also fraught with difficulties. In the first place, it is often only when a building is being disassembled that it is possible to find enough evidence to reach meaningful conclusions; if a building is in good condition, the really important evidence may be covered by relatively modern additions. In the present case, the most indicative feature, to be mentioned below, could only have been discovered when the house was being disassembled. In the second place, any house that has been lived in over a period of years has undergone many changes and additions. Doors and windows, for example, are added and removed, new floors are laid over old, rooms are remodeled, and so on. Moreover, some portions of a building, especially the roofing, are naturally subject to wear and have to be replaced from time to time. In the third place, it was much more common in the past than it is today to use materials salvaged from other buildings either in the original construction of a building or in later repair and remodeling. Hence, it is possible to find materials much older than the building itself incorporated into it. House logs, especially, can easily be used over and over again since it is mainly the corner notches and their own weight that hold them together. Time after time I have been told that log buildings, or parts of them, have been taken down, moved, and reassembled or added to other structures, and I have no doubt that these reports are substantially correct.

To deal point by point with the various features of the Whitaker-Waggoner house from the standpoint of dating would be fruitless. Most features of the construction could have been used at almost any time in the nineteenth century, not to mention the early part of the twentieth century, or even the eighteenth century, although the history of Indiana largely precludes this last possibility. One of the reasons for this state of affairs is that which attracts the folklorist to folk architecture: tradition exerts a powerful sway in the choice of building materials and in building techniques, and tradition in this case is buttressed and reinforced by functional considerations. For example, hewn logs were used in the construction of this house, we might say, because this was a traditional way of building. But we must also add that the materials were readily available for this type of construction, that the builder was familiar with the required building techniques and had the necessary tools, and that the finished building was staunch, commodious, and pleasing to the eye, required a minimum of upkeep, and was superbly insulated against both the cold of Indiana winters and the heat of Indiana summers. Other types of construction were theoretically possible. Grafton Whitaker might have built a stone house. The materials for a stone house were at hand and superb masonry skills were also at hand; witness the stone fireplaces and chimneys. The materials for a frame house were also at hand, and the skills needed, while of a slightly different order, are no more demanding than those required for a log house of this sort. In the last analysis, the folklorist must probably fall back upon the comfortably vague word *tradition*. Whitaker probably built the kind of house he did because it was the kind he was familiar with. He knew that type of house and he knew its very obvious virtues. He wanted a house that was substantial and enduring and chose not to experiment with unfamiliar types—a wise choice, I might add, in the light of hindsight.

But to return to the features of the house that might help in dating it, most of the features cannot allow one to be very exact. Many features tell us at once that we are dealing with early rather than contemporary construction: the logs, sills, plates, rafters, and studs are hewn rather than sawed; hand-molding planes, rather than material from a planing mill, were used for decorating the interior; and clay was used in the masonry rather than modern mortar. As it happens, however, it is the hardware to which we must turn for more exact evidence, to be more specific, the door hinges and the wood screws that hold them on. The paneled doors in the front of the house, I assume, are original. They are handmade of yellow poplar with through-mortice-and-tenon joints pinned with wooden trunnels, and they harmonize with the rest of the interior woodwork. I believe they were made by the same carpenter who made the mantelpieces, for instance. The hinges appear to be original, for they exactly fit the only mortices on the doors and door frames. If hinges have been replaced on a door, it is very rare to find them fitting the mortices exactly. The hinges in question are butt hinges of cast iron and obviously of an early type in that the pin was an integral part of the casting rather than a separate part as in modern, so-called loose-pin hinges. The cast-iron butt door hinge was patented in England in 1775 and rapidly replaced other types of hinges.[4] The hinges were held to the doors and frames with flat-headed, blunt-ended wood screws. Henry Mercer tells us that the wood screw in use in the early nineteenth century was "invariably blunt-ended," that a machine to point the ends of wood screws was patented in New York in 1846, and that the pointed variety of screw "universally superseded the pointless screw."[5] The hinges and their screws show that the house was probably built after 1775 and before 1846. The history of settlement in Indiana allows us to be more precise: after 1820 and before 1846. Greater precision than this we probably cannot obtain. The rest of the hardware in the house would agree in a general way with these dates. No eighteenth-century hand-made nails were found, for instance, but there were great quantities of machine-made cut nails of the type manufactured after 1820.[6] Although many of the original door latches had been replaced by modern knobs, several cast-iron latches of an early-nineteenth-century type were on the doors.

A brief summary of the history of the house may close this discussion. The main part was built probably in the late 1820's and the rear wing shortly thereafter. The rear wing used partly logs from some other building. At the time the house was built, or very soon thereafter, it was covered with clapboard siding. Although a number of minor changes and additions were made over the course of the years, the only significant one was the removal of two small front porches, until the fall of 1966 when the house was disassembled to be rebuilt eventually in the Outdoor Museum of Folk Life at Indiana University.

NOTES

1. Mr. J. B. Whitaker of Paragon, Indiana.

2. See Henry J. Kauffman, "The Riddle of Two Front Doors," *Dutchman* 6, no. 3 (Winter 1954–1955): 27.

3. This type of barn has been discussed in Henry Glassie, "The Pennsylvania Barn in the South," *Pennsylvania Folklife* 15, no. 2 (Winter 1965–1966): 12–16.

4. Henry C. Mercer, *Ancient Carpenters' Tools*, p. 259.

5. Ibid., p. 256.

6. Ibid., p. 246. Mercer errs in stating that the machine-pressed wire nail "revolutionized the nail industry by driving the cut nail out of the North American market, about 1890" (p. 238). The cut nail is presently available at any Indiana lumberyard, for it is still widely used for nailing hard woods, such as oak flooring. Being brittle, it will not bend in such applications as will a wire nail. It has other practical advantages, too. Being rectangular in cross section, if it is driven into the wood with its long axis parallel to the grain it is less likely to split the wood than would a round nail of comparable size. Moreover, since it tapers on two surfaces from the head to the point, it can more easily be removed from wood than can the wire nail.

BIBLIOGRAPHY

Erixon, Sigurd. "Är den nordamerikanska timringstekniken överförd från Sverige?" *Folkliv* 19 (1955): 56–68.

Glassie, Henry. *Pattern in the Material Folk Culture of the Eastern United States*. University of Pennsylvania Monographs in Folklore and Folklife, no. 1. Philadelphia: University of Pennsylvania Press, 1968.

———. "The Pennsylvania Barn in the South." *Pennsylvania Folklife* 15, no. 2 (Winter 1965–1966): 8–19; 15, no. 4 (Summer 1966): 12–25.

———. "The Types of the Southern Mountain Cabin." In *The Study of American Folklore: An Introduction*, edited by Jan H. Brunvand, pp. 338–370. New York: W. W. Norton, 1968.

Fife, Austin, Alta Fife, and Henry Glassie, eds. *Forms upon the Frontier: Folklife and Folk Arts in the United States*. Monograph Series, 16, no. 2. Logan: Utah State University Press, 1969.

Kauffman, Henry J. "Literature on Log Architecture: A Survey." *Pennsylvania Dutchman* 7, no. 2 (1955): 30–34.

———. "The Riddle of Two Front Doors." *Dutchman* 6, no. 3 (Winter 1954–1955): 27.

Kniffen, Fred. "Folk Housing: Key to Diffusion." *Annals of the Association of American Geographers* 58 (1965): 549–577.

———, and Henry Glassie. "Building in Wood in the Eastern United States: A Time-Place Perspective." *Geographical Review* 56 (1966): 40–66.

Mercer, Henry C. *Ancient Carpenters' Tools*. 3d ed. Doylestown, Pa.: Bucks County Historical Society, 1960.

Roberts, Warren E. "Folk Architecture." In *Folklore and Folklife: An Introduction*, edited by Richard M. Dorson, pp. 281–293. Chicago: University of Chicago Press, 1972.

Shurtleff, Harold R. *The Log Cabin Myth: A Study of the Early Dwellings of the English Colonists in North America*. Cambridge: Harvard University Press, 1939.

Wacker, Peter O., and Roger T. Trindell. "The Log House in New Jersey: Origins and Diffusion." *Keystone Folklore Quarterly* 13, no. 4 (Winter 1968): 248–268.

Weslager, Clinton A. *The Log Cabin in America from Pioneer Days to the Present*. New Brunswick, N.J.: Rutgers University Press, 1969.

———. "Log Houses in Pennsylvania during the Seventeenth Century." *Pennsylvania History* 22 (1955): 256–266.

———. "Log Structures in New Sweden during the Seventeenth Century." *Delaware History* 5, no. 2 (September 1952): 77–95.

9. Tollgate Lore from Upstate New York

A Contribution to Folk-Cultural Studies

David J. Winslow

This study of tollgate lore is essentially a folk-cultural study in that it sheds light on many aspects of the total culture of the Upstate New York region in the nineteenth century. Historically, this investigation offers information on the modes of transportation and the early transportation routes that linked rural areas to each other and to the cities. It also becomes involved in examining such cultural patterns as architectural differences of tollhouses, the conduct of farming, the amusements of rural people, religion, superstitions, place names, folktales, and other elements relating to folklife studies. Parallels from the British Isles were found in many instances, and these are offered for comparative purposes. In addition to the historical approach, contemporary informants offer oral material on the subject, and, whenever possible, the relevance of tollgates to present-day life and thought has been noted.

The spiritual heritage of Yorkers was in evidence, too, even if some of their material culture was destroyed when an angry mob gathered near Waterford on a hot day in July 1863 and tore down the last remaining tollgate on the Stillwater-Waterford Turnpike. Public antagonism to the turnpike company reached a climax in this act and reflected a burgeoning discontent with most turnpike and plank-road companies throughout Upstate New York during the last half of the nineteenth century. Probably this was one of only a handful of cases where a tollgate was torn down as a result of public violence, but nearly all the rustic structures have disappeared in one way or another from the landscape. The tollhouses are fascinating for the antiquarian, but most travelers on the old roads thought of them only as places to be detained while on a journey and where "you had to show the color of your money," as one old-timer put it.[1] For a few, the old tollhouses were places for conversation, companionship, and recreation. Quite a few of the original structures still survive in New York State, but they either have been abandoned and moved or have been drastically renovated to serve other purposes. A few old photographs and pictures from rare postcards are still extant to show how the once-common landmarks appeared.

Most persons would agree that there was good reason for the angry crowd to tear down the tollgate on the Stillwater-Waterford Turnpike (originally the Waterford-Whitehall Turnpike), which stretched for approximately sixty-four miles. In February 1849 the turnpike company was indicted and convicted for maintaining a public nuisance. It was said to have neglected just about everything "except the taking of tolls," and over the subsequent years the road was not maintained to the satisfaction of the public, its condition becoming very bad.[2] Elsewhere violent measures were being taken against the turnpike companies, but before pointing out a few of these incidents, the functions of a turnpike company should be explained, and the concept of a turnpike company as a public utility should be clarified.

In the early years of the nineteenth century, the chartered turnpike took precedence over all other schemes for roadmaking. There was much that was substantially uniform in the charters of these old turnpike companies. To save repetition in individual cases, and because here we are not primarily interested in the technical aspects of turnpikes and their social and economic impact, some of the main points the charters possessed in common will be given. The charter was issued by the state to a number of men, whose names were given on the document; commissioners were appointed to receive subscriptions; the stock was to consist of a specific number of shares, the value of which was usually fixed at twenty dollars each, and a certain amount of it was to be paid at the time of subscribing. When subscribers had obtained a certain number of shares, the commissioners were to give notice of a meeting for the election of directors, at which meeting the commissioners would preside and the stockholders would elect nine directors. The president and the directors, who were to hold office for one year, were to call for installments on the shares of stock at their discretion, and failure on the part of the stockholders to respond within thirty days would result in forfeiture of the payment already made. The president and the directors were to enact such by-laws and regulations as they thought necessary, so long as they were not in conflict with the laws of the state or the United States. A road was to be constructed upon the most direct and convenient route practicable between two points of termination; the roadbed was to be eighteen or more feet in width, made of stone, gravel, or other hard substance, crowned in the center, and compacted so as to form a solid road with a smooth hard surface. On the completion of the whole or specified parts of the turnpike, inspectors, who were appointed for the purpose, were to issue certificates, upon which the governor of the state was to give permission for the erection of a gate or gates at points named in the charter, which points were usually ten miles apart, the first one to be four or five miles from the starting point. The direction and route of the turnpike were to be decided by the commissioners (disinterested parties) to be appointed by the governor, and, in the case of disagreement with any landowner as to the amount of damage, a jury of six disinterested freeholders was to assess the damage. The directors were to declare dividends semiannually and to render annual accounts of the finances of the company to the controller of the state. Because the turnpike companies were public-service enterprises, the public did have legal recourses if it felt it was being victimized or if the consensus was that the companies were not maintaining the roads properly. The legal guarantees and protective measures for both sides will be outlined later, but now it will be shown that occasionally the public did not negotiate but in some more cases adopted violent measures against the turnpike companies.

In Chenango County, where Samuel Lyon took a rigorous measure against a tollgate, the old turnpike to Catskill and Kingston had tollgates every few miles. It is still remembered that it cost thirty-two cents for a rig to go about ten miles. Lyon owned two farms, one on each side of a tollgate, and, though by 1835 that part of the turnpike had fallen into disrepair, the keeper not only refused to arrange for the improvement of the road but also refused to set a yearly rate. One morning Lyon sent his son, Seth, with a team of oxen from one farm to the other, with the instructions, "If you find the gate locked, hitch the oxen to a gatepost and pull it out." This was done and, as a result of the lawsuit that followed, the gate was removed.[3]

Cage Corbin drove a stagecoach from Delhi to Kingston. The stage company was behind on its toll payments, and the tollkeeper a little below Margaretville wouldn't let Cage through. Cage unhooked his leaders, took a chain and tore the gate right off, and dragged it out of the way. Then he hooked up his team and went on.[4] And near Mexico, New York, although no actual violence has been reported, "the toll-gate houses on the plank road were at times the scenes of conflicts arising from the questions regarding the payment of . . . the desired tolls."[5] There is a report of a tollkeeper someplace who awoke one morning to find the gate gone. A scrawled bit of paper read:

The man who stopped the boy
When going to the mill,
Will find his gate
At the bottom of the hill.[6]

Near the same area a woman, when the usual toll was demanded of her, drove the keeper into the house with a horse whip, and a law suit resulted.[7]

In Oswego County shortly after the Civil War, Union veterans, encouraged by townsfolk, wreaked havoc on the tollgates and tollhouses on the Rome Plank Road near Scriba, according to one old resident:

One fine afternoon the farmers of the community were discussing what could be done about getting around paying the tolls for using the Rome Plank Road. It wasn't that they minded paying for the use of a road, but they couldn't see paying for the use of an old road that was sadly in need of repair. The discussion continued for about an hour in the tavern on Scriba Corner. The resentment, during the talk of these men, increased by leaps and bounds against the unfair tolls paid to these robbers. After reinforcing their courage with liquor, the veterans marched down to the tollhouses and tore them apart, so that never again would they have to pay tolls for using roads that were beyond repair. Even today children will find and pick up some of the remains of these tollhouses that were torn down years ago.[8]

In early-nineteenth-century England, analogues to such destruction of tollgates are to be found, but there Biblical support was offered to justify the violence. Citing the blessing on Rebekah, ". . . let thy seed possess the gate of those which hate them" (Genesis 24:60), gangs of ruffians, masked and clad in white, terrorized gatekeepers by rousing them from bed with a blast on a cow horn, burning the gatehouses, and demolishing the gates. Members of these gangs called themselves Rebekahites.[9]

Bitterness against turnpike tolls in this country, of course, had its antecedents throughout the British Isles. During the mid-nineteenth century in Belfast, Ireland, for example, "protests against the turnpike system became more and more vigorous as the nineteenth century progressed. Millowners complained bitterly. Quarry owners bemoaned the fact that tolls increased their prices."[10] One Bernard Hughes, a Belfast baker, publicly denounced turnpikes as "more devilish than locusts."[11] Finally, in 1857, turnpike trusts were abolished in Ireland.

Some New York travelers didn't resort to violence in their efforts to avoid paying the toll but were more wily in their methods. Near Bearsville, where tollgates were established in 1855 on the plank road through Little Shandaken and Bristol, some people were so angry at being taxed for driving on the road that they made a "shunpike," or "dugway," up the hill and drove to Bristol another way. One tollgate on this road was at a tavern operated by a man named Harder, and another one was on top of Cooper's Hill, where a toll of eight cents was charged for a one-horse rig, and sixteen cents for a team.[12] On the Waterloo and Fayette Plank Road, which was chartered in 1850, there was an active hostility against paying the tolls and a shunpike was built to bypass the tollgate. This shunpike was near a tollhouse a short distance south of Waterloo; the tollhouse was removed in 1900 and the site converted into a private dwelling.[13]

Just over the border in Massachusetts, shunpikes were also utilized. A story is told of one man who, in complaining about toll charges, said: "Very well, then, they must make that road down the mountain so smooth that I may take a glass tumbler and roll it down from top to bottom of the hill without breaking the glass. We will make a shunpike; we'll tap the pike on one side of the gate, pass 'round and connect on the other; then where will their tolls be?"[14] However, this plan was negated because the General Court stepped in and levied fines on all shunpikers far more tyrannous than tollgate demands. At least one such shunpike in Blanford was blockaded by force and judicial authority.

Shunpikes were not unknown in Ireland. One record reveals that "for several years travellers with economy in mind eluded the various toll gates on the New Antrim Road and by using the Crumlin Road, which was free of toll houses, made their way along the old line, free of charge. However, this loophole was soon plugged by the transfer of the toll house . . . to a point controlling both the Crumlin and Shankill Roads."[15]

The term *shunpike* appears to be an Americanism, with its earliest known literary usage occurring in 1853, although it probably was in oral usage earlier. In that year the term was used in connection with the Oswego Canal: "The Oswego Canal . . . has been called a shunpike."[16] The terms *shunpike* and *shunpiker* are in current usage and often are used in connection with routes alternate to superhighways.[17]

Occasionally someone hated the whole idea of turnpikes and tolls so much that he simply ignored the entire setup, including shunpikes and other methods devised to avoid payment of tolls. An old farmer in

Oneida County objected so strongly to "shelling out" at one station on the Deansboro-Clinton Road, that in order to get to a village two miles away he would go roundaboutly some eight miles.[18] However, such passive resistance to the toll systems was rare. Much more common was the practice of "running the tollgate," which simply meant charging past the tollhouse, when the gate was up, without stopping to pay the toll. Such antics were usually overlooked, but occasionally the law was invoked. The directors of the Third Great Western Turnpike in 1813 actually did bring a lawsuit against John Curtis, accused of "running the tollgate." The charge later was withdrawn, but the directors sent him a letter telling him that he was "ungentlemanly."[19]

Another method employed to cheat the turnpike company out of its legal toll was to change the size of wagon tires when out of sight of the gatekeeper. On many turnpikes the width of wagon tires regulated the toll cost, because narrow wheels caused ruts, while wide wheels helped flatten the road. Narrow wheels would be likely to cut into planks on a plank road, too. The practice of charging more for narrow-wheeled vehicles was very common, and in some cases wagons with tires narrower than a certain width were forbidden during the winter and spring seasons or were forbidden to carry more than a specified amount. Some of the wagon-wheel tires were six or eight inches wide, designed to save tolls, and even wide detachable tires were invented to be put over narrow wheels. There were scouts who watched for those who removed their "cut-rate" detachable tires when out of sight of the toll collector, and a fine of one extra toll was collected for that offense.[20] Alan McCutcheon has found that, in Ireland, various other kinds of attempts were made to circumvent the payment of tolls. For example, two cars would be tied together so that they could pass as one vehicle, bribes would be paid to turnpike officials so that overladen vehicles could pass, and farmers ran up accounts with gatekeepers and never paid them.[21]

In connection with the methods used by travelers to cheat the turnpike companies, it should be mentioned that it was fairly easy to pass counterfeit bank notes at the tollgate. On February 5, 1810, the directors of the Third Great Western Turnpike noted that counterfeit bank notes were being passed at the gates and decided that thereafter the gatekeepers should not take any bank notes, except at their own risk. The records of the Coxsackie Turnpike Company reveal that on September 1, 1815, the company had to make good for a counterfeit bank note received by William Field, a gatekeeper. Bogus bank notes turned up at tollgates on this road with increasing regularity over the next twenty-five years. On March 18, 1840, for the sum of two dollars, the company purchased one "Day's Counterfeit Detector," a series of facsimiles of counterfeit bank notes to be used for comparative purposes. This move apparently was successful, for on July 6, 1841, another one of these detectors was purchased for the same price. After this no more counterfeit notes turned up at the tollgates, or at least no more were recognized.[22]

Although the public was generally irked at the idea of paying for the privilege of traveling on certain roads and therefore contrived many methods of avoiding this payment, the travelers were guaranteed a certain amount of legal protection against being victimized by unscrupulous tollkeepers and turnpike companies. On the Great Northern Turnpike, for example, gatekeepers who demanded more than the legal amount were required to forfeit ten dollars for each offense. Still another measure taken to protect the public from being exploited at the tollgate was a state law requiring the appointment of road inspectors in every county having toll roads. It was the duty of these inspectors to examine the roads periodically, and, when the roads were judged by them to be unsafe or difficult on which to travel because of neglect or any other cause, the tollgates would be ordered thrown open. When tollgates were thrown open, it meant simply that there could be no tolls collected from travelers. There must have been teeth in this law because records show that numerous tollgates were thrown open. For example, on the Branchport and Penn Yan Plank Road, where John Nickerson and John Clark were keepers at gates one and two, respectively, people complained about the condition of the road. The state rescinded the company's charter and the tollgates were thrown open.[23] If the tollkeeper failed to obey the order to open the gates, he was liable to fine or imprisonment. During the war years of 1812–1814, the Oswego and Ithaca Turnpike was not kept in proper repair because of heavier traffic, and as a result the gates were ordered thrown open. The following table shows the number of days the north and middle gates of the turnpike were forced open and the collection of tolls suspended.[24]

Suspension of Tolls on the Oswego and Ithaca Turnpike

Year	Number of Days Closed Middle Gate	North Gate
1813	142	118
1814	65	101
1815	32	74

Some turnpike companies hired their own inspectors to make sure by daily inspection tours that the roads were in good condition. These conscientious companies probably thought such a move to be in their own interests, in addition to creating a good public image. In 1813 each director of the Third Great Western Turnpike Road Company was given the authority to settle with travelers who had sustained damages on the road.

In addition to attempting to keep the public honest, the problems of the turnpike companies were compounded by the fact that a small minority of tollkeepers were dishonest in their dealings with them. One case in point is that of Simeon Parkhurst, a tollkeeper on the Rome and Oswego Plank Road, which was organized in 1847. Parkhurst, who was a stagecoach driver before becoming a tollgatherer at gate nine, collected $85 in tolls during the month of September 1868, according to company records. However, he didn't turn over the funds to the company treasurer, was caught, and lost his job. Solomon Matthews bought the account, so it is said, and collected it at his own pleasure.[25] The fact that the turnpike companies didn't consider all tollgatherers completely trustworthy is borne out further by two other illustrations. Gaylord N. Sherwood, a turnpike company director at Camillus, recorded in his diary in 1851 that he removed temptation from the gatekeepers as soon as possible by going himself to the gatehouses to pick up the tolls that had been collected. It is of interest to note that a former tollhouse on this turnpike is still standing near Isaac Dixon Road in Camillus but has been moved back from the present highway.[26]

In an effort to ensure that the gatekeeper turned over the correct amount of funds to the corporation, the employers required the tollgatherers to swear to an oath, before a justice of the peace, that they, the tollgatherers, would handle the money honestly. An oath of this type, signed by William Knapp, a gatekeeper on the Otsego Lake Turnpike, carries the following text:

I William Knapp, do solemnly swear, that I will
honestly and faithfully keep separate and apart
all the monies I shall receive from all and every
person travelling on or passing the Otsego Lake
Turnpike Company Gate, and that I will keep the same in
a box provided for that purpose, and will render
a faithful and just account of the same, once a
month, to the Treasurer of said Turnpike Company,
and will in all things appertaining to the duties
of a Toll Gatherer, conform myself to the laws of the
State, as far as I am able, and to the Instructions I
may receive from time to time, from the President,
Directors and Company of the said Turnpike.
                    William Knapp
Sworn and Subscribed Before me this 19th Day of
Dec. 1825
                    Isaiah Newcomb, Justice of Peace[27]

In the eyes of the public, most tollkeepers were suspect, although not justifiably so. Ulysses P. Hedrick, writing in his informative *History of Agriculture in the State of New York*—a somewhat misleading title, for the book encompasses a much wider range of material—wrongly asserts that "most of the toll-gate keepers retired as rich men—it was said that they made an equal division of the monies received for the toll companies."[28] This policy may have been true in a few cases, but rich retired tollkeepers certainly were atypical. For example, the Coxsackie Turnpike Company, in its early years, used this method of division of money received. The records of this company show that on May 5, 1814, Daniel Miller, a gatekeeper, received half the toll collected at "the new gate."[29] Profits usually were small for the turnpike and plank-road companies, and the directors of the companies were beset perennially by financial difficulties. A large percentage of these companies failed. The mistaken notion that tollkeepers were a rich group apparently prevailed early in the nineteenth century: "The travelers may have envied the gate-keeper's lucrative opportunities, for they divided with the employing companies a constantly growing revenue,"[30] one person observed.

A more truthful view is presented by Anne Gertrude Sneller in her charming *A Vanished World*, which describes rural life in Upstate New York in the late nineteenth century: "Much of the profit for the company depended on the honesty of the gatekeepers. A strict oversight was kept by the directors. A very old gentleman once told me that at a meeting of the directors where he was present, one of them demanded that a certain gatekeeper be dismissed. He knew for a fact, he said, that the gatekeeper's family had had *oysters* twice that winter, and he couldn't have bought oysters out of his wages without cheating."[31]

In reality the tollkeeper usually was underpaid, and he or she, as the case might have been, had to be a combination public relations expert, bookkeeper, policeman, friend, and something of a mathematical wizard. The gatekeeper was bound by an oath to a long list of rules and regulations imposed by the turnpike company, and he was fair game for robbers. As indicated above, sometimes these tollgatherers were women, but more often they were men. The records of the Trenton-Prospect Plank Road Company reveal that a woman, Mrs. Sharp, collected $12.50 for tending a tollgate on this road for a period in 1856, and in the same year a Mrs. Slicher received a like amount for collecting tolls. In 1853 on this road a gatekeeper, Robert Billbarrow, was paid $25.00 for tending a gate from May 11, 1852, to May 11, 1853. This could hardly be described as a lucrative position. On this particular plank road the usual salary of gatekeepers was $12.50 for each quarter, making a total yearly salary of $50.00, hardly enough to retire on as a rich man.[32] In 1904, according to the records of the company, a man by the name of Houghtaling, a gatekeeper on the Delaware Turnpike, was paid the sum of $1.70 for working ten days.[33] On the Owego and Ithaca Turnpike, gatekeepers at first were paid $10 per month, which was raised to $12.50 in 1814. In 1825 they were receiving $8.33 and this was still further reduced to $8.00 in 1826,[34] again illustrating the fact that it would have been almost impossible to accrue any fortune on this salary schedule alone. Another example of the paltry salaries received by gatekeepers is an entry in the records of the Coxsackie Turnpike Company, showing that in 1884 a gatekeeper was paid his year's wages in a lump sum—$240. This method of payment was a frequent practice of this company.[35]

For some tollkeepers the job was only a part-time venture. Isaac Russell, a pioneer on the Old Turnpike near Cooperstown, operated a farm as well as officiating at the tollhouse on the turnpike.[36] However, this practice was forbidden by the Third Great Western Turnpike Road Company. Number one on its list of rules and regulations for gatekeepers was that "it is expected and required that every gatekeeper will give his personal attention to the business of his office; and not leave the gate to the care of his family, or any other person, more than is unavoidably necessary.—Farming and gate tending are incompatible."[37]

Tollkeepers actually had some unofficial "police" duty besides gathering tolls. There was a $25.00 fine for conviction on a charge of defacing a milestone, and gatekeepers were required to report suspected violators. Their bookkeeping duties involved keeping a daily record of those persons who passed through the gate, as well as the amount of toll paid. These reports were to be turned in to the company at the end of each month.

Even though some tollgatherers didn't have strict consciences about overcharging travelers or cheating their employers, generally they were known as good neighbors; they knew everybody who lived and everything that happened within five miles of the gate in either direction. They were one of the chief sources of news for travelers. It should be pointed out that not all tollhouses were as unpopular and disliked as much as the one at Waterford and a few other places. For example, the tollgate south of South Trenton was at a hotel operated by Isaac Curry in 1812. Here was a place to hear the latest news of the war; since Curry was an assemblyman, he would be one of the first to learn of any important happenings.[38] Turnpike companies encouraged tollgatherers to be hospitable to travelers, and sometimes the gatekeepers were censured for not being so. In February 1813, a tollgatherer on the Third Great Western Turnpike was advised by the directors "to be more accommodating to travelers," after a committee investigated a complaint against him. However, the committee found that his "conduct generally met with approbation."[39] Apparently, gatekeepers were prone to lend company funds to needy travelers, because the directors of this turnpike company instructed gatekeepers "not to lend money, on any pretext."[40]

A romantic portrait of a tollgatherer has been penned by Nathaniel Hawthorne and appears as "The Toll-Gatherer's Day: A Sketch of Transitory Life," in *Twice-Told Tales*. Hawthorne shows that the tollgate is an excellent place to observe the range of human life, and that the tollgatherer is a "sage old man." He is able to distinguish the weight of every vehicle through his practiced ear. Farmers, peddlers, preachers, newlyweds, and other persons pass the gate each day, and the tollgatherer has his thoughts about each. As the day ends, "the old tollgatherer looks seaward, and discerns the lighthouse kindling a far island, and the stars, too, kindling in the sky, as if but a little way beyond; and the mingling reveries of heaven with remembrance of earth, the whole dusty procession of mortal travelers, all the dusty pilgrimages which he had witnessed, seem like a flitting show of phantoms for his thoughtful soul to muse on."[41]

In many cases the gatekeeper had a dwelling place at the gate, the dwelling having been built specifically for this purpose. Typical dwelling places were on the plank road between Cooperstown and Fort Plain, where each of the three tollgates on this road had a dwelling place for the gatekeeper. These may have been considered as "fringe benefits" and made up somewhat for the gatekeepers' poor pay. The toll was ten cents at each of the gates on this road. One was located near the Fenimore Farm, approximately three-quarters of a mile north of Cooperstown; another was near the head of Otsego Lake; and the third was about two miles north of Springfield Center. There was another tollgate on the east side of the lake, about two miles north of Cooperstown. It is said to have been operated by a man named Olive.[42]

Some turnpike companies chose to lease out the turnpike, gate, toll-house, and "all appertenances" to an individual for a term of years. An indenture would spell out the terms of the lease, which would be signed by the lessee and officials of the turnpike company. The Otsego Lake Turnpike Company practiced this policy, and a substantial part of the document follows:

This Indenture, made the fifth day of February in the year of our Lord, 1841, Between the President, Directors and Company of the Otsego Lake Turnpike, by their committee, Ellery Corey, William Nichols and Henry Phinney, of the first part, and Levi Gray, of the town of Springfield, of the second part. Witnesseth, that the said parties of the first part, for and in consideration of the Rents, covenants and conditions herein after contained, on the part of the said party of the second part, his heirs, Executors administrators and assigns, to be paid, kept and performed have demised, leased, unto the said party of the second part, All of the Otsego Lake Turnpike Road, with the gate and Toll House, and Tolls.

To have and to hold the said Turnpike, Gate, Toll-House and Tolls, with the appertenances, for and during the term of six years, from the first day of January last, yielding and paying therefore unto the said parties of the first part, the yearly rent of One Hundred and eighty-six Dollars and fifty cents, payable on the first day of January in each and every year hereafter. And the said party of the second part, covenants and agrees to keep the said Road, Gate and Toll-House, and Bridges, Causeways, Throughways, Water-Courses etc. in a complete state of repair, during the continuance of this Lease, at his own proper cost, expense and charge, and will also save harmless the said parties of the first part, from all damages, costs, suits or expenses, which they may sustain or be put to, by reason or means of the same being out of repair, at any time during the said six years.

And it is also agreed between the parties to these presents, that in case said rent of One hundred and eighty-six Dollars and fifty cents, or any part thereof, shall be behind or unpaid, for the space of ten days next and after the same should have been paid, that then, and in each case, the said parties of the first part, may re-enter, and occupy the said premises, provided no distress can be found to make the said rent.

The lease further provided that Gray was to spend six hundred dollars on the road during the term of the lease, and that he was to provide an accurate accounting of all the income and expenses. This lease then was signed by all the parties in the presence of a justice of the peace. The latter then affixed his signature, making the document binding.[43] This appears to be typical of such transactions in the United States. However, in Ireland, for example, the right to operate tollgates was auctioned off yearly to the highest bidder.[44]

In the days of the toll roads, it was commonly agreed that payment of tolls must be waived if the traveler could show that he was on his way either to or from a gristmill or church. One wonders what method of divination the turnpike directors expected the tollgatherers to use when deciding who was out for a Sunday drive or who was going to or from a religious meeting. Regardless of the complexities possible, that old phrase "to mill or meeting" had a definite quasi-legal connotation.[45] On the Gouverneur and Antwerp Plank Road, where "loud were the anathemas at having to pay," the tollgates were four miles apart, rather close compared to the usual ten miles between gates. In 1850, a citizen from Scotch Settlement complained at the cost of driving over only one mile of hemlock plank when coming "to mill or meeting," and a reduction was made in his behalf.[46] There were other valid reasons, too, for being exempted from paying tolls.

Typical of the turnpikes was the Great Northern Turnpike, where tollgatherers were given authority to detain travelers until they paid the toll, unless they were traveling to or from public worship, farm, funeral, gristmill, blacksmith shop, polling place, or a physician's office. Midwives were exempt along with jurors, witnesses, troops of the United States, artillery wagons, and persons residing within two miles of the tollgate. If one were driving a carriage with a tire track of less than twelve inches in width, he didn't have to pay.[47] Physicians apparently were exempted from paying toll on some turnpikes, including the Third Great Western Turnpike. At a meeting of the board of directors of this company on February 6, 1809, it was agreed that Dr. David Little could commute free of toll between the towns of Springfield and Cherry Valley. His family also could commute freely with him.[48]

Baptist and Methodist ministers, however, were not as fortunate as some physicians regarding free passage on the turnpikes, even though they wore "the cloth" and were on their way to a religious meeting. The Reverend David Marks, a Freewill Baptist circuit rider, wrote in his autobiography that, on November 15, 1821, he "came to a turnpike gate in Camillus, and after telling the gate keeper my situation and business, I requested a free passage. Being denied, I offered my hat, coat, or shoes, for security. He replied he wanted money; but after detaining me half an hour, let me pass, with a charge never to come to that gate again with a horse and no money."[49] In the summer of 1833, the Reverend James Erwin, a Methodist itinerant preacher, was on his way to Hammond to conduct a religious service. In his autobiography he remarks that "there were two toll gates on the way and it would require twelve cents to pay our tolls both ways."[50]

Stagecoaches generally didn't stop at the tollgates, for stage companies commonly paid their toll charges every three months so that the stages need not be stopped on their way but could sweep straight through the tollgates with swaying grandeur.[51] The turnpike companies apparently worked out various plans with the stage companies regarding tolls. On July 5, 1814, the directors of the Third Great Western Turnpike repealed a rule that stages could travel at one-half rate. This was in effect for one year, but on August twelfth of the same year it was ruled by the directors that stages could travel free of toll.[52]

Turnpike tolls were at one time so complicated that the collector, especially on the heavily traveled roads, almost had to be a mathematical wizard to survive. A percentage sometimes was added to the toll in winter months, yet sleighs went by for a cent less than did wagons on most roads. In addition to yearly passes being issued to make things a little simpler for the tollgatherer, some turnpike companies in New York State, as well as those in Connecticut and probably elsewhere, issued tickets for travelers, who could turn them in at the tollgates. The Southport Plank Road Company, organized in 1848, issued simple tickets, on which was printed: "The Southport Plank Road Company / TWO CENTS / Good for One Passage."[53] Tickets for the Hartford and New Haven Turnpike in Connecticut are extant, and these tickets of various price denominations each bear a quaint woodcut of the type of conveyance or animal for which each was issued. The twenty-five–cent ticket bears a cut of a stagecoach, while the ticket for a sleigh bears a nice woodcut of a one-horse cutter. There was a charge for driving cattle, pigs, or other livestock through the tollgate, and tickets for this purpose, bearing likenesses of the respective types of livestock, were issued.[54] It is probable that at some time tickets of this type will turn up for New York State tollgates.

Because of the ephemeral nature of tickets, it is difficult to offer much comparative material. In Somerset, England, we know that, on the Shepton Mallet Turnpike, tickets were used to pass at the various gates. There were different prices for "waggons," cars, chaises, horses, asses, beasts, sheep, and pigs. Tickets also bore this notice: "This ticket clears either of the undermentioned gates, but not more than any one of them: Chelynch, Long-Cross, Dean, Charlton."[55]

The complexity of computing toll charges is well illustrated by the various rates in effect on the Schenectady and Utica Turnpike (approximately sixty-eight miles long) in the early nineteenth century.[56] According to the following table, which shows the rates to be paid for each ten miles traveled, the cost for a horse and rider over the whole distance

Toll Charges on the Schenectady-Utica Turnpike

Type	Toll	Type	Toll
Sheep, per score	8 ¢	Two-horse wagons	12½¢
Hogs, per score	8 ¢	Three-horse wagons	15½¢
Cattle, per score	18 ¢	Four-horse wagons (tires under six inches)	75 ¢
Horses, per score	18 ¢	Five-horse wagons (tires under six inches)	87½¢
Mules, per score	18 ¢	Six-horse wagons (tires under six inches)	$1.00
Horse and rider	5 ¢	One-horse cart	6 ¢
Tied horses, each	5 ¢	Two-ox cart	5 ¢
Sulkies	12½¢	Three-ox cart	8 ¢
Chairs	12½¢	Four-ox cart	10 ¢

Chariots	25 ¢	Six-ox cart	14 ¢
Coaches	25 ¢	One-horse sleigh	6 ¢
Coachers	25 ¢	Two-horse or ox sleigh	6 ¢
Phaetons	25 ¢	Three-horse or ox sleigh	8 ¢
Two-horse stages	12½¢	Four-horse or ox sleigh	10 ¢
Four-horse stages	18½¢	Five-horse or ox sleigh	12 ¢
One-horse wagons	9 ¢	Six-horse or ox sleigh	14 ¢

from Schenectady to Utica would be about thirty-four cents, approximately one-half cent per mile. A private coach would be charged nearly three dollars. The cost for the same trip today on the State Thruway is slightly more than one dollar. In the early days a stage would be charged from about sixty cents to one dollar and a quarter, and the charge for animals would be from fifty cents to one dollar and a quarter per score. On the Seneca Turnpike, the Old Genesee Road, over which an enormous amount of westward travel passed, the fares were about the same, a rate of six cents per score for cattle being the only radical difference. In 1813, the directors of the Third Great Western Turnpike raised the rate of toll for Pennsylvania wagons.[57]

On some turnpikes, weighing machines apparently were installed at tollhouses, and the rate of toll was regulated by the amount of weight on each conveyance. Although the details of such a system are sketchy, some light is shed upon it by an editorial that appeared in the *American Farmer* on July 12, 1882:

In looking over the proposed new turnpike bill, presented this season, we find the clause relating to roads and wheels, very properly omitted; the weighing machines are proposed to be continued, which we also consider as very proper, if it be only to prevent cruelty to animals, which might otherwise be induced by gain. It is, however, doubtful whether any allowance in toll ought to be made for wheels more than six inches wide; because the wheels themselves are part of the load, and the improved method of making turnpikes does suppose the utility of rollers that will nearly cover the stones each eight inches across, or go between them without making them lift up at either end. Wheels of six inches might pay according to weight and horses, (six to eight horses and four to six tons), and narrow wheels (1-1½″) not to be allowed to carry more than a given load—suppose four horses and three tons—exclusive of the carriage. One thing of peculiar importance the act provides, namely, that the soles of the wheels, of whatever width, shall be even and flat: this, we believe, will soon put an end to very broad wheels; for unless by shoeing them with a central thick sole, or by making the rim barrel-shaped, they could have made them run almost as easy as narrow wheels, they could not have availed themselves of the advantages of heavy lading, and exemptions from weighing.[58]

Definite information on the use of weighing machines at tollgates comes from England in the form of a humorous anecdote:

At one end of the farm was a turnpike gate, kept by a very bad-tempered and abusive old fellow. The road in those days was very largely used by coal-haulers with whom he was always at feud, and they, on their part, did their best to make his life a burden. Tolls were fixed on a basis of number of wheels and weight. If the old fellow thought one of the haulers had more than his allowed weight, he would make him drive on to his weighing machine. In the early 1870s the first traction engine, then called a road-steamer, came his way. It was a weird object with an upright "coffee-pot" boiler and either three or five wheels: at any rate there was an odd one in front. He was not going to be bested by this new-fangled invention, so he ordered the driver to go on the weighing machine. In vain the man assured him it would smash the machine: he had to go. Of course there was a frightful wreck which took a long time to repair, whilst the haulers loaded their carts as much as they liked without his being able to check them, and greeted him with cheerful remarks such as, "Who weighed the devil?"[59]

An official receipt, which also served as a pass, was issued to William Campbell, upon payment of one dollar, for "one years' commutation, for himself and family only, at the most Westerly Gate, on the Turnpike Road, belonging to the President, Directors and first Company of the Great Western Turnpike Road, from 24 May 1829 till s[ame] t[ime] of May 1830." The document, owned by me, is signed by George Dollar, the gatekeeper. Campbell, the author of *Annals of Tryon County*, was a stockholder in the turnpike company, the one dollar charge probably being the special rate for stockholders.

As if the tollgatherer didn't already have enough to keep him busy, some companies, the Third Great Western Turnpike Road Company, for example, made him dispenser of scrip, a type of currency that could be exchanged for merchandise. In 1816 one type of scrip was receivable at the Western Turnpike gates for three cents and payable at one of Pinney's stores at Middlefield or Worcester. A similar type of scrip was payable at the post office in Cooperstown.[60]

Broadly speaking, tollhouses in Upstate New York fell into three architectural types: (*a*) the inn or tavern where tolls were collected; (*b*) the village residence or farmhouse that served as a tollhouse, and (*c*) the simple structure built specifically for a tollhouse and usually occupied by only the gatekeeper and his family. The first type is exemplified by the hotel near South Trenton and the Mansion House near the Old Erie Canal south of Rome.[61] The second type is illustrated by the tollhouse near Oneonta (9.1) where a barn is connected to a house with

9.1

Tollgate near Oneonta, postcard view.

9.2

Tollgate, Fort Plain, postcard view.

Old Toll Gate near Oneonta, N.Y.

Old Toll Gate, Fort Plain, N. Y.

COEYMANS, N. Y.----THE TOLL-GATE C. & W. P. R. CO.

an adjoining orchard, while an example of the simple structure may be seen in (9.2), the tollhouse near Fort Plain. This type of simple structure was purely functional and was constructed at a minimum cost. According to the records of the Coxsackie Turnpike Company, it cost $669.51 to erect a new tollhouse in 1889. This cost included all the hardware and labor. (More than a score of years earlier this same company spent $2.11 for yellow paint for a tollhouse, giving some indication that the little houses could be seen fairly easily by travelers.)[62] In 1810, a tollhouse was constructed on the Third Great Western Turnpike at a cost of $71.00. John Burgess was the carpenter.[63]

Some of the tollhouses included rather elaborate archways over the road (9.3 & 9.4), while others had only a simple roof extension a few feet over the road (9.5). It was not uncommon for commercial advertising to be plastered on the tollhouse or a nearby building, and sometimes the rates of toll appeared on a sign hanging near the gate (9.6). The sign on the barn near the gatehouse at Peterboro advertises liver pills (9.7), while signs on the gatehouse near Hudson advertise a worm killer and a

9.3

Tollgate C.& W.P.R. Co., postcard view.

9.4

Tollgate, Ravena, postcard view.

TOLL GATE, RAVENA, N.Y.

remedy for "female complaints" (9.8). Horses usually could get a drink of water at the tollhouse as may be seen by the convenient rain barrels near the gatehouse at Peterboro. Doubtless, the traveler, too, could obtain a drink of water from the gatekeeper. And perhaps the gatekeeper kept something a little stronger for travelers who were his friends. The tollhouse that was at a site in the vicinity of New Scotland Avenue in Albany was operated for many years by the Fivey family. The archway over the road from the house was connected to a two-story ice house, from which ice was sold to travelers and neighbors.[64]

I have found no record of elaborate tollhouses, such as might have been found in the Middle Atlantic states or Virginia, in Upstate New York. The elaborate types were built of stone, some having been fashioned in the octagon mode, which had some popularity in the mid–nineteenth century. One has only to read descriptions of tollhouses in England to discover that the tollhouses in Upstate New York had little in common with their counterparts in the British Isles. In one area of England, the tollhouses have been described as follows:

They are sometimes Gothick as at Chilcompton, or classical as at Kilmersdon, or even Regency as at Churchill. These, however, are touches of fancy: as a rule one need only describe their architecture as vernacular. They are built of local material, they are simple and functional and generally unmistakable, though sometimes their proportions have been spoiled by later additions to provide more spacious living quarters. Yet there is almost infinite variety in their design, sometimes one-

9.5

Tollgate near Coxsackie, postcard view.

9.6

Tollgate, Hudson, postcard view, 1909.

9.7

Tollgate, Peterboro, postcard view.

storeyed, sometimes two-storeyed, sometimes flush with the road, sometimes oddly shaped to give a view of traffic approaching a road junction at an awkward angle, sometimes with sturdy little porches or deep overhanging eaves, to give some shelter to the gatekeepers.[65]

Once a tollhouse was built on a turnpike, it virtually took an act of the state legislature for it to be moved to another site. So we can see how these gatehouses became established landmarks. After the legislators passed a bill approving the moving of a tollhouse site, the judges of the county in which the gatehouse was located had to approve the change. An example of this action is illustrated by the following text from a contemporary document:

Whereas the Legislature of the State of New York, by an act passed April 25, 1832, gave authority "to the President, Directors and Company of the Otsego Lake Turnpike, to remove their toll gate from the place where it now stands to such other place as should by the Judges of the County Courts of the County of Otsego be deemed most suitable and proper." Now therefore we the subscribers, Judges of the County Court of the County of Otsego, by virtue of the authority given us by the said act, deem a place a few rods northerly from the house of F. Pegg, Innkeeper, as the most suitable and proper place for the location of the said toll gate, in case the said President, Directors and Company think proper to remove the same from where it now stands. Given under our hands at Cooperstown this thirteenth day of February, One thousand eight hundred and forty one.

J. D. Hammond
Hiram Kinne
J. C. Wentworth
Levi Stewart
Seth Chase[66]

At many of the tollhouses in New York State, a bar was used to block the road until the toll had been paid. The bar was raised and lowered by the gatekeeper. This type of barricade may be seen in (9.9), the old tollgate near Monticello. Another type of barricade often used may be seen in (9.10), the old tollgate at Pawling, comprised of a kind of fence that could be raised and lowered. This type may also be seen in (9.11), the old tollgate near Hillsdale. An Englishman, John Fowler, writing about his tour through the state in 1830, said, "I noticed a peculiarity in the toll-gates as we passed along (which articles are much less frequent than in England) namely their drawing up in portcullis fashion, instead of opening as ours do."[67] In many places no physical means of blocking the road was used. It is doubtful if actual pikes were ever used for this purpose in New York State, although it is possible they were used in New England or Virginia, where the first tollgates in this country were erected.[68] The authority to charge tolls brought to such roads the familiar name, the turnpike, sometimes shortened to pike. The pike, originally the weapon of the foot soldier in European armies, was the customary weapon of the guards of the American colonial governors. It consisted of a long wooden staff with a pointed steel head. At the entrances to forts and other official entrances, soldiers barred the way by crossing their pikes in front of the parties seeking entrance until satisfactory explanation had been given of the right to pass. The pike was adapted in the government-authorized barring of the road, until the toll had been paid, by placing a pike or wooden bar (the steel head was not necessary) on a turnstile or gate. It was called a turnpike from the device for ensuring the collection of tolls, and, by folk etymology and natural abbreviation, the roads became known familiarly as pikes. As was indicated above, the types of devices used to bar the road ranged from complicated turnstiles to simple bars which could be raised or lowered. The latter type was used to keep pigs and other livestock from scuttling through until the driver had paid the required toll. One traveler through

Old Toll Gate, Hudson, N. Y.

9.8

Tollgate, Hudson, postcard view.

875. THE OLD TOLL GATE NEAR MONTICELLO, N.Y.

Old Toll Gate, Pawling, N. Y. 1906

THE OLD TOLL-GATE NEAR HILLSDALE, N. Y.

9.9

Tollgate near Monticello, postcard view.

9.10

Tollgate, Pawling, postcard view, 1906.

9.11

Tollgate near Hillsdale, postcard view.

New York State found that in many instances gatekeepers left the gate open most of the time, "except . . . when a tough customer comes along that they think likely'll kick up a row."[69]

Tollgates have had some impact on the names of places and establishments in New York State. Doubtless there are numerous instances, but only a few are cited here. Among the places that have derived their names from tollgates is the Toll-Gate School District in the town of New Haven in Onondaga County. This district is named after a tollgate that once stood on the Rome and Oswego Plank Road, organized in 1847, nearest Mexico on the West.[70] Small towns were known frequently as "tollgate towns" or "tollgate hamlets." Just about their only distinction was that they were places where tolls had to be paid. Wilmington in the Adirondacks has been described as this type of town.[71] Fort Hunter was designated as a "two-cent town" because it cost two cents to travel on the road through the village.[72] The old tollhouse on Route 30-A be-

9.12

Tollgate, Cherry Valley, postcard view, 1907.

tween Johnstown and Fonda was until recently the Toll-Gate Tavern, while an old tollhouse near Albany still serves this purpose. However, the name "toll-gate" attached to an establishment can be very misleading. A case in point is the Toll-Gate Restaurant on Route 20, the Old Cherry Valley Turnpike, between Richfield Springs and West Winfield. According to the owner, this building never was a tollhouse. "We just had to think of a name in a hurry so we called it the Toll-Gate Restaurant," he said. Actually, there once was a tollhouse a mile or so east of the restaurant. After the demise of the turnpike, it was torn down.

Among old tollhouse structures that are still standing is the gatehouse at Cherry Valley (9.12). This building has been moved back from the road and is unoccupied. An old tollhouse on the Great Northern Turnpike in Glens Falls is a residence just off Route 9 at the north end of the city. The tollhouse at Vail Mills has been moved to a site near the Kennyetta Creek, Sir William Johnson's favorite fishing spot, and converted into a camp. The tavern Jack's Place on U.S. Route 20, just east of Nassau in Rensselaer County, is the former Coldwater Tavern. This old tavern once served the dual purpose of being a tollhouse and providing a place for the dispensement of refreshment of the nonalcoholic variety.[73] During the temperance frenzy of the nineteenth century, the term "coldwater" was used freely to describe persons, organizations, and places identified with the temperance movement.

There is a good tollhouse story told about the architectural historian who was traveling through the country in search of interesting architectural examples. Having spotted a little house next to the road, and believing that it once may have been a tollhouse, he went to the door and rapped. An old lady opened the door and the historian asked, "Did this used to be a toll-house?" "No," the old woman replied, "it ain't never been no toller than it is now."[74]

There were sinister whisperings about the old south tollhouse on the Owego and Ithaca Turnpike. The house was formerly located on the east side of the highway at the foot of a hill as one drives into Catatunk, a small hamlet approximately three miles south of Candor. The gate was across the road just west of the house. In its heyday, balls were held at the house. One night at the height of a ball, a woman remarked that she hoped, when her time came to die, she would be dancing on that floor. Before the evening had passed, her wish came true. Her lifeless body was carried into another room and the ball went on. It was rumored that men had later visited the house at times and were never heard from again. This tollhouse was said to have been a very "tough" place. Counterfeit money was found in the rafters when the house was torn down. It has been said that some of the same kind of money was found in the ground in the vicinity of the house.[75]

Another tollgate story was told by an Englishman who visited New York State in 1833–1834. An unlettered man named Judge Sterling was appointed arbitrator between settlers and squatters from the East. He put a chain across the road in front of his home on Sunday and exacted toll for traveling on the Lord's Day. One westbound Yankee demanded a receipt so that he would not have to pay another toll in that Central New York district. The almost illiterate Sterling let him write the acknowledgment and then painfully added a signature. At a store in the next village the Yankee traveler cashed his "receipt," which read, "Please to pay the bearer the sum of $100."[76]

And still another tollhouse tale, which may be the tallest of all, concerns farmers in southern New York State who at one time generally took their produce and livestock to market via the Newburgh-Cohocton Turnpike. Turkeys and pigs were among the common types of livestock driven along the turnpike. At night, on the turnpike, the turkeys would roost in the trees while the drover would stay at one of the inns that served the dual purpose of also being used as a tollhouse. It is told that one time two drovers were at one of these tollhouse inns, becoming mellow over their ale before starting the drive to Newburgh. These men made a bet: the one driving the turkeys said that he would get to Newburgh first, while the one driving the pigs said that he would be the winner. It turned out that the one driving the pigs won the race because the other drover had forgotten that his birds would fly up into the trees at night and roost, while the pigs could be driven night and day. The following year—so the story goes—the man driving the turkeys won back his money in a similar bet, for he had crossed the turkeys with owls.[77]

A numskull tale, centering around a tollhouse formerly located near Brewerton, involves the one-armed gatekeeper, Cyrus Hurd, and one of his "three strapping daughters." There was a prevalence of cholera in 1832–1833, but Brewerton thus far had escaped the dread plague. However, the citizens were on the lookout for any possible sign of it. One day, so the story goes, an elephant attached to a traveling show passed down the road toward the tollgate. One of Hurd's daughters went to the gate and espying the elephant—it being the first of its kind she had ever seen—ran back into the house crying, "The cholera has come, the cholera has come!" Fortunately, no other case of the disease was recorded.[78]

Tollgate lore has been incorporated into at least one folksong, in addition to the above tales and anecdotes. In the 1850's, young people on their way to camp meeting would sing:

The man at the turnpike bar
Never ask'd for his toll,
But rub'd his auld poll,
And look'd after the low-back'd car . . .[79]

A final interesting bit of lore associated with the turnpike era is an advertisement that appeared in the New Baltimore, N.Y., *Recorder* on June 9, 1807: "Wanted at New Baltimore, 20 miles above Catskill, by subscriber, 10 or 15 SWORN TURNPIKERS to work on the Baltimore and Renssellaer [*sic*] Turnpike, to whom good wages will be given. No Dutchman need apply unless he is pretty well Yankeyfied; and no Irishman unless he can demolish a quart of rum a day. [signed] Daniel Ives."

It has been more than a century and a half since the erection of the first tollgate in New York state. Most of the old tollhouses have disappeared, but the lore associated with them is viable. Persons who never passed through one of the old gates and had to "shell out," relate tales about them; the gamut of human emotion is remembered at the old tollhouse. Conviviality and kindness, shrewdness and chicanery, violence and even death are woven into tollgate lore, which probably never will be forgotten.

NOTES

1. Mrs. Robert Cleaver, *The History of the Town of Catherine, Schuyler County, New York*, p. 59.

2. Sydney Hammersley, *The History of Waterford, New York*, p. 106.

3. Harold W. Thompson, *Body, Boots, and Britches*, p. 162.

4. Norman Studer, "Yarns of a Catskill Woodsman," *New York Folklore Quarterly* II, no. 3 (Autumn 1955): 191. This story was told to Studer by Mike Todd, an old-time hunter of the Catskills.

5. Elizabeth M. Simpson, *Mexico*, p. 286.

6. Alice Morse Earle, *Stage Coach and Tavern Days*, p. 240.

7. Gilbert Sumner Wood, *The Taverns and Turnpikes of Blanford, 1733–1833*, p. 256.

8. Informant, Mrs. H. W. Bales, Oswego. She heard the tale from "Grandma" Kocher of Oswego in 1950 and recalled it for the collector, Thomas Geary, on May 25, 1954. From the Folklore Archives, English Department, State University College, Oswego, New York.

9. M. Lovett Turner, "Stories in Stones," in *Countryside Mood*, edited by Richard Harmon, pp. 134–135.

10. Alan McCutcheon, "Roads and Bridges," *Ulster Folklife* 10 (1964): 79.

11. *Belfast News-Letter*, September 24, 1857.

12. Anita Smith, *Woodstock*, p. 25.

13. J. E. Becker, *History of the Village of Waterloo*, p. 160.

14. Wood, *Taverns and Turnpikes of Blanford*, p. 256.

15. McCutcheon, "Roads and Bridges," p. 78.

16. Mitford M. Mathews, *A Dictionary of Americanisms on Historical Principles*, p. 1536.

17. Based on a personal communication with Dr. Mitford M. Mathews, who cited the following sources: *Lamp*, June 1952, pp. 6–10; and *New Yorker*, December 8, 1951, pp. 80–83. He added that the term still survives on maps and in local parlance near Madison, N.J., and Sharon, Conn.

18. Thompson, *Body, Boots, and Britches*, p. 163.

19. Manuscript records of the Third Great Western Turnpike Road Company, New York State Historical Association Library, Cooperstown (hereafter cited as NYSHA).

20. Eric Sloane, *Our Vanishing Landscape*, p. 83.

21. McCutcheon, "Roads and Bridges," p. 79.

22. Manuscript records of the Third Great Western Turnpike Road Company and the Coxsackie Turnpike Company, NYSHA.

23. Miles A. Davis, *History of Jerusalem*, p. 62.

24. Informant, Crede D. Hagerty, 1947, Harold W. Thompson archives, NYSHA (hereafter cited as HWT). Note that two different turnpikes with similar names will be mentioned in the text: the Oswego and Ithaca, from Lake Ontario south to Ithaca, and the Owego and Ithaca, from the Chemung River north to Ithaca.

25. Simpson, *Mexico*, pp. 327–328.

26. Mary Maxwell, *Among the Hills of Camillus*, p. 28.

27. Manuscript records of the Otsego Lake Turnpike Company, NYSHA.

28. Ulysses P. Hedrick, *A History of Agriculture in the State of New York*, p. 176.

29. Manuscript records of the Coxsackie Turnpike Company, NYSHA.

30. Herbert B. Howe, *Jedediah Barber, 1787–1876*, p. 32.

31. Anne Gertrude Sneller, *A Vanished World*, p. 15.

32. Manuscript records of the Trenton-Prospect Plank Road Company, NYSHA.

33. Manuscript records of the Delaware Turnpike Company, NYSHA.

34. Informant, Crede D. Hagerty, 1947, HWT.

35. Manuscript records of the Coxsackie Turnpike Company, NYSHA.

36. [Duane H. Hurd], *History of Otsego County*, p. 248.

37. Broadside from the Manuscript Division of the New York Public Library.

38.   Samuel W. Durant, *History of Oneida County*, p. 540.

39.   Manuscript records of the Third Great Western Turnpike Road Company, NYSHA.

40.   Ibid.

41.   Nathaniel Hawthorne, *Twice-Told Tales*, p. 286.

42.   Manuscript record of the recollections of Harvey I. Russell, founder of the *Otsego Farmer* newspaper, NYSHA.

43.   Manuscript records of the Otsego Lake Turnpike Company, NYSHA.

44.   McCutcheon, "Roads and Bridges," p. 79.

45.   Jared Van Wagenen, *The Golden Age of Home-spun*, p. 116.

46.   J. S. Corbin, *History of Gouverneur*, p. 43.

47.   George Brown, *Pleasant Valley*, p. 122.

48.   Manuscript records of the Third Great Western Turnpike Road Company, NYSHA.

49.   Marilla Marks, ed., *Memoirs of the Life of David Marks, Minister of the Gospel*, p. 54.

50.   James Erwin, *Reminiscences of Early Circuit Life*, p. 134.

51.   Marion Rawson says in *From Here to Yender* (p. 25), "Stagecoaches paid their toll by the year, but passengers within many a coach paid every time they came within the clutches of the gatekeeper, and none dared hide beneath the wolfskin seat to avoid the gouging."

52.   Manuscript records of the Third Great Western Turnpike Road Company, NYSHA.

53.   David Teeter of Elmira, in 1947, reported the ticket owned by M. O. Force of Elmira (HWT).

54.   Information supplied by Abraham Slepak, Colchester, Conn., the owner of the tickets.

55.   Robin Atthill, *Old Mendip*, pp. 127–128.

56.   Archer Hulbert, *Historic Highways*, XIII, 111.

57.   Manuscript records of the Third Great Western Turnpike Road Company, NYSHA.

58.   *American Farmer*, July 12, 1882, p. 127.

59.   Atthill, *Old Mendip*, p. 126.

60.   Specimens at NYSHA.

61.   Durant, *History of Oneida County*, p. 386.

62.   Manuscript records of the Coxsackie Turnpike Company, NYSHA.

63.   Manuscript records of the Third Great Western Turnpike Road Company, NYSHA.

64.   *Albany Times Union*, May 16, 1965.

65.   Atthill, *Old Mendip*, p. 121.

66.   Manuscript records of the Otsego Lake Turnpike Company, NYSHA.

67.   John Fowler, *Journal of a Year in the State of New York in the Year 1830*, p. 70.

68.   Frederick James Wood, *The Turnpikes of New England and the Evolution of the Same through England, Virginia, and Maryland*, p. 7.

69.   Clifton Johnson, *New England and Its Neighbors*, p. 161.

70.   Simpson, *Mexico*, p. 328.

71.   Alfred L. Donaldson, *A History of the Adirondacks*, I, 343.

72.   Informant, Carl Kaufman, Tribes Hill, N.Y., July 18, 1965.

73.   Informant, Paul Huey, Massac, N.Y., October 13, 1964.

74.   Informant, Clyde R. Jones, Concord, Mass., October 20, 1964.

75.   Collected from Mrs. Clarence Knapp, Newark Valley, N.Y., by Crede D. Hagerty (HWT). Hagerty noted that he "visited Mrs. Knapp numerous times and her authority on the subject seemed to be sound. I would approximate Mrs. Knapp's age at 70 [in 1947] and she learned a great deal about the material by visiting the old residents."

76.   Edward S. Abdy, *Journal of a Residence and Tour in the United States of North America*, I, 265.

77.   Informant, Crede D. Hagerty, 1947.

78.   Informant, Elet Milton of Central Square who heard the tale from Edward Emmons, Brewerton. Collected by Mrs. Bertha Murphy, Central Square, in January 1963 (from the Folklore Archives, English Department, State University College, Oswego, N.Y.).

79.   Daniel Carter Beard, *Hardly a Man Is Now Alive*, p. 68.

BIBLIOGRAPHY

Abdy, Edward S. *Journal of a Residence and Tour in the United States of North America*. 3 vols. London: J. Murray, 1835. Reprint, New York: Negro Universities Press, 1969.

Albany Times Union, May 16, 1965.

American Farmer, July 12, 1882.

Atthill, Robin. *Old Mendip*. London: Routledge and Kegan Paul, 1964.

Beard, Daniel Carter. *Hardly a Man Is Now Alive: The Autobiography of Dan Beard*. New York: Doubleday, Doran, 1939.

Becker, J. E. *History of the Village of Waterloo*. Waterloo, N.Y.: Waterloo Library and Historical Society, 1949.

Belfast News-Letter, September 24, 1857.

Brown, George. *Pleasant Valley: A History of Elizabethtown*. Elizabethtown, N.Y.: Post and Gazette Press, 1905.

Cleaver, Mrs. Robert. *The History of the Town of Catherine, Schuyler County, New York*. Rutland, Vt.: Tuttle Publishing Co., 1945.

Corbin, J. S. *History of Gouverneur*. Waterford, N.Y.: Hungerford, Holbrook Co., 1905.

Coxsackie Turnpike Company. Manuscript Records. New York State Historical Association Library, Cooperstown.

Davis, Miles A. *History of Jerusalem*. Penn Yan: H. C. Earles, 1912.

Delaware Turnpike Company. Manuscript Records. New York State Historical Association Library, Cooperstown.

Donaldson, Alfred L. *A History of the Adirondacks*. 2 vols. New York: Century Co., 1921.

Durant, Samuel W. *History of Oneida County*. Philadelphia: Everts and Fariss, 1878.

Eager, Samuel W. *An Outline History of Orange County*. Newburgh, N.Y.: S. T. Callahan, 1846–1847.

Earle, Alice Morse. *Stage Coach and Tavern Days*. New York: Macmillan, 1915.

Erwin, James. *Reminiscences of Early Circuit Life*. Toledo: Spear, Johnson & Co., 1884.

Fowler, John. *Journal of a Year in the State of New York in the Year 1830*. London: Whittaker, Treacher & Arnot, 1831.

Gray, Kate M. *History of Springfield*. Cooperstown, N.Y.: General James Clinton Chapter, DAR, 1935.

Greene, Nelson. *History of the Mohawk Valley: Gateway to the West*. 4 vols. Chicago: Clarke, 1923.

Hammersley, Sydney. *The History of Waterford, New York*. Waterford, N.Y.: Privately printed, 1957.

Hawthorne, Nathaniel. *Twice-Told Tales*. Boston: Houghton, Mifflin and Co., 1903.

Hedrick, Ulysses P. *A History of Agriculture in the State of New York*. Albany: J. B. Lyon Co., 1933.

History of Greene County. New York: J. B. Beers and Co., 1884.

Howe, Herbert B. *Jedediah Barber, 1787–1876: A Footnote to the History of the Military Tract of Central New York*. New York: Columbia University Press, 1939.

Hulbert, Archer Butler. *Historic Highways of America*. 16 vols. Cleveland: Arthur H. Clark Co., 1902–1905.

[Hurd, Duane H.] *History of Otsego County*. Philadelphia: Everts and Fariss, 1878.

Johnson, Clifton. *New England and Its Neighbors*. New York: Macmillan, 1902.

Langdon, William C. *Everyday Things in American Life, 1776–1876*. New York: Charles Scribner and Son, 1941.

McCutcheon, Alan. "Roads and Bridges." *Ulster Folklife* 10 (1964): 73–81.

Marks, Marilla, ed. *Memoirs of the Life of David Marks, Minister of the Gospel*. Dover, N.H.: Free Will Baptist Printing Establishment, 1846.

Mathews, Mitford M. *A Dictionary of Americanisms on Historical Principles*. Chicago: University of Chicago Press, 1951.

Maxwell, Mary. *Among the Hills of Camillus*. Syracuse: Privately printed, 1952.

Meyer, Balthasar H. *History of Transportation in the United States before 1860*. New York: Peter Smith, 1948.

Otsego Lake Turnpike Company. Manuscript Records. New York State Historical Association Library, Cooperstown.

Rawson, Marion. *From Here to Yender*. New York: E. P. Dutton Co., 1932.

Russell, Harvey I. Manuscript Record of the Recollections of Harvey I. Russell. New York State Historical Association Library, Cooperstown.

Schoharie County Historical Review, May 1956.

Searle, Mark. *Turnpikes and Toll-Bars*. 2 vols. London: T. Fisher Unwin [1930].

Seaver, Franklin. *Historical Sketches of Franklin County*. Albany: J. B. Lyon, 1918.

Simpson, Elizabeth M. *Mexico: Mother of Towns*. Buffalo: J. W. Clement Co., 1949.

Sloane, Eric. *Our Vanishing Landscape*. New York: Wilfred Funk, 1955.

Smith, Anita. *Woodstock: History and Hearsay*. Saugerties, N.Y.: Catskill Mountain Publishing Corp., 1959.

Smith, John. *Our Country and Its People*. Boston: Boston Historical Co., 1899.

Sneller, Anne Gertrude. *A Vanished World*. Syracuse: Syracuse University Press, 1964.

Studer, Norman. "Yarns of a Catskill Woodsman." *New York Folklore Quarterly* 11, no. 3 (Autumn 1955): 183–192.

Third Great Western Turnpike Road Company. Manuscript Records. New York State Historical Association Library, Cooperstown.

Thompson, Harold W. *Body, Boots, and Britches*. Philadelphia: J. D. Lippincott, 1940.

Trenton-Prospect Plank Road Company. Manuscript Records. New York State Historical Association Library, Cooperstown.

Turner, M. Lovett. "Stories in Stone." In *Countryside Mood*, edited by Richard Harmon. London: Odhams Press, 1946.

Van Wagenen, Jared. *The Golden Age of Homespun*. Ithaca: Cornell University Press, 1953.

Wood, Frederick James. *The Turnpikes of New England and the Evolution of the Same through England, Virginia, and Maryland*. Boston: Marshall Jones Co., 1919.

Wood, Gilbert Sumner. *The Taverns and Turnpikes of Blanford, 1733–1833*. Blanford, Mass.: Gazette Press, 1908.

10. Ethnic Tensions in the Lower Rio Grande Valley to 1860

James L. Evans

The term *Lower Rio Grande Valley* refers to a limited area in the south-eastern part of Texas. It has no specific boundaries, but most persons living in that part of Texas restrict the term to the area within counties bordering the Rio Grande and within a hundred miles of the Gulf of Mexico. The term applies only to the land in the United States; residents of neither the United States nor Mexico use the term to refer to the area on the Mexican side of the river. The area is really a delta, not a valley at all. Today it includes more than a normal portion of well-to-do persons, many of them the owners of fine homes and massive citrus lands that cause the casual tourist to consider the Valley affluent. But many of the residents are of Mexican ancestry and are very poor. In Texas, persons of Mexican ancestry are generally called *Mexican Americans*, *Latin Americans*, or *Latins*, and all others except Negroes are called *Anglos*. These terms are used merely to distinguish the two groups; they have no connotations of discrimination. The Latins, whether their ancestors came to the locale two hundred years ago or in the early 1900's, usually speak Spanish in their homes today; and perhaps more than half of the ones past middle age can speak only Spanish. At the time of the 1960 census, the one Standard Metropolitan Statistical Area in the Lower Valley had the highest fertility ratio of any in the entire United States. The 1970 census shows that the two Standard Metropolitan Statistical areas in the Lower Valley ranked third and fourth among 243 in the entire nation in fertility rate.[1]

Some Latin Americans are found in almost every profession, but the majority must earn their livelihood by manual labor. Many families are migrant laborers who yearly follow the harvests in other states and then take whatever jobs they can get upon their return to the Valley each autumn. The plight of these Latins repeatedly causes the area to be mentioned as one of poverty. When in April of 1968 a Citizens' Board of Inquiry in Washington listed 256 counties in the United States where persons suffered from "chronic hunger," it included all three of the most southeastern counties in Texas.[2] Conditions in the area, however, have improved considerably since 1968.

Writers, whether dime novelists of the 1870's or historians, have often accepted and promoted the myth that the history of the locale is largely one of Mexican bandits lurking somewhere out of sight but ever alert to stab or shoot the innocent, virtuous American and to steal what-ever he had. Many writers either state or imply that not only was Juan Cortina the bandit leader *par excellence*, but also that until World War I all or nearly all Mexicans in the United States were bandits eager to attack Americans and to take their property and lives. History does not support this myth, however. As one Texas folklorist has said, just as the white plantation owners forced the Negro women into sexual rela-

239

tions and then established the myth of the Negro as a sex fiend, so the Anglos, after depriving the Mexicans of their land, cattle, and lives, established the myth of the border Mexican as a bandit.[3]

The Spaniards were late in settling northeastern Mexico, making no efforts to move into the section until the 1740's. Then, officials in Central Mexico appointed José de Escandón to explore the region on both sides of the Rio Grande. Shortly afterward, they commissioned him to colonize the area; and with a few soldiers who were to become colonists, some other colonists of all social classes, and a caravan of supplies, he started northward for settlement in 1747. Within a decade he had founded numerous towns, several of which are today important towns on the Mexican bank of the Rio Grande.[4] In addition to the Indians in the area, there was also one settlement of perhaps two hundred Negro males who had mated with Indian women.[5] Most of the settlers in later years came from Mexico.

In the towns first established by Escandón, persons ordinarily held the land in common; within a few years, however, grants of various sizes were often given to leaders of the new communities, and in the next generation these grants were divided among the heirs. Many of the towns that began in the 1700's were on the south bank of the Rio Grande in what is now Mexico, but the land grants were often north of the river in present-day United States. Because the life was basically agricultural and pastoral, the grants were often elongated rectangles, less than a mile in width but extending inland, often northward, for several miles. Thus, each grant had access to the river, making irrigation and crop production possible; the land unsuited for crops was used for grazing.[6]

Although the Spanish settlers determined the mores and customs of the region, in the late 1700's all persons, regardless of race or class, were readily accepted into the society. Negroes, Indians, and the hybrids already there; full-blooded Spaniards from both Mexico and Spain; non-Spanish Europeans; mestizos from the interior of Mexico; Indians of various tribes—all were accepted with hardly any signs of discrimination. Intermarriage among the races and classes was common, thus causing a compatible society that was a mixture of various bloods.[7] Specific individuals often owned the land, but these landholders were largely patriarchal in nature, and anyone was regarded as having the right to settle permanently on any unused portion of a grant. The poorest immigrants to this region had a chance to improve their condition, and they realized that a good life for their children was possible.

Geographical factors tended to influence the life and to make the area more cohesive. Though life was primitive, food was plentiful. The climate and soil caused some foods to grow easily, and the abundance of land made grazing profitable. Then, too, the river itself was a major factor in uniting the society of the Lower Rio Grande. Especially because many persons lived on one side of the river but sometimes worked on the other side, the river tended to unite the people both to the locale and to each other. And the region was isolated from densely populated areas to the north and south.

Thus, by the early 1800's, the people in the area had developed a self-

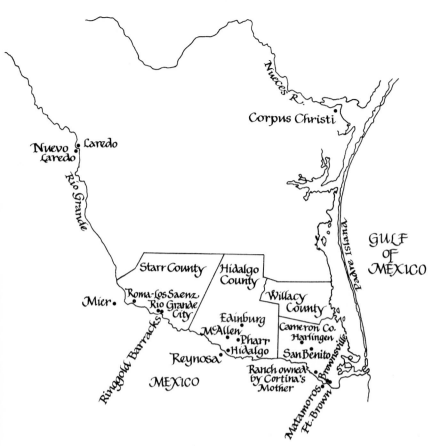

sufficient, patriarchal, though crude and primitive, society. They had no interest in what went on in the land to the north, and, though originating mostly from Spanish Mexico and maintaining its customs, they really cared very little more about the events in the country to the south. Unlike the destitute peons elsewhere in Mexico, the lowest persons in the society were secure and contented.[8]

Besides the towns, many ranch settlements developed, each one largely a community to itself; in time more people lived on these ranches than in the towns along the river. Many of the persons moved farther north of the Rio Grande, sometimes as far as the Nueces River, which in places is over 150 miles from the Rio Grande. Those settlers nearer the Nueces were engaged mainly in grazing sheep or cattle.[9]

The Lower Rio Grande Valley itself was hardly affected by the events

10.1

Map of Lower Rio Grande Valley. The four counties shown are those generally regarded as the Lower Rio Grande Valley area today. McAllen and Harlingen, the largest towns other than Brownsville, today, were not founded until well after 1900.

or the outcome of the Mexican War for Independence. The war was not fought in the area, and the self-contained society continued its ways as a part of independent Mexico much as it had earlier as a part of the Spanish possession.

Soon afterward several things endangered the life of the Valley. Unknown to the inhabitants at the time, the American argument of manifest destiny caused people in the United States to think of annexing the region. The movement to establish a Republic of the Rio Grande, a country to be composed of several states of northern Mexico and that part of Texas south of the Nueces, revealed that outsiders in Mexico were also considering the area as part of a larger one. The War for Texas Independence, though not fought in the Valley, did take many Americans to Texas, many of whom were restless adventurers with very little consideration for a dark-skinned person. Usually these persons considered the Negro inferior to the whites, and often they considered the Mexican—a dark-skinned hybrid of the Spaniard and the Indian— parallel to the offspring of a Negro and a white. Residents of the Lower Valley were oblivious of the Alamo and most other battles of the war, but tales of these events and of Mexicans were circulated in the United States, thereby increasing anti-Mexican feelings and causing Americans throughout the country to consider the Mexican not only racially inferior but also cowardly and treacherous.

During the decade between the War for Texas Independence and the Mexican War (1836–1846), numerous filibustering expeditions penetrated the land south of the Nueces, making the area between the two rivers a no man's land. The men not only stole cattle, but also, and perhaps more significant, terrified residents, causing many to abandon their lands and livestock and to leave for the interior of Mexico. The cattle abandoned in this area formed the basis for some of the Anglo cattle empires that later developed there. These filibusterers also sent back north unfavorable accounts of the Mexicans. The most noted of these filibusterers was Ewen Cameron, an immigrant from Scotland, who from 1836 until 1842 led a band that harried the ranches and stole cattle to drive to the market at Galveston.[10]

The last of these raids—the one that resulted in the Mier Expedition—was really the first battle of the Mexican War. When one leader realized that his group had failed and that additional plundering would probably not be profitable, he ordered a return to Central Texas. Dissatisfied with the orders to return and eager to slaughter more dark-skinned Mexicans, supposedly to get revenge for the defeat at the Alamo, many of the men, including Cameron, established a small group of their own, crossed the Rio Grande, and raided towns to secure horses and cattle. On December 23, 1842, they entered the town of Mier without opposition, but the arrival of more Mexican troops caused the Texans, greatly outnumbered, to surrender on December 26.[11] The captured Americans were marched through the river towns on the south side as far as Matamoros;[12] they were later kept as prisoners in Central Mexico; as punishment for an attempted escape, one-tenth of the group was selected by lottery and executed. Perhaps the Americans, acting without sanction of any government, had no motive more honorable than raiding and looting a weaker nation, but reports were told of their being marched through the Mexican towns as a spectacle for an inferior population of darker skin and mixed bloods. Also circulated were accounts of prolonged captivity within Mexico where they experienced forced labor, hunger, and, in some cases, execution. These reports intensified the belief that Mexicans were cruel and treacherous, and, consequently, Americans intensified their hatred of the Mexicans en masse.

More than anything else, the Mexican War and its outcome changed the life in the Lower Valley. Matamoros, a town some twenty miles from the Gulf, was on the south bank of the river, but it had claimed a large portion of land north of the town as the town common. This common, used for grazing, was on a grant made back in 1782 and still owned by members of the family of the original grantee.[13] As stated by one of his contemporaries, in 1846 President Polk ordered General Zachary Taylor to begin "*a war of defence*, although not a Mexican shot had been fired" and "to capture the city of Metamoros [*sic*], and to carry the war into the interior of Mexico."[14] In the spring of 1846, Taylor and his troops erected Fort Brown on the land used as the Matamoros common; from this fort they went out on the early skirmishes of the Mexican War. Thus, the eastern part of the Lower Rio Grande Valley became a meeting place for the armies of two nations; it also became the gateway to Mexico or to the United States for adventurers, smugglers, and other unscrupulous people, whether they traveled by land or by sea. In his diary for May 8, 1847, the day after soldier payday, Oliver Hazard Perry indicated the type of soldier stationed there: "Whiskey is playing the very devil with the Troops[.] I never saw a more Drunken set of men than was exhibited by the 1st Mass Infantry."[15] He added that the inhabitants said these soldiers "act[ed] about as bad as other Volunteers did before them."[16] When the Mexican War ended, the inhabitants of the Valley could neither accept nor even comprehend the treaty provision that the Rio Grande was an official boundary dividing the land and its inhabitants. For generations, the river had united the settlements and the people. Furthermore, since most of the persons as far north as the Nueces were Mexicans, they naturally believed that the Nueces River should be the logical boundary.

Even more disruptive to the way of life in the Valley was the type of immigrant from the North who came to the area and stayed. About 1849 the worst of all societies came to the Rio Grande, especially to Brownsville, which aptly became known as the "sewer" of both Europe and America. Unlike those few of European descent who had come during the 1700's, the new ones did not blend into the native society. Whether irresponsible adventurers or opportunists eager for wealth, they almost always regarded the Mexicans as racially inferior creatures whose inferiority was evidenced and/or caused by their ancestors' having mated with another race. These new Americans also felt that, since the United States had defeated Mexico in the recent war, any American was justified in treating any person of Mexican ancestry however he chose. Greedy for power, wealth, and land, they often made claims to land north of the river that had belonged to a Latin family for nearly a century. Latins who attempted to save their land found litigation costly and useless. If the American claimant did not get the land, an American

10.2

The Execution of Captain Ewen Cameron,
April 25, 1843. Cameron County, Texas, in
which Brownsville is located, was named for
him. (From Thomas J. Green, *Journal of the
Texian Expedition against Mier.*)

lawyer probably did. Thus, the 1850's were very disturbing to the earlier residents of the Valley. They saw the new Americans steal their land, and they saw the new Americans assault and kill their relatives and friends. Still they attempted to preserve their old ways; still they accepted honest immigrants who made no effort to exploit them.

In the 1850's, as racial bitterness increased, the town of Brownsville, a port and periodical smuggling center, flourished, much of the prosperity no doubt resulting from the presence of troops at Fort Brown. Whenever federal authorities talked of removing soldiers from various points along the Rio Grande, Anglos in Brownsville protested that troops were essential there.[17] Federal officers, perhaps aware that these Anglos desired troops mainly to improve the local economy and to protect their power as a dominating minority, withdrew forces from Fort Brown in early 1859.

By then the racial situation had become very tense. The new American had no respect for the Mexican, and the Mexican both resented and feared the new American. When land-greedy Americans claimed the townsite of Brownsville, the family to whom the land had been granted in 1782 carried the case, *Patrick Shannon* v. *Cavazos*, to the United States Supreme Court, where it was dismissed, supposedly for lack of jurisdiction, thus leaving the land in the hands of the new Americans.[18]

Like many others, Juan Cortina, who was a direct descendant of the original grantee, became very bitter over the treatment that Latins received from Anglos. When, in July of 1859, he saw an Anglo marshal in downtown Brownsville mistreating a peon who had formerly worked for the Cortina family, Cortina shot and wounded the marshal, rescued the peon, and crossed the river to Mexico. In late September of that year, Cortina returned to Brownsville with a band of Mexicans variously estimated at thirty to two hundred, seeking vengeance on a few specific Anglos who had habitually mistreated Latins. The group killed three Anglos and, unintentionally, two Latins; they spent several hours looking for specific other Anglos; and they freed all persons in the local jail, most of whom were held there for minor offenses or because they were Mexicans.[19] The *Brownsville Flag* put out a special issue (October 1, 1859) bearing the caption:

Guerrilla Attack upon Brownsville!
Five men killed! An armed Guerrilla Band in Possession
of the City! More lives threatened! Threats to burn
the City! The Guerrillas yet in camp on the American
side of the river!! The excellent conduct of our
neighbors, the Authorities and People of Matamoros!!
No American Protection!!!

The County Court, composed mostly of Anglo opportunists, later referred to this raid as "an invasion of American territory by armed Mexicans under the Mexican flag with hostile intentions against the constituted authorities of our State and country,"[20] and newspapers included such reports as that in the *Texas State Gazette* (October 15,

10.3

Juan N. Cortina, photographed in his
uniform of brigadier general in the Mexican
army, about the year 1864. (From José T.
Canales, *Juan N. Cortina: Bandit or
Patriot?*)

1859), which said: "The Lower Rio Grande has lately been the scene of a Mexican invasion." In the Texas State Archives are numerous letters written to the governor of Texas by Anglo businessmen in Brownsville, a typical one being that of E. R. Hood, who stated: "I am at Brownsville, and Brownsville was yesterday captured, and captured by Mexicans. . . . Five men of ours were killed, one of theirs [*sic*]. They had possession until mid-day. The jailer was slain, the prisoners were liberated & armed, men were robbed. . . . Are we to be left to the mercy of bandits?"[21] These Anglos also sent a petition to both the governor and President Buchanan, saying that "an armed body of Mexicans, somewhere about 100 strong" and headed by Juan Cortina, had attacked the town, aroused "from their slumber several innocent and inoffensive citizens, and in the most brutal and ruthless manner began to shoot them down, and in several instances to mutilate their persons in a most beastly manner." The petitioners added: "We have seen that a single Mexican outlaw can raise a crowd in our midst of several hundred desperate, lawless, and licentious beings, and offend with impunity the most sacred laws of security, peace, public order, and civilization itself."[22]

Meanwhile, Cortina and his group retired to his mother's ranch several miles from Brownsville. Newspapers, letter writers, and later historians repeatedly emphasized that Cortina had issued a proclamation including the words "our personal enemies shall not possess our lands until they have fattened it with their own gore."[23] Very few, however, mentioned that he had stated in the same proclamation that their "oppressors number but six or eight."

Then the erroneous report reached the state capital that Cortina had captured Corpus Christi, located on the Gulf of Mexico over 150 miles from the Rio Grande. According to rumors, the attack was a part of a Mexican plan to recover all land to the Nueces and to destroy maliciously all the American property possible. Upon hearing this rumor, the governor sent the Texas Rangers to the Rio Grande.

In spite of the rumors, Cortina's men had made no attack whatever since that of September 28. Tomás Cabrera, who was said to be one of Cortina's leaders, was held captive by the Anglos, but they had promised him a fair trial. Nevertheless, the night after the Texas Rangers arrived —November 10, 1859—"an unknown and lawless mob" took Cabrera out of jail and hanged him. Not until this lynching did Cortina make his first attack after the September raid.[24] Since the Texans were not overly successful in their first skirmishes, citizens throughout the state made the claim that Cortina and the Mexicans were so treacherous that not even the Texas Rangers could defeat them.

But not until later did the federal government feel any concern. Then, upon discovering that there had been no attack whatever on Corpus Christi and that there was no basis at all for the recent report that one hundred Americans had been slain in a later battle, federal officers began to ignore the situation. Finally, though, after more incidents between Texan forces and the ones of Mexican ancestry, federal troops arrived and drove Cortina across into Mexico, where he remained for over a year. All winter Americans in the area sent out complaints of danger, trying thereby to create hysteria, to secure the permanent return of troops, and to portray the Mexicans as bandits. They glossed over the fact that the early raid was simply a personal conflict; they presented it as evidence that Cortina as an individual and the Mexicans en masse were bandits. As is often true among groups that are the victims of prejudice, the misdeeds of one individual were regarded as characteristic of the entire group.

Apparently many Texans were influenced by the reports about the Mexicans on the Rio Grande; the file of correspondence to the governor that winter includes numerous semiliterate letters from throughout the nation asking to raise or join a force to go to the Rio Grande. Some letters indicate a desire for high pay; others merely indicate a desire to kill Mexicans. A typical letter in the Texas State Archives is the one from Wiley Morgan, Jr. of Liberty, Mississippi:

---

th

March 24

Liberty Amite Co Miss

Hon Sam Houston

Sir I offer you

my services to Join any
company to fight those
dam Mexicans if you
except my Services you will
please write to me, So my
expences are paid. Thats all
I care for, Write to me and
Let me Know if you want
me and where I shall come
too   Yours Respectfuly
                    Wiley Morgan Jr[25]

A more literate letter and one of the many that had several signatures is the following one from Macon, Georgia:

Macon Ga Mch 14th 1860

To His Excellency
        Sam Houston
                Dear Sir.
                        The
undersigned, having read Your recent
Communication to the Secritary of War,
transmitted by Genrl Britton and also
accounts of the frequent outrages
committed by the Mexicans and Indians
upon the Citizens of Texas and Sympathi-
sing with Sufferings of the latter.—
respectfully offer you their Services
to assist in defending the frontier

and if necessary carrying the War into
the heart of Mexico itsself.

　　If a Company would be acceptable
to you for such Service we have
little doubt but that we could
Speedily organise one here which
Would do its utmost in any
Service to protect the Citizens
or defend the honor of the State
of Texas. We have been lead to
make this offer from the seeming hesitency
of the Federal Government in affording that
assistance which you So earnestly request
and the exrgincy of the case, absolutely
requires.

　　With Sentiments of respect and Esteem
We remain Very
　　　　Truly yours
　　　　　Jno G Patton
　　　　　Jno M Stubbs
　　　　　Chas E Ross
　　　　　W. W. Lancy[26]

The originals of many such letters are in the file of correspondence sent to Governor Houston during the winter of 1859–1860.

By the late 1860's the traditional story stated that Cortina's criminal career dated back to the 1840's and that he had been a continual trouble-maker in Brownsville for years; yet, as late as January 14, 1860, the marshal that Cortina had wounded in July, 1859, testified that he had never known of Cortina prior to that July day.[27] I have encountered dozens of newspaper accounts written about Cortina in late 1859, and not one of them has given any account of criminal activity by Cortina prior to 1859. W. P. Reyburn, the appraiser general, pointed out in his report made in November of 1859 that during the raid in September, the raid that was the basis of such erroneous accounts and such a terrible aftermath, Cortina was merely seeking vengeance on a few individuals.[28] Maj. S. P. Heintzelman, head of the U.S. troops sent to the area, stated in his official report that the "sole object [of the September raid] appeared to be revenge" and that the party "did not make any attempt to plunder or rob."[29] Reyburn also said that weeks later Cortina, to feed his men, brought into his camp eleven beeves belonging to a certain man, then notified the man of what he had done, and sent him a due bill for the eleven he had taken.[30] Capt. James B. Ricketts, in his communication to the adjutant general of the United States in December of 1859, declared: "The origin of the difficulty is owing to a falling out between parties mixed up with private affairs, and is so complicated that it is difficult to ascertain the truth, no doubt much exaggerated, and not improved by demonstrations on the part of some rangers and citizens who have effected nothing as yet."[31] Robert Taylor, one of the commissioners sent by Sam Houston, who had become governor of

10.4

John Salmon "Rip" Ford of the Texas
Rangers. (Courtesy Barker Texas History
Center, University of Texas at Austin.)

Texas in December, 1859, stated in a confidential reply: "I am sorry to
say a good many of the latter [Anglos] in fact some of them who have
been burning ranches & Hanging and shooting Mexicans without
authority of Law are more dreaded than Cortina."[32] In filing claims, F.
M. Campbell, an Anglo who had been held prisoner by Cortina, supposedly to serve as interpreter, stated that Texas Rangers had burned up
his "pens and fences for firewood, and one horse by accident" and that
the Texas Rangers had used hogs and goats and fifty barrels of sweet
potatoes for which the commander refused to pay. He estimated the
value of the property taken or destroyed by Cortina at two hundred
dollars and that taken or destroyed by Rangers at one thousand dollars.[33] And a female missionary who conducted a school in Brownsville
stated in her diary: "For two weeks after the assault by Cortina I remained in my house and continued my school, as I knew his murderous
designs were only against his enemies. As long as he had his own band
of men, who were fully instructed upon whom to commit violence, I felt
no apprehension that any harm would befall me."[34]

One newspaper in southern Texas, the *Matagorda Gazette* (November 19, 1859), pointed out that Cortina was not conducting a war against
the United States or a "massacre of the innocent." It mentioned that
in September he wreaked his vengeance against only a few personal
enemies and then "departed without further molestation of any one."
The *Gazette* also reminded its readers that Cortina had refused to fight

the Texas Rangers in Brownsville because he did not want to endanger lives and property by fighting there. And, although Gen. Rip Ford of the Texas Rangers tried to point out the danger of Cortina by stressing that Cortina and his men knew about and could easily have captured wagons with more than $160,000 in goods and money en route to Brownsville from the coast,[35] the fact that Cortina's men made no attempt to attack these wagons is further evidence that Cortina was not a bandit leader at that time.

But, while the Anglos in Brownsville were keeping themselves in a frenzy and sending out to the world all sorts of statements about Mexican banditry, the Mexicans, realizing the American attitude toward them and filled with the resentment that had been seething for more than a decade, began to regard Cortina as their leader. By early 1860 they considered him as the leader who would right the wrongs they had suffered from Americans, the leader who would drive the Americans back to the Nueces, the leader who would enable them to return to the peaceful way of life they had enjoyed in the past. And Cortina, selected by the people as their leader, accepted that position. Seeing that open warfare existed between Anglos and Latins and that Mexicans could best carry on this warfare by looting the property of Anglo invaders, he accepted the role previously erroneously assigned to him by the Americans and became a bandit leader commanding lesser bandits. Certainly, banditry in the area continued for years, but no doubt the accounts were often as misleading and exaggerated as were those of Cortina's first raid. For example, in the spring of 1875, when reports of Mexican banditry in the Lower Rio Grande Valley were at their peak, the officer in charge of the Frontier Forces that were sent to the area stated in correspondence to his superior officer: "There are so many false reports circulated in this country, it is difficult to know when they are true—It is astounding to know what effrontry Some of the people of this border have—They are continually writing articles—which they know to be false—."[36] And a few days later this same officer wrote: "If we find thieves we have to go to the newspapers for them—."[37] Regardless of the extent of Mexican banditry from 1860 until 1920, the peaceful and simple way of life of the Lower Rio Grande Valley in the late eighteenth and early nineteenth centuries was replaced by racial hatred and discrimination and by indiscriminate and unlimited mistreatment of persons known as Mexicans.

NOTES

1. Fertility ratio is the number of children under 5 per 1,000 women aged 15 through 49. Brownsville-Harlingen-San Benito, the only Standard Metropolitan Statistical Area in the Lower Rio Grande Valley in 1960, had a fertility ratio of 664; the next highest of the 212 SMSAs in the United States was Ogden, Utah, with 648; next were Laredo with 646 and El Paso with 633. Both Laredo and El Paso are located on the Mexican border, and both are composed largely of Latin Americans. (See *U.S. Census Population 1960, United States Summary*, Table 63 on pp. I-176 through I-178.) In the 1960's, McAllen-Pharr-Edinburg was made into an SMSA, and at the time of the 1970 census it ranked third among the 243 SMSAs in the United States in fertility rate. Brownsville-Harlingen-San Benito ranked fourth in 1970 and Laredo ranked first, but El Paso had dropped to seventeenth. The fertility rate in the nation as a whole had declined greatly in the 1960's, and the rate for Laredo, though the highest in the country in 1970, was only 477. (See *U.S. Census of the Population 1970, United States Summary*, Table 66 on pp. I-314 through I-316.)

2. *Brownsville Herald*, April 23, 1968. The counties of Hidalgo and Cameron are the two most southeastern ones of the Valley. Willacy County, the third one named, is north of Cameron and does not border Mexico; thus, not always is it considered a part of the Lower Valley. Civic organizations were quite resentful of the publicity. The Commissioners' Court of Cameron County declared a "Frijole and Tortilla Day" to emphasize that the Latin diet of frijoles (beans) and tortillas (a type of bread made from corn) was of "high nutritive value," not an indication of poverty. (See *Houston Chronicle*, June 9, 1968.)

3. Américo Paredes, *"With His Pistol in His Hand,"* p. 20.

4. James Lee Stambaugh and Lillian J. Stambaugh, *The Lower Rio Grande Valley of Texas*, pp. 27–31; Frank Cushman Pierce, *A Brief History of the Lower Rio Grande Valley*, pp. 17–18.

5. Stambaugh and Stambaugh, *Lower Rio Grande Valley*, p. 29; Oran Randolph Scott, "History of Hidalgo County," M.A. thesis, p. 2.

6. Stambaugh and Stambaugh, *Lower Rio Grande Valley*, p. 34.

7. Paredes, *"With His Pistol in His Hand,"* pp. 8–9.

8. Ibid., pp. 10–11.

9. Ibid., p. 9.

10. Maurice S. Pipkin, "An Early History of Cameron County," M.A. thesis, p. 42. Cameron County, Texas, is named in honor of Ewen Cameron.

11. "Mier Expedition," *The Handbook of Texas*, ed. Walter Prescott Webb, I, 189. Ewen Cameron was one of the leaders of the Mier Expedition and the one who led the ill-fated escape in Central Mexico.

12. Thomas J. Green, *Journal of the Texian Expedition against Mier*, pp. 118–124; Thomas W. Bell, *A Narrative of the Capture and Subsequent Sufferings of the Mier Prisoners in Mexico*, ed. James M. Day, pp. 22–23. Both of these are reprints of books written by members of the expedition and originally published in the 1840's.

13. Pierce, *Brief History of the Lower Rio Grande Valley*, p. 34.

14. William Jay, *A Review of the Causes and Consequences of the Mexican War*, pp. 131–132.

15. Oliver Hazard Perry, Diary, p. 16.

16. Ibid.

17. "Difficulties on Southwestern Frontier," *House Executive Document 52*, 36th Cong., 1st sess., pp. 12–14. One letter of March 9, 1859, was sent to the secretary of war; it had 103 signatures. *Document 52* consists of 147 pages dealing with Cortina and/or the trouble on the border in 1859 and 1860.

18. Pipkin, "Early History of Cameron County," p. 74; Pierce, *Brief History of the Lower Rio Grande Valley*, p. 35.

19. Charles William Goldfinch, *Juan N. Cortina, 1824–1892*, p. 22.

20. *Document 52*, p. 93.

21. Letter to Gov. Hardin R. Runnels, Hardin R. Runnels Correspondence, 1859, Texas State Archives.

22. *Document 52*, pp. 20–23.

23. Ibid., p. 72.

24. Ibid.

25. Letter to Gov. Sam Houston, Sam Houston Correspondence, 1860, Texas State Archives.

26. Ibid.

27. *Document 52*, p. 129.

28. Ibid., p. 65.

29. "Troubles on Texas Frontier," *House Executive Document 81*, 36th Cong., 1st sess., p. 4. This 105-page document has copies of numerous papers and letters concerning the trouble on the border.

30. *Document 52*, p. 66.

31. Ibid., p. 75.

32. Letter to Sam Houston, Sam Houston Correspondence, 1860, Texas State Archives.

33. *Document 81*, p. 91.

34. Melinda Rankin, *Twenty Years among the Mexicans*, p. 83.

35.   John Salmon Ford, *Rip Ford's Texas*, pp. 268–269. This book, edited by Stephen Oates, is made up of Ford's writings.

36.   Report from Neal Coldwell to Major John B. Jones, April 30, 1875, John B. Jones Correspondence, Adjutant General Papers, Texas State Archives.

37.   Ibid., May 4, 1875.

BIBLIOGRAPHY

Adjutant General Papers, 1870–1875. Texas State Archives, Austin.

American Flag (Brownsville), January 26, 1859; October 1, 1859.

Bell, Thomas W. *A Narrative of the Capture and Subsequent Sufferings of the Mier Prisoners in Mexico*. Edited by James M. Day. Waco: Texian Press, 1964. [Facsimile reprint of 1845 edition, "printed for the author at the press of R. Morris & Co., DeSoto County, Mississippi."]

Brownsville Herald, April 23, 1968.

Bryant, Katharine Louise. "Friction along the Rio Grande Border after the Mexican War, 1848–1859." M.A. Thesis, University of California, Berkeley, n.d.

Canales, José T. *Juan N. Cortina: Bandit or Patriot?* An address by J. T. Canales before the Lower Rio Grande Valley Historical Society, at San Benito, Texas, October 25, 1951. San Antonio: Artes Gráficas, 1951.

Castañeda, Carlos E. *Our Catholic Heritage in Texas*. Vol. 3. Edited by Paul J. Foik. Austin: Von Boeckmann-Jones Co., 1939.

Chatfield, W. H., comp. *The Twin Cities (Brownsville, Texas; Matamoros, Mexico) of the Border and the Country of the Lower Rio Grande*. New Orleans: E. P. Branado, 1893.

Crawford, Polly Pearl. "The Beginnings of Spanish Settlement in the Lower Rio Grande Valley." M.A. Thesis, University of Texas, Austin, 1925.

Daily Picayune (New Orleans), October, 1859.

Daily Review (Edinburg, Tex.), December 7, 1952.

Davenport, Herbert. Papers. Texas State Archives, Austin.

Dobie, J. Frank. *A Vaquero of the Brush Country*. Dallas: Southwest Press, 1929.

Ferguson, Keene. "The Development of the Image of the Racially Inferior Mexican." Paper in files of the History Department, University of Texas, Austin.

Ford, John Salmon. Papers, vols. 4–5. University of Texas Archives, Austin.

———. *Rip Ford's Texas*. Edited by Stephen B. Oates. Austin: University of Texas Press, 1963.

Galveston Weekly News, October–December, 1859.

Goldfinch, Charles William. *Juan N. Cortina, 1824–1892: A Re-Appraisal*. Brownsville: Bishop's Print Shop, 1950.

Graf, LeRoy P. "The Economic History of the Lower Rio Grande Valley, 1820–1875." 2 vols. Ph.D. Thesis, Harvard University, 1942.

Green, Thomas J. *Journal of the Texian Expedition against Mier*. Austin: Steck Co., 1935. [Facsimile reproduction of 1845 edition.]

Houston, Sam. Correspondence. Texas State Archives, Austin.

Houston Chronicle, June 9, 1968.

Jay, William. *A Review of the Causes and Consequences of the Mexican War*. Boston: Benjamin B. Mussey & Co., 1849.

Matagorda (Texas) *Gazette*, November 19, 1859–February 15, 1860.

Mexico. *Reports of the Committee of Investigation Sent in 1873 by the Mexican Government to the Frontier of Texas*. New York, 1875.

Paredes, Américo. *"With His Pistol in His Hand": A Border Ballad and Its Hero*. Austin: University of Texas Press, 1958.

Peavey, John R. *Echoes from the Rio Grande*. Brownsville: Springman-King Co., 1963.

Perry, Oliver Hazard. Diary. Bancroft Library, University of California, Berkeley.

Pierce, Frank Cushman. *A Brief History of the Lower Rio Grande Valley*. Menasha, Wis.: George Banta Publishing Co., 1917.

Pipkin, Maurice S. "An Early History of Cameron County." M.A. Thesis, Texas College of Arts and Industries, Kingsville, 1940.

Ranchero (Brownsville and Matamoros), 1865–1870.

Rankin, Melinda. *Twenty Years among the Mexicans: A Narrative of Missionary Labor*. Cincinnati: Chase & Hall, Publishers, 1875.

Rippy, J. Fred. *The United States and Mexico*. New York: Alfred A. Knopf, 1926.

Runnels, Hardin R. Correspondence. Texas State Archives, Austin.

Scott, Florence Johnson. *Historical Heritage of the Lower Rio Grande*. San Antonio: Naylor Co., 1937.

Scott, Oran Randolph. "History of Hidalgo County." M.A. Thesis, Texas Christian University, Fort Worth, 1927.

Shearer, Ernest Charles. "Border Diplomatic Relations between the United States and Mexico, 1848–1860." Ph.D. Thesis, University of Texas, Austin, 1939.

Smithwick, Noah. *The Evolution of a State.* Austin: H. P. N. Gammel, 1900.

Stambaugh, James Lee, and Lillian J. Stambaugh. *The Lower Rio Grande Valley of Texas.* San Antonio: Naylor Co., 1954.

Texas State Gazette (Austin), October 15, 1859.

United States. "Difficulties on Southwestern Frontier." *House Executive Document 52.* 36th Cong., 1st sess. SS1050.

————. "Hostilities on the Rio Grande." *Senate Executive Document 21.* 36th Cong., 1st sess. SS 1031.

————. "Troubles on Texas Frontier." *House Executive Document 81.* 36th Cong., 1st sess. SS 1056.

————. *U.S. Census of the Population 1970, United States Summary.* Washington, D.C.: G.P.O.

————. *U.S. Census Population 1960, United States Summary.* Washington, D.C.: G.P.O.

————. U.S. Census Records, Texas: Hidalgo County, 1860, 1870, 1880.

Viele, Mrs. Egbert L. *"Following the Drum": A Glimpse of Frontier Life.* New York: Rudd & Carleton, 1858.

Webb, Walter Prescott. Collection. University of Texas Archives, Austin.

————, ed. *The Handbook of Texas.* 2 vols. Austin: Texas State Historical Association, 1952.

————. *The Texas Rangers: A Century of Frontier Defense.* Austin: University of Texas Press, 1965.

Woodman, Lyman. *Cortina, Rogue of the Rio Grande.* San Antonio: Naylor Co., 1950.

11. Wishing in and Shooting in the New Year among the Germans in the Carolinas

Walter L. Robbins

The German American custom of wishing in and shooting in the New Year consists, typically, of the following: Beginning at sunset on New Year's Eve a group of men known as New Year's shooters, carrying guns loaded only with gunpowder, make the rounds of the homes in their community. When they arrive at a home, one of the group, the wisher, calls out to the man of the house and, when he hears an answer, addresses a New Year's wish to him. After the wish the shooters fire their guns and are then invited in for refreshments. After a short stay, they proceed to the next home on their rounds, which last until dawn of New Year's Day. The present article deals with the custom as practiced in areas of North and South Carolina settled by Germans and Swiss in the eighteenth century.[1]

The North Carolina Germans were part of that mass of settlers who, before the Revolution, moved south from Pennsylvania in search of cheap land, first into the Shenandoah Valley and later into the areas of the Yadkin and Catawba rivers in North Carolina.[2] In turn, North Carolina Germans migrated to southeast Missouri in about 1800 and after.[3] Besides the Lutheran and Reformed settlers in the Yadkin and Catawba areas of North Carolina, there were also Moravians, who settled in the area of present-day Winston-Salem.[4] It is from manuscript records kept by the Moravians that the oldest accounts of the custom in North Carolina come. Ludolf Backhof taught school in the Moravian settlement of Friedberg and lived in the schoolhouse there.[5] On January 1, 1774, Backhof noted in the "Friedberg Diary" that, after the customary watchnight service around midnight on New Year's Eve, "everyone went home and could have had the pleasure of lying down to rest for a few hours, if they had not been hindered in this by the plot of the young men and big boys of the neighborhood, who, led by Friedrich Läkel, went from farm to farm to shoot the New Year in. To be sure, they did not come to the schoolhouse. But we heard shooting all night until dawn, so that we felt just as if the whole area were full of Indians. When everyone arrived at noon for today's services, they could not say enough of what a turbulent night it had been and how they had been disturbed."[6] There are later reports of shooting at New Year's from Moravian communities, but it is not clear whether only shooting, pure and simple, was involved or an actual procession of shooters from house to house. Like the shooters in 1774, the shooters in the later accounts are, when identified, always boys or young men in their late teens or early twenties. In 1806, the Aufseher Collegium, one of the governing bodies of elders in Salem, complained of "repeated shooting" on the previous New Year's Eve and expressed the intention of seeking out the culprits.[7] In 1810, five young men were expelled from the Salem congregation for shooting on New Year's Eve and thus causing "a general sensation

257

among the brothers and sisters."[8] This penalty suffered by the shooters, together with additional steps taken by the authorities, prevented a recurrence of shooting on New Year's in 1811.[9] On New Year's Eve, 1831, in Bethània, there was some shooting at the time of the watch-night services.[10] Young shooters suffered powder burns in New Year's accidents in Bethabara in 1834,[11] and in either Friedberg or Hope in 1835.[12] The attitude of these Moravian accounts is a hostile one and is typical of the attitude of the "Plain Dutch" toward the custom, familiar also from accounts of the custom from Mennonite and Brethren areas of the Shenandoah Valley.[13]

In contrast, the attitude of the "Church Dutch" in North Carolina, the Lutherans and Reformed on the Yadkin and Catawba rivers, was a friendly one. In the vicinity of Rockwell, Rowan County, in the Yadkin River area, people who were not visited by the shooters felt offended. Here, in the 1880's and 1890's, the young men went from house to house, carrying heavily loaded muzzle-loaders, and shot against the chimneys to make a loud noise. They would be invited in, and, while the wife went to the kitchen to get food for them, the man of the house would bring out his brandy jug and "set up" the shooters.[14] In the 1880's and 1890's, in the area of Mount Pleasant, Cabarrus County, also near the Yadkin, people went from house to house, shooting the old year out and the New Year in and serenading their neighbors. The people in the house would give the group a "treat," and then the group would move on.[15] In 1914, William Alexander Graham described "New Year's Shooting" as he knew it in his home area of Iron Station, Lincoln County, west of the Catawba River. The shooters assembled about midnight and went from house to house until sunrise. They would creep up to a home, and the wisher, or "preacher" as he was called, would call out to the man of the house three times, the man answering at the third call. Then the "preacher" would deliver the wish or "sermon," after which the shooters would fire one after another. The "preacher" would then say to the man of the house: "If you are a man of grace, / Come to the door and show your face." (This rhyme may be an English version of a Pennsylvania Dutch original ending in the rhyme words *bischt* and *Gsicht*.) In response to the rhyme, the man of the house would then open the door, and the shooters would enter and have refreshments. At sunrise, after the rounds, the shooters would breakfast at a designated place.[16] In 1958, William Brannon, of Davidson, North Carolina, wrote to me of another instance of the custom in Lincoln County, as related to him by his grandfather, who was in his eighties: The shooters would creep up to a home. One of them would start playing a fiddle; "then, after starting very quietly, they would all join in playing and singing to the family as they stood outside the house." When the people of the house came to the door, the shooters would fire their muzzle-loaders one after another and then would go inside and have refreshments.[17] The custom still survives today in the Catawba River region, namely in Cherryville, a small town located in the northwest corner of Gaston County, which borders Lincoln County on the south. There are two groups of shooters in Cherryville: The older group, the "Cherryville New Year's Shooters," is descended from the shooters of yore, while the newer group, the "Traditional New Year's Shooters," seems to have been formed in the late 1950's. Both groups have members ranging in age from the young to the elderly. The "Cherryville New Year's Shooters," whom I observed on New Year's, 1967, assemble at the Wayside Inn Café, a grill on the outskirts of town on the road to Lincolnton. For the most part, they use old muskets loaded with black powder. In 1967, there were two wishers, or "speech criers," J. C. Beam and E. G. Green, who alternated in chanting the wish known as the "New Year's Speech" at the various stops. At midnight J. C. Beam chanted the "New Year's Speech" to the owner of the grill, after which the shooters, one by one, went out into the road and fired. Most of them avert their heads when firing. They fire with one hand on the trigger and the other against the base of the stock of the gun, some of them turning their bodies with the recoil. After this round, another "speech crier," Vance Sellers, about seventy-five years of age, delivered the wish known as the "Ladies' Speech" to the wife of the owner of the grill. Each of the shooters then fired again. The shooters then continued on to the next stops, at which the procedure was shorter—the "New Year's Speech" followed by shooting. The Cherryville shooters no longer have refreshments at each home visited, as was formerly the case. One exception is the home of elderly "Aunt Violet" Carpenter, who has served refreshments to the shooters for years and whose home is still a traditional stopping place for both groups of shooters. The shooters no longer walk, as formerly, but travel in automobiles, and their rounds no longer end at dawn but rather in the late afternoon of New Year's Day.[18]

The term *New Year's shooters*, used for the participants in the Catawba River region, Pennsylvania, the Shenandoah Valley, and Illinois, is probably derived from the Pennsylvania Dutch *Neijohrschitz* or its European equivalent *Neujahrsschütze*.[19] Some of the participants had a special function, the wisher, for instance. Both at Iron Station, Lincoln County, North Carolina, and in Bollinger County, Missouri, he was termed the "preacher" and his wish the "sermon."[20] Nowadays, in Cherryville, North Carolina, the wisher is known as the "speech crier," who delivers a "speech," probably derived from the German word *Spruch*, used to denote the wish both in Pennsylvania and in Europe.[21] Besides the wisher, there were musicians in the group. Musicians, including a fiddler, took part in the custom in Lincoln County, according to Brannon's account.[22] The shooters also used musical and noise-making instruments in the Shenandoah Valley, Pennsylvania, and Europe, violins being especially prominent in Berks County, Pennsylvania.[23]

The Lincoln County practice, mentioned by Brannon, of drawing the attention of the family by singing and playing music has a parallel in Towamencin Township, Montgomery County, Pennsylvania, where, in about 1834, young shooters sang "an enlivening song sufficiently loud to waken the family."[24] In the Swabian settlement of Neu-Posttal, Bessarabia (U.S.S.R.), the shooters crept up to the house and sang folksongs.[25] The practice of calling out to the person to be honored was also common.[26] The fact that, at Iron Station, the "preacher" called three times to the man of the house, the man replying at the third call,[27] may have to do with the belief found in the German-speaking area of Europe that one should reply to someone calling from outside at night only at the third call. Otherwise one may meet with an accident, die, or be struck dumb, for the caller may be an evil spirit. But, when one's name is called three times, one may answer or go out, because the caller is a pure spirit or a human being.[28] According to both accounts from Lincoln County—Graham's and Brannon's[29]—the shooters tried to take the family by surprise, a trait reported also from Pennsylvania, Indiana, and Europe.[30]

We have seen that in Cherryville, North Carolina, there are actually two wishing ceremonies, one for the man of the house, to whom the "New Year's Speech" is addressed, and one for the housewife, to whom the "Ladies' Speech" is addressed. However, the wish to the housewife was originally addressed to the daughter of the house, as is apparent from the words *miss* and *lovers* occurring in such texts. In fact, these two ceremonies correspond to the traditional double aspect of wishing in and shooting in the New Year as both a household custom and a courtship custom. The household wish addressed to the man of the house was often solemn in tone, while the wish addressed to the daughter was a love poem. In the area of Egypt, Lehigh County, Pennsylvania, in about 1913, the wisher first chanted a wish to the man of the house and, at one home where there was an eligible daughter, chanted a second wish to her.[31] In the village of Datzeroth, in the Westerwald section of Germany, the young wisher similarly delivered a household wish for the parents and then a wish for his sweetheart.[32] In Europe, where the shooters were young men, the courtship aspect of the custom flourished.[33] But in America, where older men also participated in the rounds,[34] the ceremony for the daughter lost its courtship aspect. In 1833, in Kempton, Berks County, Pennsylvania, it was still a younger member of the party of shooters who wished for the daughter.[35] In the 1880's and 1890's, at Bower's Station, Berks County, and, around 1913, in the area of Egypt, the older wisher wished for both the family and the daughter.[36] In Cherryville, North Carolina, nowadays, the wisher, invariably a middle-aged or elderly man, wishes for someone closer to him in age, the housewife. This change in the role of the wisher may also be reflected in the texts addressed to the daughter from Pennsylvania and North Carolina, where the lover is sometimes referred to in the second or third person, rather than the first.[37]

There were also traditions connected with the actual shooting. At Iron Station, Lincoln County, "beginning at the head of the line each one fires until all have shot."[38] According to Brannon's account from Lincoln County, one member of the group of shooters shouted: "One! Two!," and so on, each shooter firing as his number was called.[39] Similar quasi-military attempts at firing at particular intervals or in particular formations took place in the Shenandoah Valley, Pennsylvania, Germany, and Austria. For instance, in the area of Egypt, Lehigh County, the wisher touched each shooter on the back, one after another, so that the shots came in succession.[40]

The North Carolina shooters attempted to make a loud noise when shooting. As already mentioned, they shot against the chimney in Rockwell, Rowan County.[41] At Iron Station, Lincoln County, they pointed the muzzles of their guns at the ground.[42] But the most common way of making a loud noise was by overloading one's gun, a practice found at Rockwell and Iron Station,[43] as well as in the Shenandoah Valley, Pennsylvania, and Europe.[44] Overloading sometimes led to accidents caused by the bursting of the gun barrel. Such an accident at Faulkner's Swamp, Pennsylvania, figures in the oldest American report of shooting at New Year's, that by Christoph Saur of Germantown, Pennsylvania, in 1753.[45] A similar accident in southwestern Lincoln County, North Carolina, at New Year's, 1879, gave rise to the oldest account of the custom from the Catawba River area: "Jacob Metcalf, a youth who lives four miles southwest of town, narrowly escaped instant death while out New Year's shooting. The gun had been loaded for a 'big crack,' as the New Year's shooter is pleased to call the hideous report, and the discharge was followed by the bursting of the gun. One fragment of the gun hit the youth's hat, while another struckk [*sic*] his chest, inflicting a painful, though not dangerous wound. In our opinion, the folly of New Year's shooting will never be fully understood until all who engage in the dangerous sport are either killed or maimed for life."[46]

William Brannon's grandfather told how the Lincoln County shooters fired the anvil: "They would take an anvil placed in a wheelbarrow for mobility and place an amount of black powder in a hole in it. Over this hole was placed a rock, and a fuse of powder led a short distance from the powder. Someone would put a wire on the end of a long pole and get this red hot in a fire. He would touch this hot wire to the crude fuse and everyone would run like the devil. Grandpa said you could hear the blast for miles."[47] The Pennsylvania shooters also fired the anvil, a practice they called *ambosschiesse*.[48] Although I have found no evidence of this practice in the German-speaking area of Europe, I suspect that a wider search would yield some. It was definitely practiced in Canada on the Queen's birthday and in England, both on the Queen's birthday and at weddings.[49]

Two terms for shooting were also applied to the custom as a whole: "New Year's shooting" in Rockwell, Rowan County, and in Iron Station, Lincoln County,[50] and "New Year's Shoot" at Cherryville, Gaston County. Both these terms were probably derived from the term *Neijohrschiessa*, used in Pennsylvania, or the corresponding *Neujahr(s)schiessen*, used in Europe.[51] In Mount Pleasant, Cabarrus County, North Carolina, the custom was called "shooting the old year out and the New Year in," possibly derived from the German expression "das alte Jahr ausschiessen und das Neujahr einschiessen," used, for instance, in dialect form for the rounds in Upper Austria.[52] Similarly, Backhof used the term "das Neujahr einschiessen" for the celebration in the Moravian settlement of Friedberg, North Carolina, in 1774.[53] Two other Moravian accounts use still another term: Of the young shooter Heinrich Stöhr at Bethabara, at New Year's, 1834, the author of the account says, "This brother had been occupied even yesterday in shooting—as is the custom in many places—in order to announce the New Year, or as the expression goes, to shoot the New Year in."[54] A group of young shooters at either Friedberg or Hope, at New Year's, 1835, were engaging in "Shooting in of the New Year."[55] The term used in the original German of both these accounts is "das Neujahr anschiessen," which, in its dialect form, was also used as a term for wishing in and shooting in the New Year in Pennsylvania and which is the most common term for this custom, or for the shooting part of it, in Europe.[56]

At Iron Station, Lincoln County, according to Graham, "a large attendance at New Year's shooting was considered a good omen for the next wheat crop," because the powder smoke settling on the ground increased the ground's fertility.[57] A similar belief used to exist in Cherryville.[58] Shooting at New Year's as fertility magic is found throughout the German-speaking area of Europe, specifically, shooting into and under the branches of fruit trees.[59] In nine Pennsylvania German counties, it was believed that trees would not bear if people did not shoot the New Year in for them.[60]

The Catawba River custom of the shooters breakfasting together after the rounds, reported as early as the 1870's and 1880's, has Pennsylvania parallels and may be in the tradition of the gatherings celebrated by the European shooters at the local inn after the rounds.[61] Similarly, the parties held by the European shooters and their girls after the rounds may be the origin of the celebration in the Iron Station area, Lincoln County, which occurred at the place where the shooters had breakfast after the rounds. Graham says: "Here the preacher left and the others, principally the young people, spent some time in drinking, dancing, prize shooting and other festivities common to the Christmas season in those days."[62]

Now, some words about the wishes. The "speeches" in Cherryville, North Carolina, are chanted nowadays, and the evidence is that this was the case elsewhere in America, at least in Pennsylvania.[63] For instance, a wisher in the area of Egypt, Lehigh County, chanted a household wish in a celebration around 1913.[64] In about 1949, William Brown, of Hepler, in the Mahantongo Valley of Pennsylvania, was still making the rounds chanting a wish. The text and melody of Brown's wish were given by Boyer, Buffington, and Yoder in their book, *Songs along the Mahantongo*.[65] In 1958, I recorded two "speeches" as chanted, both to the same melody, by "Uncle Sid" Beam, a Cherryville "speech crier."[66] The three "speech criers" who took part in the 1967 celebration in Cherryville also seemed to be making use of the same melody. Whether the North Carolina and Pennsylvania melodies are connected, I must leave to those qualified to judge, but certainly the practices are. The European background of chanting is not clear. Some wishes used by European shooters were sung, but the only one, to my knowledge, that was chanted, strictly speaking, was a wish used in Vorderstoder, Upper Austria.[67]

There are seven American texts in English that are similar in wording, with the same formulas and quoted hymn lines recurring frequently.[68] Five of them are from the Catawba River area of North Carolina, two from Lincoln County,[69] and three from Cherryville, in Gaston County.[70] The sixth text is from an area settled by North Carolina Germans, Bollinger County, Missouri.[71] The seventh text, from southern Ohio, actually a one-line fragment consisting only of an English version of a German formula enumerating blessings, appears similar to the Catawba

River texts and, like the Missouri text, may have been brought to the midwest by North Carolina Germans.[72]

We can form some idea of how the North Carolina English texts were derived from their German originals by comparing them to the fourteen German texts, plus their variants, that we have from Pennsylvania. In form, both the English and the German texts are similar. Like other German folk poems, they are iambic in meter, with three or four beats to the line, and are in couplet form. They differ from other folk poetry in having, most of them, concluding stereotyped formulas referring to the shooting to follow the reciting or chanting of the wish (called by me "shooting" formulas).[73] A good many of the German and English texts used in Pennsylvania, the Shenandoah Valley, North Carolina, and Missouri were also lengthy, a trait apparently peculiar to texts used by settlers in the eighteenth-century stream of migration.[74] As already pointed out, in Pennsylvania there were two types of wish: (*a*) the household wish addressed to the man of the house, which survives in North Carolina, and (*b*) the wish for the daughter, which in North Carolina has been transformed into a wish addressed to the housewife. Some attention to the wording of one example of each of these types can give us an idea of how the English wishes arose. Our household wish is a text from Iron Station, Lincoln County, published in 1914 by William Alexander Graham:

1   Good morning, Landlord and Landlady!
      Sons and daughters and all who are within your house.
      I wish you all a happy New Year in this year of our Lord 1914.
      I wish you all great health, long life, which God will bestow you on,
5   Keep joy, peace and encouragement and God will bless your whole
          intent.
      On your house and all therein
      I wish you all a blessing.
      Praise Him in times of all
      Who gives you houses, lands and all.
10   The poor and needy praise the Lord
      Who blessings need of every sort.
      In every part I wish you ease,
      That God may give you luck and peace.
      God preserve the house that you are in,
15   Where you go out, where you come in.
      In this world both man and wife
      Grow tired of this earthly life
      And seek an eternal rest,
      Choosing some other subject for the best.
20   And I wish from my heart
      From this world we do depart
      We may all sing new hymns
      Like David did in former times.
      But you are like that frail flower,
25   Born to flourish but an hour,

That with the sun does uprise,
Unfolds, and with the evening dies.
Such and so withering are our earthly joys
Which time and sickness soon destroys.
30 A thousand wretched souls have fled
Since the last setting sun;
But the Lord hath lengthened out our thread
And still our moments run.
Great God, let all our hours be thine,
35 Then shall our sun in smiles decline.
Never build your hopes too high,
But keep God always before your eye,
And that you and I are born to die.
Time by moments steals away,
40 First the hour and then the day,
Small the daily loss appears,
But soon it doth amount to years.
Sad experience may relate
What a year the last has been;
45 Crops of sorrow have been great
In this vain world of sin.
That they must lie within the tomb
The sons of Adam know is their certain doom.
As runs the glass, man's life does pass.
50 Xerxes the Great did surely die;
This must be the case with you and I.
I have this New Year's morn called you by your name,
Disturbed you of your rest, meant no harm by the same;
Here we stand upon your land
55 With guns and pistols in our hand.
And when we pull trigger and powder burn,
You'll hear the roaring of our guns.
Here we are in your yard,
A little distance all apart.
60 And, as it may be your desire,
Our guns shall either snap or fire.
As I hear no objection,
63 We'll now proceed to your protection.[75]

Lines 20–29, 36–46, and 49 are of unknown origin. The others have parallels or definite sources, as follows. Lines 1–5: Of these lines, lines 1–2 enumerate the various people in the house. Joined to this "household" formula is a formula enumerating blessings. We often encounter the same combination in the Pennsylvania texts, for instance in the beginning of an undated broadside text:

Ich wünsche euch und euren lieben Hausfrau, Söhne und Töchter, Knechte und Mägde, und alle wie ihr im Hause seyd, Gross und Klein, und alle wie ihr zu eurem Hause aus und ein gehet, ein glückselig neues Jahr, Friede Freud und Einigkeit, und auch die Ewige Seligkeit.[76]

There are also European parallels, for instance, lines 2–3 of a wish used by shooters in Datzeroth, Westerwald:

2   Wir wünschen Euch und Allen, die im Hause sind, ein glückselig
        neues Jahr, Friede und Einigkeit, Gesundheit und ein langes
        Leben,
3   Das mög Euch der liebe Gott geben.[77]

Lines 6–9 are an English rendering of stanza 6 of "Nvn wölle Gott, das vnser gsang" by Johannes Zwick (ca. 1496–1542), a New Year's hymn frequently quoted in the Pennsylvania texts.[78] Stanza 6 is quoted in lines 74–77 of the Pennsylvania broadside wish just mentioned:

74   Einem jeden Haus und was darin,
        Dem wünschen wir den rechten Sinn—
        Zu Gottes Preis und Ehr allzeit,
77   Der Haus und Hof und alles gibt.

Lines 10–11 may have a connection, though only a tenuous one, with stanza 14 of Zwick's hymn, if these lines about "the poor and needy" are indeed a very garbled rendering of stanza 14, addressed to *den Armen*, "the poor." If there is a connection between "luck and peace," on the one hand, and *Glück* and *Frieden*, on the other, lines 12–13 may be from lines similar to lines 70–73 of a Pennsylvania text gathered by John Baer Stoudt in Berks or Lehigh County before 1910:

70   So wünsch' ich euch nun Gottes Segen
        Und dazu ein gutes Glück,
        Gott lass euch in Frieden leben
73   Alle Stund und Augenblick.[79]

Lines 14–15 are a rendering of what I call an "in-and-out" formula, such as that in lines 74–75 of Stoudt's text:

74   Gott segne euch und euer Haus,
75   Wo Ihr gehet ein und aus.

Lines 16–19 are a rendering of lines similar to those found in America only in lines 64–67 of Stoudt's text:

64   Weil wir allhier auf dieser Erden
      Das Leben satt und müde werden,
      Begehren auch die ewige Ruh'
67   Und eilen nach dem Grabe zu.

Lines 30–35 come from stanzas 5 and 6 of a morning hymn by Isaac Watts, "Once More, My Soul, the Rising Day":

(5)
1   A thousand wretched souls are fled
    Since the last setting sun,
    And yet thou lengthen'st out my thread,
4   And yet my moments run.
(6)
1   Dear God, let all my hours be thine,
    Whilst I enjoy the light;
    Then shall my sun in smiles decline,
4   And bring a pleasant night.[80]

Lines 47–48 may possibly be from stanza 1, lines 7–8, of a New Year's hymn: "Ach wie laufen doch die jahre!"[81] The lines in question read:

7   Alles, was von Adams erben,
8   Gross und kleine müssen sterben.

Lines 50–51 may be from the sixteenth-century hymn, "Allein auff Gott setz dein vertrawn,"[82] which was also known as the "Golden ABC," since each of its stanzas began with a different letter of the alphabet. Stanza 22 of the hymn, beginning with X, reads:

1   Xerxes verliess sich auf sein Heer,
    Darüber wart geschlagen sehr:
    So du most kriegen, Gott vertraw,
4   Sonst alle zeit den frieden baw.

This hymn is connected to New Year's by its use in soothsaying at that time. During New Year's Eve in Silesia and East Prussia, people wrote the letters of the alphabet on slips of paper and drew three of them. The three corresponding stanzas of the "Golden ABC" were significant for the coming year.[83] Because of its use at New Year's, the stanza relating to Xerxes, like other hymn lines, may have found its way into a German New Year's wish and then, in an English rendering, into the North Carolina text. Another example of the Xerxes motif is found in the Shenandoah Valley, namely in the rhyme for "X" in an ABC book by Ambrosius Henkel, published in the early nineteenth century by the Henkel Press, New Market, Virginia. This rhyme seems to be derived from or parallel to the hymn stanza just quoted. It reads:

1   Xerxes der König hat regier't,
     Mit grossem Volk den Krieg geführt:
     Er ward dennoch geschlagen sehr,
4   Trotz seiner Macht und grossem Heer.[84]

Lines 52–63 consist of concluding "shooting" formulas. Lines 52–53 are akin to lines 96–99 of the first New Year's wish in the popular Pennsylvania anthology *Der Lustige Sänger*:

96   Dieweil wir euch nun diese Nacht,
      Von eurem süssen Schlaf aufwecken,
      So nehmet ihr euch wohl in acht,
99   Und thut vor unsern Schüssen nicht erschrecken,[85]

Lines 54–55 are akin to another Pennsylvania formula, found, for example, in lines 81–83 of Stoudt's text:

81   Wir steh'n all hier auf eurem Land,
      Haben die Gewehre all in der Hand,
83   Und die Hähne sind schon gespannt![86]

Lines 56–57 are a rendering of a formula found, for instance, in lines 12–13 of a text from Womelsdorf, Berks County, Pennsylvania:

12   Jetzt thun wir die Hahnen rücken,
13   Den Pulverdampf solt ihr erblicken.[87]

Lines 58–59 are akin to a formula found, for instance, in lines 102–103 of the first text in *Der Lustige Sänger*:

102   Wir stehen alle hier zur Seiten,
103   Und schiessen ab mit Freuden.[88]

Lines 60–61 are akin to a "verdriessen-schiessen" formula—for instance, that in lines 70–71 of the third text in *Der Lustige Sänger*:

70 Wanns dich aber thut verdriessen,
71 So musst du es sagen ehe wir schiessen,[89]

Lines 62–63 are akin to a "Verdruss-Schuss" formula, such as that in lines 72–73 of the third text in *Der Lustige Sänger*:

72 Dieweil wir hören kein Verdruss,
73 So sollst du hören unsern Schuss,[90]

Since the same formulas and quoted hymn lines recur in many German texts, we cannot, as a rule, connect any particular North Carolina English text with any particular Pennsylvania German text. But the text from Iron Station, Lincoln County, just analyzed, is an exception to this rule. It has a block of lines, namely, lines 12–19, that is particularly close to a virtual block of lines in Stoudt's text from Berks or Lehigh County, namely, lines 64–67, 70–75. The Iron Station text, with its strong German connections, confirms Graham's statement regarding the wishes used in the Catawba River area: "The original sermon was in German, and in many places it was preached in that language prior to 1860."[91] But the longevity of the German traits in the Iron Station text is exceptional, because, while German wishes did exist side by side with English wishes as late as the Civil War, the actual change-over from German to English in North Carolina took place much earlier,[92] as is illustrated by a New Year's wish in German from as early as the year 1812: "Appended to a rather lengthy but almost illegible 'New Year's Wish for the Old and the Married,' penned on October 10, 1812, by a poetically inclined German of Alamance County, is the following German note: 'If you ever write something again, by all means do better. This is an evil thing. Such poor spelling! It is a disgrace. It is not written evenly and the words are not properly placed.' This cruel review would indicate that to the sorrow and disgust of the older people the ability to write good German was gradually fading out."[93] The early disappearance of German traits from most of the wishes is seen in the other five English texts from North Carolina and Missouri, which, unlike the Iron Station text, contain lines of German origin, not in their middle portions, but rather only in their introductory formulas enumerating blessings and in their concluding "shooting" formulas, for instance, lines 1–8, 37–42, of the wish chanted by Vance Sellers of Cherryville to the housewife:

1　Good morning to you, Miss.
　　I wish you a Happy New Year,
　　Great health, long life which God may bestow
　　As long as you are here below.

5　I wish you part in ev'ry ease,
　　And God will 'stow you luck and peace.
　　God will preserve the house you are in,
　　Where you go out and you go in.

　　I wish you lovers of every kind
10　To suit your heart and please your mind,
　　Whose hearts are pure, whose hands are clean,
　　Whose tongue still speaks the thing it means.

　　No slander dwells upon your tongue.
　　He hates to do his lover wrong,
15　Or should we trust in ill report
　　And venter to our lover's heart.

　　And then my hopes and wishes meet
　　And make my meditation sweet.
　　The very frost that spews the ground
20　And the hail that sends a dreadful sound.

　　Icy bond the river hold
　　Our tender arms the winter's cold,
　　Board the vine your face to see
　　And dwell forever in love with me.

25　If our branches are in danger, shoot
　　From Jacob's staff to David's root.
　　False are the men of high degree
　　To a better sort of vanity.

　　Laid in a balance both appear
30　Light as a puff of empty air,
　　The sun and moon with bearing light
　　And all the sparkling eyes at night.

　　What we begin or what we do,
　　Let this be right and prosperous, too.
35　Or let this in our names be done
　　Until our earthly race is run.

　　Now here we are standing in your yard,
　　Just a little distance all apart.
　　When we pull trigger and powder burns
40　You shall hear the roaring of our old guns.
　　We hope this may be your desire
42　That all our guns and pistols, they shall fire.[94]

269

Among the lines of German origin absent from the middle portions of the other five texts (the other four texts from North Carolina and the Missouri fragment), in contrast to the Iron Station text, are English renderings of lines from German hymns. The reason for this is that, before the nineteenth century was very old, the North Carolina Germans were not only speaking English but also worshipping in English. Gehrke traces the influx of English into the Lutheran and Reformed churches and notes of Lincoln County: "Of four services conducted on Synodical Sunday in St. Paul's Church in Lincoln County in 1827, three were held in the English language."[95] The German hymns used in church services were thus replaced by English hymns, and the quotations of German hymn stanzas characteristic of the Pennsylvania household wishes were replaced, in the North Carolina household wishes, by quotations from English-language hymns. We have already encountered in the Iron Station household text some lines from a hymn by Isaac Watts, the most popular English-language hymn writer of the period.[96] The remaining hymn lines in the other five texts are all, not from the hymns, but rather from the psalms of Watts. Of the five texts, the psalms are most prominent in three: Two of the three texts are from Cherryville (one of them Sellers's "speech" quoted above), are addressed to the housewife (and, historically, to the daughter), and are, therefore, in part love poems—the love lyrics including reworded versions of some, but not all, of the psalm quotations. The same is true of the third text, namely that from Lincolnton, Lincoln County, which, while addressed to the household, nevertheless contains lines similar to those of the two Cherryville texts just mentioned. There is evidence that the texts quoting the psalms were formerly household wishes: The fourth and fifth texts are household wishes, and a two-line formula found in them may derive from a psalm. Lines 14–15 of the Cherryville "New Year's Speech" read:

14 But if it brings our promises good,
15 As the year before the flood,[97]

Lines 4–5 of the Missouri fragment read:

4 And if our wishes find you good,
5 'Tis better than the year before the flood.[98]

The words "promises good" in the version of the formula in the "New Year's Speech" suggest that these lines may be very garbled versions of stanza 4, lines 1–2, of Watts's psalm 15:

1 Firm to his Word he ever stood,
2 And always makes his Promise Good;[99]

The text from Lincolnton, Lincoln County, which is addressed to the household but is worded in part like the present-day Cherryville "speeches" to the housewife, may represent a hypothetical "transition" from the use of such texts quoting the psalms in the household ceremony to their exclusive use nowadays in the housewife's ceremony. In addition, there is the fact that not all of the psalm lines in the housewife's or daughter's texts have been adapted as love lyrics. Some of them still retain their religious solemnity. But solemn lines, in the Pennsylvania and European background, were characteristic of the household wishes but not of the wishes to the daughter, which were love poems.[100] The two Pennsylvania texts addressed to the daughter that have come down to us contain love formulas paralleled in Europe by formulas in verse love letters and Easter egg inscriptions.[101] But there is no trace, in the North Carolina wishes to the housewife or the daughter, of English renderings of the Pennsylvania love formulas. Perhaps it was to replace these poems containing love formulas that household wishes containing lines from Watts's psalms were adapted as love poems for the daughter. The psalm lines quoted in the North Carolina texts have undergone changes due not only to their conversion into love lyrics, but also to distortion from oral transmission. It may also be the case that the psalm texts, in whatever hymnal or hymnals the North Carolinians quoted them from, differed somewhat from the texts in the first edition of Watts's psalms, which I quote here. Thus, lines 11–16 of Sellers's text read in the original psalm 15, stanza 2 and stanza 3, lines 1–2:

(2)

1   Whose Hands are pure, whose Heart is clean;
    Whose Lips still speak the thing they mean:
    No Slanders dwell upon his Tongue:
4   He hates to do his Neighbour wrong.

(3)

1   Scarce will he trust an ill Report,
2   Nor vents it to his Neighbour's Hurt:[102]

Lines 17–18 of Sellers's wish contrast with stanza 27, lines 1–2, of psalm 104, where they are addressed to the deity:

1   In Thee my Hopes and Wishes meet,
2   And make my Meditation sweet:[103]

Lines 19–22 of Sellers's wish contrast with stanza 4 of psalm 147:

1   With hoary Frost he strows the Ground;
    His Hail descends with clattering Sound:
    Where is the Man so vainly bold
4   That dares defy his dreadfull Cold?[104]

Lines 23–24 of Sellers's wish are derived from stanza 7, lines 3–4, of psalm 15:

3   This is the Man thy Face shall see,
4   And dwell for ever, Lord, with Thee.[105]

Lines 25–26 of Sellers's wish are derived from stanza 10, lines 1–2, of psalm 80:

1   Fair Branch, ordain'd of old to shoot
2   From David's stock, from Jacob's Root;[106]

Lines 27–30 of Sellers's wish come from stanza 3 of psalm 62:

1   False are the Men of high Degree,
    The baser Sort are vanity;
    Laid in the Ballance both appear
4   Light as a Puff of empty Air.[107]

Lines 31–32 of Sellers's wish are possibly derived from psalm 136, either from stanza 3, lines 1, 3, of the common meter version:

1   The Sun supplies the Day with Light;
    How bright his Counsels shine!
    The Moon and Stars adorn the Night:
4   His Works are all divine.[108]

or from stanza 4, lines 1–2, of the long meter version:

1   He fills the Sun with Morning-Light,
    He bids the Moon direct the Night:
    His Mercies ever shall endure
4   When Suns and Moons shall shine no more.[109]

Thus, both the custom and the wishes in North Carolina show parallels with their German background in America and Europe. The texts of the wishes also show the changes that came about during the period of transition from German to English.

The evidence for the custom of wishing in and shooting in the New Year in South Carolina is much sparser than the North Carolina evidence but also points to a German origin. It all comes from the "Dutch Fork," an area between the Broad and Saluda rivers just northwest of Columbia. Germans and Swiss settled here in the colonial period, most of them apparently coming directly from Europe, although some did come to South Carolina overland from Pennsylvania and may therefore, like the North Carolina Germans, have felt the influence of Pennsylvania German culture.[110] On June 7, 1937, Daniel Boland, age eighty-five, of Little Mountain, Newberry County, told George Leland Summer in an interview, "On Christmas and New Year's shooting parties would go out, and the host would have good suppers for them."[111] The only other, somewhat fuller, account of these rounds is not of the rounds at New Year's but rather of those at Christmas. In 1892, John A. Chapman wrote:

Sixty years ago, the young men of the Dutch Fork retained many of the wild, frolicksome habits which their forefathers brought with them from the Fatherland. Perhaps the wildest of these customs was, to ramble throughout the night of Christmas Eve, in companies of a dozen persons, from house to house, firing heavily charged guns, and having thus aroused the family they would enter the domicile with stamping scramble to the blazing fire, greedily eat the *praetzilies* and *schneck-ilies*, imbibe, with many a rugged joke and ringing peal of laughter, heavy draughts of a compound liquor made of rum and sugar, butter and alspice stewed together, and then, "With monie an eldritch screetch an' hollo," rush out into the night to visit the next neighbor.[112]

We find in this account elements similar to those in the accounts of the New Year's custom from North Carolina and elsewhere: the shooters making the rounds at night with heavily loaded guns and having refreshments. This is actually the only detailed description that we have from the Carolinas of the refreshments consumed by the shooters. The suffix *-lies* on the German words for the cookies eaten suggests that they are of southern German or Swiss origin, as were, indeed, the South Carolina German-speaking settlers. Pretzels are common at New Year's in the German-speaking area of Europe. The *schneckilies* were snail-shaped cookies, which are common, under various names, during the German Christmas season. The Swiss *Schnëggli*, for instance, is baked at New Year's.[113]

NOTES

1. This article, based on a paper read November 9, 1969, at the annual meeting of the American Folklore Society in Atlanta, was drawn from my doctoral dissertation, "The German-American Custom of Wishing in and Shooting in the New Year" (hereafter cited as Robbins).

2. See Albert Bernhardt Faust, *The German Element in the United States*, I, chaps. 5–8; Elmer L. Smith, John G. Stewart, and M. Ellsworth Kyger, *The Pennsylvania Germans of the Shenandoah Valley*, chaps. 1–4; Robert W. Ramsey, *Carolina Cradle*, chaps. 7, 13.

3. See Robert Sidney Douglass, *History of Southeast Missouri*, I, 79–80; Jonas Viles, "Population and Extent of Settlement in Missouri before 1804," *Missouri Historical Review* 5 (1910–1911): 198–199; Timothy Flint, *Recollections of the Last Ten Years*, ed. C. Hartley Grattan, pp. 225–231.

4. Faust, *German Element*, I, 231–233.

5. Adelaide L. Fries et al., trans. and eds., *Records of the Moravians in North Carolina*, II, 657, 781.

6. L[udolf] C. Backhof, "Diarium von Friedberg vom Jahr 1774," January 1, 1774, Archives of the Moravian Church in America, Southern Province, Winston-Salem, N.C. (hereafter cited as Moravian Archives); cf. Fries et al., *Records of the Moravians*, II, 836–837.

7. Aufseher Collegium, Salem, *Protocoll*, January 7, 1806, Moravian Archives (hereafter cited as Auf. Coll.).

8. Aelteste Conferenz, Salem, *Protocoll*, January 4, 1810, Moravian Archives (hereafter cited as Aelt. Conf.); cf. Fries et al., *Records of the Moravians*, VII, 3117. Auf. Coll., January 9, 1810. Aelt. Conf., January 10, 1810.

9. Auf. Coll., December 11, 1810. Aufseher Collegium, Minutes, December 27, 1810, on an index card: "New Year Celebration," in a file of translations at the headquarters of Old Salem, Inc., Winston-Salem, N.C. Aelt. Conf., January 4, 1811; cf. Fries et al., *Records of the Moravians*, VII, 3141. Auf. Coll., January 8, 1811.

10. "Diarium der Gemeine Bethanien 1830," December 31, 1830, Moravian Archives; cf. Fries et al., *Records of the Moravians*, VIII, 3950.

11. "Bethabara Diary," January 1, 1834, Moravian Archives; cf. Fries et al., *Records of the Moravians*, VIII, 4138. "Schrift von Bethabara, vom Januar 1834," January 1, 1834, Moravian Archives.

12. "Bericht von Friedberg und Hope vom Jahr 1835," January 1, 1835, Moravian Archives; cf. Fries et al., *Records of the Moravians*, VIII, 4204.

13. Smith, Stewart, and Kyger, *Pennsylvania Germans*, p. 102.

14. Notes from two interviews with Robert Holshouser, age eighty-one, Rockwell, Rowan County, N.C., March 23 and April 13, 1958.

15. Notes from an interview with Thomas Rhinehart, age eighty-six, Rockwell, Rowan County, N.C., April 13, 1958.

16. William Alexander Graham, "New Year's Shooting: An Ancient German Custom," *North Carolina Booklet* 13, no. 3 (January 1914): 147–148, 149–150.

17. Letter from William E. Brannon, Davidson, N.C., October 28, 1958.

18. See Robbins, pp. 42–44, 177–179, 182–183, 184, and also Arthur Palmer Hudson, "The New Year's Shoot," *Southern Folklore Quarterly* 11 (1947): 235–243; Donald W. Crawley, "The New Year's Shoot at Cherryville," *North Carolina Folklore* 10, no. 2 (December 1962): 20–27; Harnett T. Kane, *The Southern Christmas Book*, pp. 97–103.

19. See, for example, Edwin M[iller] Fogel, "Twelvetide," *Pennsylvania German Folklore Society* [Yearbook], VI, 15; Adam Wrede, *Eifeler Volkskunde*, p. 204.

20. Graham, "New Year's Shooting," pp. 147, 148. H. M. Belden, ed., *Ballads and Songs Collected by the Missouri Folk-Lore Society*, p. 514.

21. See, for example, William J. Buck, "Manners and Customs—Sports and Pastimes—Local Superstitions—Inns," in *History of Montgomery County, Pennsylvania*, ed. Theodore W. Bean, p. 336; Walter Diener, *Hunsrücker Volkskunde*, p. 223.

22. Brannon, letter.

23. See, for example, an account by the Bechtelsville (Pa.) correspondent, *Reading (Pa.) Weekly Eagle*, January 7, 1882, reprinted in [Alfred L. Shoemaker, ed.], "New Year's Eve in the Olden Time," *Pennsylvania Dutchman* 2, no. 15 (January 1, 1951): 1.

24. Brannon, letter; Buck, "Manners and Customs," p. 336.

25. Emil Ziemann, "Neu-Posttal zwischen Neujahr und Silvester," *Heimatbuch der Gemeinde Neu-Posttal, Kreis Akkerman, Bessarabien*, p. 138.

26. See, for example, Smith, Stewart, and Kyger, *Pennsylvania Germans*, pp. 101, 103; Theodor Wolff, "Volksleben an der oberen Nahe," *Zeitschrift des Vereins für Volkskunde* 12 (1902): 419.

27. Graham, "New Year's Shooting," pp. 147–148.

28. F. Ranke, "Ruf, rufen," *Handwörterbuch des deutschen Aberglaubens*, VII, col. 848.

29. Graham, "New Year's Shooting," p. 147; Brannon, letter.

30.   See, for example, [B. Bausman], "New Year's Eve," *Guardian* (Philadelphia) 19, no. 1 (January 1868): 6–7, reprinted as [Alfred L. Shoemaker, ed.], "'Shooting in the New Year,'" *Pennsylvania Dutchman* 5, no. 9 (January 1, 1954): 3; Franz Lipp, "Das Neujahransingen von Vorderstoder (Oberösterreich)," *Jahrbuch des österreichischen Volksliedwerkes* 8 (1959): 120–121.

31.   Leonard L. Leh, "Shooting in the New Year," *Pennsylvania Dutchman* 4, no. 9 (January 1, 1953): 3.

32.   Ludwig Petry, "Neujahrsnacht in einem Westerwälder Dorfe," *Zeitschrift des Vereins für rheinische und westfälische Volkskunde* 12 (1915): 52–53.

33.   See Robbins, pp. 100–110.

34.   See, for example, Edward C. Smith and Virginia van Horn Thompson, *Traditionally Pennsylvania Dutch*, p. 46.

35.   Nathan Bachman, account (1893), published or reprinted in [Alfred L. Shoemaker, ed.], "Shooting in the New Year," *Pennsylvania Dutchman* 1, no. 21 (December 1949): 2.

36.   John Baer Stoudt, *The Folklore of the Pennsylvania Germans*, pp. 103, 108; Leh, "Shooting in the New Year," p. 3.

37.   See the third New Year's wish given in the popular anthology, *Der Lustige Sänger*, pp. 162–164, lines 2–3, 5–7, 12–13, 19–24 (also in Robbins, pp. 208–210, text no. 3); a text from Lincolnton, Lincoln Co., N.C., given by Graham, "New Year's Shooting," pp. 150–151, lines 7–8, 12 (also in Robbins, pp. 225–226, text no. 18); a version of the "Ladies' Speech" as chanted by the Cherryville "speech crier," "Uncle Sid" Beam and recorded by me (in Robbins, p. 227, text no. 20; see also below, notes 66, 70), lines 8, 29; and Vance Sellers's version of the "Ladies' Speech" (see below, note 70), as given below, line 9.

38.   Graham, "New Year's Shooting," p. 149.

39.   Brannon, letter.

40.   Leh, "Shooting in the New Year," p. 3.

41.   Holshouser, interview.

42.   Graham, "New Year's Shooting," p. 149.

43.   Holshouser, interview; Graham, "New Year's Shooting," p. 149.

44.   See, for example, Fogel, "Twelvetide," p. 15.

45.   *Pensylvanische Berichte*, January 16, 1753.

46.   *Lincoln Progress*, January 4, 1879.

47.   Brannon, letter.

48.   H[enry] A. Schuler, "Shooting-In the New Year: A Peculiar Pennsylvania-German Custom," *Pennsylvania-German* 8 (1907): 16; Fogel, "Twelvetide," p. 15.

49.   W[illiam] J[ohn] Wintemberg, "Folk-Lore Collected in the Counties of Oxford and Waterloo, Ontario," *Journal of American Folk-Lore* 31 (1918): 139; *Notes and Queries* 168 (January–June 1935): 350, 394, and 169 (July–December 1935): 141.

50.   Holshouser, interview; Graham, "New Year's Shooting," p. 147.

51.   Schuler, "Shooting-In the New Year," p. 16; Robbins, p. 127.

52.   Rhinehart, interview; Robbins, pp. 128–129.

53.   Backhof, "Diarium von Friedberg," January 1, 1774.

54.   "Bethabara Diary," January 1, 1834.

55.   "Bericht von Friedberg und Hope," January 1, 1835.

56.   See, for instance, Fogel, "Twelvetide," p. 15, and Robbins, pp. 127–128.

57.   Graham, "New Year's Shooting," p. 149.

58.   Notes from an interview with the "speech crier," A. Sidney ("Uncle Sid") Beam, age eighty-five, Cherryville, N.C., August 28, 1958.

59.   See, for example, Adolf Wuttke, *Der deutsche Volksaberglaube der Gegenwart*, ed. Elard Hugo Meyer, p. 65 (par. 75), p. 426 (par. 668).

60.   Edwin Miller Fogel, *Beliefs and Superstitions of the Pennsylvania Germans*, p. 208 (no. 1042).

61.   Crawley, "New Year's Shoot," p. 24; Beam, interview; Robbins, pp. 151, 163–164; [C. Kleeberger], *Volkskundliches aus Fischbach i. d. Pfalz*, p. 27.

62.   See, for example, Wolff, "Volksleben," p. 420, and Robbins, pp. 165–166; also Graham, "New Year's Shooting," p. 147.

63.   Fogel, "Twelvetide," p. 15.

64.   Leh, "Shooting in the New Year," p. 3.

65.   Walter E. Boyer, Albert F. Buffington, and Don Yoder, comps. and eds., *Songs along the Mahantongo*, pp. 191–196 (also quoted in Robbins, pp. 374–377).

66.   Texts nos. 19 and 20 in Robbins, pp. 226–227, 378–383; melody in ibid., p. 378. No. 19, the "New Year's Speech," can also be found in Hudson, "New Year's Shoot," pp. 238–239; Crawley, "New Year's Shoot," p. 23; and Kane, *Southern Christmas Book*, pp. 98–100.

67.   Lipp, "Das Neujahransingen," pp. 121, 123.

68. Two English texts from Pendleton County, W.Va., given by Smith, Stewart, and Kyger (*Pennsylvania Germans*, pp. 103–105), are probably descended from Pennsylvania German texts as are our seven English texts. The West Virginia texts, however, show no similarities in wording to the seven texts but present rather an independent rendering into English and an independent line of development as English texts.

69. Robbins, pp. 224–226 (texts nos. 17 and 18). Text no. 17, from Iron Station (Graham, "New Year's Shooting," pp. 148–149), is quoted below. Text no. 18 is from Lincolnton (Graham, "New Year's Shooting," pp. 150–151).

70. Robbins, pp. 226–228 (texts nos. 19–21); see also note 66, above. Text no. 21, Sellers's version of the "Ladies' Speech" (Kane, *Southern Christmas Book*, pp. 101–102), is quoted below.

71. Belden, *Ballads and Songs*, p. 514; see also Robbins, p. 229 (text no. 24).

72. [H(oward) W(iegner) Kriebel, ed.], "The Forum," *Pennsylvania-German* 10 (1909): 43; see also Robbins, p. 229 (text no. 22).

73. Robbins, pp. 276–277.

74. Ibid., pp. 269–270.

75. Graham, "New Year's Shooting," pp. 148–149.

76. *Ein Neujahrs Wunsch*; see also Robbins, pp. 218–220 (text no. 13).

77. Petry, "Neujahrsnacht," p. 51.

78. Text in Philipp Wackernagel, comp. and ed., *Das deutsche Kirchenlied von der ältesten Zeit bis zu Anfang des XVII. Jahrhunderts*, III, no. 680 (pp. 606–607); see also Robbins, pp. 289–292.

79. Stoudt, *Folklore of the Pennsylvania Germans*, pp. 112–114 (also in Robbins, pp. 212–214, text no. 9).

80. Text in Isaac Watts, *The Psalms and Hymns of the late Dr. Isaac Watts*, ed. Robert Goodacre, II, 151 (Bk. II, hymn 6). On Watts (1674–1748), see Arthur P. Davis, *Isaac Watts*.

81. Text in *Vermehrtes Lüneburgisches Kirchen-Gesang-Buch*, no. 89 (pp. 49–50).

82. Text in Wackernagel, *Das deutsche Kirchenlied*, V, no. 516 (pp. 327–328).

83. Wuttke, *Der deutsche Volksaberglaube*, pp. 242–243 (par. 349).

84. Ambrosius Henkel, *Das kleine ABC-Buch oder erste Anfangs-Büchlein, mit schönen Bildern und deren Namen, nach dem ABC, um den Kindern das Buchstabiren leichter zu machen*, p. 33.

85. *Der Lustige Sänger*, pp. 156–159 (also in Robbins, pp. 204–206, text no. 1).

86. Stoudt, *Folklore of the Pennsylvania Germans*, pp. 112–114.

87. L[udwig] A[ugust] Wollenweber, ed., New Year's Wish, *Banner von Berks* (Reading, Pa.), reprinted in [Shoemaker, ed.], "Shooting in the New Year," *Pennsylvania Dutchman* 1, no. 21 (December 1949): 2.

88. *Der Lustige Sänger*, pp. 156–159.

89. Ibid., pp. 162–164.

90. Ibid.

91. Graham, "New Year's Shooting," p. 150.

92. William H. Gehrke, "The Transition from the German to the English Language in North Carolina," *North Carolina Historical Review* 12 (1935): 1–19.

93. Ibid., p. 7.

94. Kane, *Southern Christmas Book*, pp. 101–102 (also in Robbins, pp. 227–228, text no. 21).

95. Gehrke, "The Transition from the German to the English Language," p. 15.

96. Davis, *Isaac Watts*, pp. 212–213.

97. Text no. 19 (see above, notes 66, 70).

98. Belden, *Ballads and Songs*, p. 514.

99. Text in Isaac Watts, *The Psalms of David Imitated in the Language of the New Testament*, pp. 38–39.

100. On the solemn lines in the household wishes, see Robbins, pp. 368–369. On the wishes to the daughter, see ibid., pp. 370–371 (three wishes for the daughter from Germany), and below, note 101.

101. The third wish in *Der Lustige Sänger* (see above, note 37), and the fourth wish in *Der Lustige Sänger*, pp. 164–165 (also in Robbins, pp. 210–211, text no. 4). On the formulas, see Robbins, pp. 317–319, 321–323, 324–326.

102. Text in Watts, *The Psalms of David*, pp. 38–39.

103. Text in ibid., pp. 269–274.

104. Text in ibid., pp. 386–387.

105. Text in ibid., pp. 38–39.

106. Text in ibid., pp. 206–208.

107. Text in ibid., pp. 156–157.

108. Text in ibid., pp. 357–358.

109. Text in ibid., pp. 362–363.

110. On the German and Swiss settlements in South Carolina, see Robert L. Meriwether, *The Expansion of South Carolina, 1729–1765*.

111. G[eorge] Leland Summer, notes from an interview with Daniel Boland, age eighty-five, Little Mountain, Newberry County, S.C., June 7, 1937, "Project 1835–1, Folklore, Dutch Fork: Customs—Traditions —Festivals," folklore collected in South Carolina by the Federal Writers' Program, typewritten ms., cabinet H, drawer 4, folder 3, Manuscripts Division, South Caroliniana Library, University of South Carolina, Columbia, S.C.

112. John Belton O'Neall and John A. Chapman, *The Annals of Newberry in Two Parts*, p. 660. The quotation within the excerpt is from "Tam O'Shanter" by Robert Burns, in *The Poems and Songs of Robert Burns*, ed. Andrew Lang and W. A. Craigie, p. 443.

113. *Schweizerisches Idiotikon*, IX, cols. 1190–1191. On the "schneckilies," see also *Rheinisches Wörterbuch*, VII, col. 1579; *Schwäbisches Wörterbuch*, V, col. 1046; and F. Eckstein, "Weihnachtsgebäck, Weihnachtsbrot," in *Handwörterbuch des deutschen Aberglaubens*, IX, cols. 256–283. On the pretzel, see F. Eckstein, "Bretzel," in *Handwörterbuch des deutschen Aberglaubens*, I, cols. 1561–1573.

BIBLIOGRAPHY

Since writing this article I have collected more copies of Pennsylvania German New Year's wishes (mainly broadsides) and will take this material into account in the published version of my dissertation. Of these wishes, the most interesting in the context of this paper is an undated 22.7 x 28.4 mm broadside, "Neujahrs Wunsch," no. H 271 of the Unger-Bassler Collection, Vault, Fackenthal Library, Franklin and Marshall College, Lancaster, Pa., two lines of which (a shooting formula), "Dann können wir unser Pulver sparen, / Und unser Werk im Sack nachtragen," may be (if tenuously) related to two lines of the Lincolnton, N.C., text: "That we may hold our credit by / And burn our powders in aegy sly—." In his twenty-three–page pamphlet, *New Year Serenades: Greetings Gathered from Reliable Sources* (Macungie, Pa.: Progress Printing House, 1945) (copies at Chester County Historical Society, West Chester, Pa., and Historical Society of Pennsylvania, Philadelphia), Jacob Hartman Rohrbach entitles a variant of the fourth wish in *Der Lustige Sänger* (see above note 101) "Greeting for Widows and Elderly Maidens." If this title is not arbitrary but reflects folk tradition, then the Cherryville housewife's ceremony may have a Pennsylvania background and not be simply an adaptation of the Pennsylvania German ceremony for a young girl. For a fuller treatment of the Christmas shooting rounds touched on in the present article, see Walter L. Robbins, "Christmas Shooting Rounds in America and Their Background," *Journal of American Folklore* 86, no. 339 (January–March 1973): 48–52. See also Walter L. Robbins, "Pastor Thomas R. Brendle's Remarks on Wishing in and Shooting in the New Year," *Schaefferstown Bulletin* 6, no. 5 (December 1972): [3]–[8]. On the diaspora from Pennsylvania (note 2) see also Klaus Wust, *The Virginia Germans* (Charlottesville: University Press of Virginia, 1969). I would appreciate receiving from readers additional information on the custom or wishes, especially regarding those lines in the two texts quoted in this article for which I have found no source or parallel.

Aufseher Collegium, Salem, N.C. Minutes, December 27, 1810. On an index card: "New Year Celebration," in a file of translations at the headquarters of Old Salem, Inc., Winston-Salem, N.C.

Bachman, Nathan. Account (1893). Published or reprinted in [Alfred L. Shoemaker, ed.] "Shooting in the New Year." *Pennsylvania Dutchman* 1, no. 21 (December 1949): 2.

[Bausman, B.] "New Year's Eve." *Guardian* (Philadelphia) 19, no. 1 (January 1868): 5–8. Reprinted as [Alfred L. Shoemaker, ed.] "'Shooting in the New Year.'" *Pennsylvania Dutchman* 5, no. 9 (January 1, 1954): 3.

Beam, A. Sidney, Cherryville, N.C. Interview, August 28, 1958.

Bechtelsville (Pa.) correspondent. Account. *Reading* (Pa.) *Weekly Eagle*, January 7, 1882. Reprinted in [Alfred L. Shoemaker, ed.] "New Year's Eve in the Olden Time." *Pennsylvania Dutchman* 2, no. 15 (January 1, 1951): 1.

Belden, H. M., ed. *Ballads and Songs Collected by the Missouri Folk-Lore Society*. University of Missouri Studies, vol. 15, no. 1. Columbia: University of Missouri, 1940.

Boyer, Walter E., Albert F. Buffington, and Don Yoder, comps. and eds. *Songs along the Mahantongo: Pennsylvania Dutch Folksongs*. Lancaster: Pennsylvania Dutch Folklore Center, 1951. Reprinted, Hatboro, Pa.: Folklore Associates, 1964.

Brannon, William E., Davidson, N.C. Letter, October 28, 1958.

Buck, William J. "Manners and Customs— Sports and Pastimes—Local Superstitions—Inns." In *History of Montgomery County, Pennsylvania*, edited by Theodore W. Bean, pp. 335–348. Philadelphia: Everts & Peck, 1884.

Burns, Robert. *The Poems and Songs of Robert Burns*. Edited by Andrew Lang and W. A. Craigie. 4th ed. New York: Dodd, Mead & Co., 1926.

Crawley, Donald W. "The New Year's Shoot at Cherryville." *North Carolina Folklore* 10, no. 2 (December 1962): 20–27.

Davis, Arthur P. *Isaac Watts: His Life and Works*. New York: Dryden Press, 1943.

Diener, Walter. *Hunsrücker Volkskunde*. Volkskunde Rheinischer Landschaften. Bonn: Fritz Klopp Verlag, 1925.

Douglass, Robert Sidney. *History of Southeast Missouri*. 2 vols. Chicago and New York: Lewis Publishing Co., 1912.

Eckstein, F. "Bretzel." In *Handwörterbuch des deutschen Aberglaubens*, I, cols. 1561–1573. Berlin & Leipzig: Walter de Gruyter & Co., 1927.

———. "Weihnachtsgebäck, Weihnachtsbrot." In *Handwörterbuch des deutschen Aberglaubens*, IX, cols. 256–283. Berlin: Walter de Gruyter & Co., 1938–1941.

Faust, Albert Bernhardt. *The German Element in the United States*. 2 vols. 2d ed. rev. New York: Steuben Society of America, 1927. Reprinted, New York: Arno Press, 1969.

Flint, Timothy. *Recollections of the Last Ten Years*. Edited by C. Hartley Grattan. New York: Alfred A. Knopf, 1932.

Fogel, Edwin Miller. *Beliefs and Superstitions of the Pennsylvania Germans*. Americana Germanica, vol. 18. Philadelphia: Americana Germanica Press, 1915.

———. "Twelvetide." *Pennsylvania German Folklore Society* [*Yearbook*] 6 (1941): 1–22.

Fries, Adelaide L., et al., trans. and eds. *Records of the Moravians in North Carolina*. Vol. 2, Raleigh: North Carolina Historical Commission, 1925; reprinted, Raleigh: State Department of Archives and History, 1968. Vol. 7, Raleigh: State Department of Archives and History, 1947; reprinted, Raleigh: State Department of Archives and History, 1970. Vol. 8, Raleigh: State Department of Archives and History, 1954.

Gehrke, William H. "The Transition from the German to the English Language in North Carolina." *North Carolina Historical Review* 12 (1935): 1–19.

Graham, William Alexander. "New Year's Shooting: An Ancient German Custom." *North Carolina Booklet* 13, no. 3 (January 1914): 147–151.

Henkel, Ambrosius. *Das kleine ABC-Buch oder erste Anfangs-Büchlein, mit schönen Bildern und deren Namen, nach dem ABC, um den Kindern das Buchstabiren leichter zu machen*. 2d ed. New Market, Va.: Salomon Henkel's Druckerey, 1820. Personal copy.

Holshouser, Robert, Rockwell, Rowan County, N.C. Interviews, March 23 and April 13, 1958.

Hudson, Arthur Palmer. "The New Year's Shoot." *Southern Folklore Quarterly* 11 (1947): 235–243.

Kane, Harnett T. *The Southern Christmas Book*. New York: David McKay Co., 1958.

[Kleeberger, C.] *Volkskundliches aus Fischbach i. d. Pfalz*. Kaiserslautern: Kgl. Bayer. Hof-Buchdruckerei Hermann Kayser, 1902. Copy at Deutsches Volksliedarchiv, Freiburg i. B., Germany.

[Kriebel, H(oward) W(iegner), ed.] "The Forum." *Pennsylvania-German* 10 (1909): 43–45.

Leh, Leonard L. "Shooting in the New Year." *Pennsylvania Dutchman* 4, no. 9 (January 1, 1953): 3.

The Lincoln Progress (Lincolnton, N.C.), January 4, 1879. Copy in North Carolina Collection, Wilson Library, University of North Carolina, Chapel Hill, N.C.

Lipp, Franz. "Das Neujahransingen von Vorderstoder (Oberösterreich)." *Jahrbuch des österreichischen Volksliedwerkes* 8 (1959): 120–123.

Der Lustige Sänger. 4th ed. rev. Allentown, Pa.: Blumer und Busch, 1846. Copies at Schwenkfelder Historical Library, Pennsburg, Pa., and Muhlenberg College, Allentown, Pa.

Meriwether, Robert L. *The Expansion of South Carolina, 1729–1765*. Kingsport, Tenn.: Southern Publishers, 1940.

Moravian Archives. Manuscripts from the Archives of the Moravian Church in America, Southern Province, Winston-Salem, N.C.:
Aelteste Conferenz, Salem. *Protocoll*, 1810, 1811.
Aufseher Collegium, Salem. *Protocoll*, 1806, 1810, 1811.
Backhof, L[udolf] C. "Diarium von Friedberg vom Jahr 1774."
"Bericht von Friedberg und Hope vom Jahr 1835."
"Bethabara Diary," 1834.
"Diarium der Gemeine Bethanien 1830."
"Schrift von Bethabara, vom Januar 1834."

Ein Neujahrs Wunsch. (*Eine genaue Abschrift des Originals—Gedruckt für Daniel Heffendräer*.). N.p., n.d. Copies at Schwenkfelder Historical Library, Pennsburg, Pa.; the Library Company of Philadelphia; Unger-Bassler Collection, Vault, Fackenthal Library, Franklin and Marshall College, Lancaster, Pa.

Notes and Queries 168 (January–June 1935): 350, 394; 169 (July–December 1935): 141.

O'Neall, John Belton, and John A. Chapman. *The Annals of Newberry in Two Parts: Part First by John Belton O'Neall, LL.D., Part Second by John A. Chapman, A.M. Complete in One Volume*. Newberry, S.C.: Aull & Houseal, 1892. Reprinted, Ann Arbor, Mich.: Edwards Brothers, 1949.

Pensylvanische [sic] *Berichte, Oder: Sammlung Wichtiger Nachrichten aus dem Natur- und Kirchen-Reich* (Germantown, Pa.), January 16, 1753. Copy at American Philosophical Society Library, Philadelphia.

Petry, Ludwig. "Neujahrsnacht in einem Westerwälder Dorfe." *Zeitschrift des Vereins für rheinische und westfälische Volkskunde* 12 (1915): 48–55.

Ramsey, Robert W. *Carolina Cradle: Settlement of the Northwest Carolina Frontier, 1747–1762.* Chapel Hill: University of North Carolina Press, 1964.

Ranke, F. "Ruf, rufen." In *Handwörterbuch des deutschen Aberglaubens*, VII, cols. 847–849. Berlin & Leipzig: Walter de Gruyter & Co., 1935–1936.

Rheinisches Wörterbuch. Edited by Josef Müller et al. Vol. 7. Berlin: Erika Klopp Verlag, 1948–1958.

Rhinehart, Thomas, Rockwell, Rowan County, N.C. Interview, April 13, 1958.

Robbins, Walter L. "The German-American Custom of Wishing in and Shooting in the New Year." Ph.D. Dissertation, University of North Carolina, Chapel Hill, N.C., 1969.

———. Personal observation of the "New Year's Shoot," practiced by the "Cherryville New Year's Shooters," Cherryville, N.C., January 2, 1967.

Schuler, H[enry] A. "Shooting-In the New Year: A Peculiar Pennsylvania-German Custom." *Pennsylvania-German* 8 (1907): 15–18.

Schwäbisches Wörterbuch. Edited by Hermann Fischer. Vol. 5. Tübingen: Verlag der H. Laupp'schen Buchhandlung, 1920.

Schweizerisches Idiotikon. Edited by Fr. Staub et al. Vol. 9. Frauenfeld: J. Huber, 1929.

Smith, Edward C., and Virginia van Horn Thompson. *Traditionally Pennsylvania Dutch.* New York: Hastings House, 1947.

Smith, Elmer L., John G. Stewart, and M. Ellsworth Kyger. *The Pennsylvania Germans of the Shenandoah Valley. Pennsylvania German Folklore Society* [Yearbook], vol. 26 (1962). Allentown, Pa.: Schlechter's, 1964.

Stoudt, John Baer. *The Folklore of the Pennsylvania Germans.* Philadelphia: William J. Campbell, 1916.

Summer, G[eorge] Leland. Notes from an interview with Daniel Boland, age eighty-five, Little Mountain, Newberry County, S.C., June 7, 1937, "Project 1835-1, Folklore, Dutch Fork: Customs—Traditions —Festivals," folklore collected in South Carolina by the Federal Writers' Program, typewritten ms., cabinet H, drawer 4, folder 3, Manuscripts Division, South Caroliniana Library, University of South Carolina, Columbia, S.C.

Vermehrtes Lüneburgisches Kirchen-Gesang-Buch. Lüneburg, 1770.

Viles, Jonas. "Population and Extent of Settlement in Missouri before 1804." *Missouri Historical Review* 5 (1910–1911): 189–213.

Wackernagel, Philipp, comp. and ed. *Das deutsche Kirchenlied von der ältesten Zeit bis zu Anfang des XVII. Jahrhunderts.* Vols. 3 and 5. Leipzig: B. G. Teubner, 1870, 1877.

Watts, Isaac. *The Psalms and Hymns of the late Dr. Isaac Watts.* Edited by Robert Goodacre. Vol. II, *Containing the Hymns and Miscellaneous Hymns.* London: Printed for Francis Westley, 1821.

———. *The Psalms of David Imitated in the Language of the New Testament, And apply'd to the Christian State and Worship.* London: Printed for J. Clark, at the Bible and Crown in the Poultry; R. Ford, at the Angel in the Poultry; and R. Cruttenden, at the Bible and Three Crowns in Cheapside, 1719. Copy at the University of Illinois, Urbana, Ill.

Wintemberg, W[illiam] J[ohn]. "Folk-Lore Collected in the Counties of Oxford and Waterloo, Ontario." *Journal of American Folk-Lore* 31 (1918): 135–153.

Wolff, Theodor. "Volksleben an der oberen Nahe." *Zeitschrift des Vereins für Volkskunde* 12 (1902): 308–316, 418–429.

Wollenweber, L[udwig] A[ugust], ed. New Year's Wish. *Banner von Berks* (Reading, Pa.). Reprinted in [Alfred L. Shoemaker, ed.] "Shooting in the New Year." *Pennsylvania Dutchman* 1, no. 21 (December 1949): 2.

Wrede, Adam. *Eifeler Volkskunde.* 2d ed. rev. Volkskunde rheinischer Landschaften. Bonn and Leipzig: Kurt Schroeder Verlag, 1924.

Wuttke, Adolf. *Der deutsche Volksaberglaube der Gegenwart.* Edited by Elard Hugo Meyer. 3d ed. rev. Berlin: Verlag von Wiegandt & Grieben, 1900. Reprinted, Leipzig: Zentralantiquariat der Deutschen Demokratischen Republik, 1970.

Ziemann, Emil. "Neu-Posttal zwischen Neujahr und Silvester." In *Heimatbuch der Gemeinde Neu-Posttal, Kreis Akkerman, Bessarabien,* pp. 138–147. N.p., 1963–1964. Copy at Institut für ostdeutsche Volkskunde, Werner-Künzig-Archiv, Freiburg-Littenweiler i. B., Germany.

12. Morality in a Yoruba Ritual in Trinidad

Jacob D. Elder

"Whoever says that African religion has no moral content (and it has been often said) does not know an African religion."[1]

More significant than the view expressed by Paul Bohannan in the above quotation from his important work on Africans is the tremendous persistence with which certain moral sanctions have survived in the religious cultic systems of some New World Negro communities. This article discusses an instance of supportive evidence in this connection and demonstrates that Dr. Bohannan's observations about Africa apply equally to Trinidad. Discussion will be based upon data presently being collected for a study of the role of African-derived ancestor cults in the maintenance of stability in a rural community in south-central Trinidad in the Caribbean.[2] This community, Gasparillo, comprises five rural localities on the edge of the Texaco oil-refinery complex at Pointe-a-Pierre and is presently undergoing rapid industrial, social, and political transition. Despite this condition, the villagers—East Indian and Negro alike—display a comparatively high level of social cohesion and inter-personal harmony. The Negroes, unlike their counterparts in other Trinidad villages, show little loss of identity, and there is no evidence of guilt feelings about admission of their genetic ancestry. In fact, every Negro spontaneously traces back his descent to one or another of the tribal traditions of ancient Nigeria—Hausa, Yoruba, and Fulani. Others recall that their great-grandparents belonged to some Congo tribe from Angola. This study is concerned with the ways in which this anchorage in the parent culture, though largely ritual, generates moral strength among this agricultural group—the ways in which the esoterics of a religious system are kept alive and functional, how the built-in moral norms manifest themselves in ritual practices, how their supporting mythology emphasizes the moral sanctions, and how by a process of emotional feedback these combine to maintain the society's moral standards.

The role of the ancestor cult in the maintenance of social cohesion in transitional societies has been amplified in several studies of the primary society.[3] In this article the focus is not upon the testing of this hypothesis but upon demonstrating that religious mythology and the associated ritual practices can provide data with which the ethnographer can generate theory about the moral sanctions enshrined in a religious system. As Bohannan remarked in his work already quoted, "A myth organizes data as narrative in order to condense mountains of facts or beliefs into recognizable forms: a theory is not a story but it does the same thing."[4]

The Yoruba cult religion of Gasparillo forms part of an extensive system of African-derived ancestor cults practiced in rural Trinidad and Tobago.[5] Sixteen years of comparative study of Trinidad folk beliefs have convinced me that consistent enculturation processes are at work in transforming what must have been the traditional forms of the Shango cult. Informants in the sixty-to-ninety-years age group have consistently insisted that incursions into the ranks of the Yoruba cultists by practitioners of *obeah* and spiritualism have tended in some localities to reduce the Shango cult to a commercial affair and to weaken the "work" of the various *orishas* (divinities or powers). Exacting a fee for spiritual healing and employing the "powers" to cure the infirm in order to gain money and status are the common practices eroding the traditional Yoruba religion in some villages. The Gasparillo Yorubas, under the leadership of a few stalwarts, have however resisted this trend. By insisting on the performance of the ceremonies in the traditional ways in which they received the knowledge from their forefathers, they refuse to syncretize the major rituals of the cult. Even opposition from the Roman Catholic church, to which the Yorubas, to a man, belong, has not succeeded in repressing the ancient rituals of the cult. Rather than capitulate, the Gasparillo Yorubas have been content to suffer expulsion from the Christian church on many occasions. The Shango cult (from the name of the Fire, "power," the chief divinity) has therefore retained its traditional cultural strength with its ancient ritual forms and belief systems intact in this community.

The conclusion about the contemporary cultural strength of the religion was dramatically demonstrated to me when the story (myth) that forms the basis of this article turned up in the Clarkes' *Introducing Folklore*—cante fable, text, music, and all—in an almost identical form.[6] My informant, Mrs. Nanine Williams, a great-grandmother from Caratal, was ninety-one years old when she related the story to me. Her memory was still exceedingly good, and recollection of dates has been her specialty. For years she accompanied her late husband, George Williams, a Yoruba from Oyo, to Shango "dances" (ceremonies), and she has been a great singer of Shango songs and an expert performer of the various dances associated with the several *orishas* in the Yoruba pantheon. In 1951 Andrew Pearse recorded prewedding Yoruba drumming at a "Feast" where George Williams was chief drummer. Now Nanine Williams's son Clermont (age 65) performs the drumming while she continues the ritual singing and dancing. It was at one of these ceremonies that I first heard Nanine Williams relate the "Myth of the Singing Skull." It is given here without any revisions and should be compared with the version in the Clarkes' work. The ritual act of which this myth is an explication follows the text. The music of the song sung by the mystical skull is also included for comparative study.

12.1

Nanine Williams, ninety-one years of age, of the village of Caratal, Trinidad, who related the "Myth of the Singing Skull."

Ogun, Ojah, and Osine
(Myth of the Singing Skull)

Three brothers—soldiers—went walking through the forests seeking a certain water. It was not long before they became very thirsty. The first brother set out from the camp to search, but he found no water. He met with trouble and had to return to his brothers. Together, then, the three brothers set out again on the search. Again they halted, and the eldest brother set out on the search alone, but after some time he again returned without any water. Then Ojah, the second brother, set out on the search for water, but he, too, returned without water—half dead with tiredness. The last brother, Osine, the one with the "broken back and crinkled fingers," decided to try. But his brothers sneered at him, called him a *bowsi* (hunchbacked) man, and asked him whether people like him could find water where healthy ones had failed. But Osine argued that it was his turn and he was going to search anyway. Osine traveled and traveled and traveled. One day, at last, he came to a great water. He was so elated that he turned back without even taking a drink, so anxious was he to give his elder brothers the good news. Having given his brothers the news, he suggested that they together set out to see the water that had given them so much trouble to find. But those elder brothers envied their younger brother and they said to themselves: "What a name will he have when we return home! He found water and we failed! We are going to kill him!"

Finally they reached the water. The eldest one, whose name was Ogun, told Osine to drink. Osine, in respect for age, allowed his eldest brother to take the first drink. Next Ojah, the second in age, drank. And then it was Osine's turn, he being the last. As Osine stooped down to drink, Ogun struck off his youngest brother's head with his sword. The head rolled slowly down into the river. Ojah, seeing it floating downstream, stuck his sword into it, and, drawing it out, he flung it into the high bush near by. The headless body was left on the river bank for the wild animals to devour.

Ogun and Ojah then filled up with water and went home to their father. They reported that they did not know where Osine had wandered to. Maybe he was lost or the lions had eaten him. The father, although glad for the water, was grieved for his lost son. He sent out searchers

12.2

Yoruba nation drummers performing at a Shango feast: Raymond Nelson (*left*) and Clermont Williams (age 65, *right*). The drums are made from old nail kegs and the heads are made of goat skin. (Courtesy *Trinidad Guardian*, January 24, 1968; Michael Ramoutar, photographer.)

into the forests, but for many a day no one came upon his son. Meantime, the wicked brothers thought that everything was over and their crime was unknown to anyone but themselves.

One day long afterward, a hunter cutting the bushes on the river bank discovered a skull. Remembering that he had heard about a man who had lost a son in the forest, he sent for the three soldiers' father, who came and recognized Osine's head at once. The father, suspecting the crime, secretly caused the skull to be brought to his house and had it hid in Osine's room. Then, summoning his two elder sons and a great congregation of the people, he asked his sons, "Should you see your brother now would you know him?"

The brothers were amused and jested: "He must be in some far country now. The lions ate him long ago." Then the skull was brought out. As the brothers looked at it, it began to sing a sad song that told all the people the story of Ogun and Ojah's crime (12.3). The father was so enraged that he "put his mouth" (a curse) upon his eldest son Ogun saying:

Oshun Mer ten Per l'Ogun or me ba

O - shun Mer ten, Per l'O - gun, or me' ba _____

Ah oo re re oh, or me ba _____

O - gun, wa - me - wa - me eh, mo ro me' _____

O - ri - sha, be' ten o - re', da co - co

O - gun mor, Dag - be' me', fo so me' _____

"In rain and storm
In thunder and lightning
You shall stand outside the gates:

As a watchman you shall stand
And eat your victuals alone
When your kinsmen hold the 'feast' for the ancestors."

Then with a big stick he drove Ogun out into the yard (compound) and left him there to be a guard forever. From that day, whenever the Yoruba people hold a feast for the ancestors and the *orishas*, they carry Ogun's meals outside the compound in the cold and rain and feed him there while the others enjoy the ritual banquet within.

This cante fable myth found in the repertory of the Gasparillo Yorubas is of crucial significance for the study of African survivals in the Caribbean as well as for generating theory about cultural persistence under conditions of technological change in general. Melville Herskovits formulated the concept of *cultural focus* in his attempt to account for the fact that some African cultural elements, when transplanted, are more resistant to variation and change than others.[7] Comparison of this tale with that reported by the Clarkes will show that, despite separation from the parent culture in Africa for nearly 150 years, this myth has retained its major literary characteristics, unchanged under the rigors of plantation slavery and the vicissitudes generated by this condition upon the original culture bearers. On the other hand, the myth represents a unique combination of a number of tale motifs,[8] the chief of which can be easily identified as:

1. Singing bone	Type 780 (Thompson)
2. Quest and tasks	Type 577 (Thompson)
3. Magical remedies	Thompson (1946, pp. 79–81)
4. Cruel brothers	Thompson (1946, pp. 79–81)
5. Cain envy	Child (vol. 1, nos. 11, 12)
6. Three knights	Child (vol. 1, pp. 141–151)

This tale, with its several versions as documented by Child and Thompson, is universally dispersed. What is significant about its occurrence in the Yoruba folk-narrative tradition in Trinidad is that this version appears to have been preserved intact within this predominantly Negro originated community. Its form may be regarded as being "fixed," since

12.3

Sung by Nanine Williams in a dialect that is apparently a mixture of French Creole and Yoruba. Nanine said that she learned the story from the old Yoruba friends who used to visit her father, Pere Legendre, at his home in Caratal, to which he had migrated from San Juan after Emancipation (1838).

any alteration would interfere with the performance and form of the supporting rituals. It may well be that we have here an insight into one of the ways by which oral traditions maintain their normative morphology under conditions of cultural migration. Under other conditions —for example, where the tale was used in secular story-telling sessions —there would have been no restriction upon the taletellers to maintain the original norms of plot and structure. It may be generalized that the myth of the Gasparillo Yorubas definitely comprises tale type 551, Water of Life, and tale type 780, Singing Bone, although the youngest son, the hero, dies, his death being avenged posthumously by his own father, whose life he saved with the magical object (water).

It is clear from the plot that it is not the admission of evidence of guilt or innocence that is crucial here. The dramatization of the tragic consequences of and the moral sanctions against killing a kinsman—the shedding of the blood of a consanguine—emphasizes the essence of the prescriptions for preservation of social harmony. Compulsory service by or other public humiliation of the criminal is sufficient compensation for this crime. The *weregild* exacted as a means of compensation for the expiation of willful murder is recorded by Robert Lowie for the Ifugao. In many regions, according to that worker, "even felonies are compounded in the interest of the public peace."[9] Exclusion from the ritual feast of the clan—social isolation—and the absolute disinheritance of a clansman, that is, deprivation of his customary tribal status and role, must carry weight of a very heavy penalty. What is emphasized here is the importance of resolving the conflict while preserving community cohesiveness, the foundations of which are based in stable family units comprising the community.

Finally, the "Myth of the Singing Skull" has theoretical significance in the context of a Yoruba religious philosophy. The particular rubric of the Yoruba morality system implicit in this tale can be regarded as being given tangible practical exposition every time, when, at a communal feast or sacrifice, the functionary is made to take the calabash containing the ritual meal and feed Ogun as he stands guard at the gates. This dramatic act of ceremonial role deprivation excluding Ogun from the feast of his own kinsmen—an "isolation ceremony"—repeated hundreds of times at the several *chapelles* from year to year and from generation to generation as an outward visible sanction, cannot fail to impress upon the community of cultists in a patriarchal culture the principle that moral condemnation must be applied to the crime of wilfully shedding the blood of a kinsman. The ritual can thus be viewed as being functional in reinforcing the concept of compulsory tribal survival through social harmony implicit in the moral rule against murder.

Regarding morality of African religions when we examine and analyze the major features of this myth, we find instances of:

1.
Rivalry over succession among kinsmen (collateral relative) for lineage headship
2.
Reversal of primogeniture through a task set by the father figure

(search for water)
3.
Cain envy[10] directed at the youngest of three brothers
4.
Murder of a tribesman and its nemesis
5.
Retribution and primitive justice dispensed by the tribal head with
popular consent and community involvement

In a society traditionally regulated by a system of religious sanctions,
where tribal cohesion is vital for the welfare of the group, the sanctions
must be restated and thus re-emphasized terminally through a regular
sequence of ritual ceremonies engaged in by all tribesmen. The man-
date proscribing the shedding of the blood of a tribesman has repercussions that go deep into the bonding system, which maintains not
only the spiritual but also the material (economic) welfare of the group.
These mandates are powerful controls that operate not only to maintain
harmony in the tribe but also as a secondary objective to control forces
that will decimate the kin group and so reduce its strength as an economic organization. As Nanine Williams explained, the ritual practice
of "feeding" Ogun outside the compound is clearly understood by all
votaries to be imperative. For those who cannot readily understand this
custom, it is to the "Myth of the Singing Skull" they turn in order to
comprehend the compulsion to avoid shedding the blood of a primary
relative.

What is still more significant for a study of the dynamics of social
cohesion at work in this community is the fact that data from the Gasparillo police show a comparatively low incidence of murder and serious
"crimes against the person" among the Negro community. It is my
postulation that an effective restraint is exerted upon deviant behavior
in the community and that interpersonal conflicts between Negroes
are effectively mediated by the obedience to the moral sanctions implicit
in the rituals of the Shango cult. In a sense it is the community that
plays the juridical role in the myth.

The Negro community at Gasparillo is one that can easily be torn
apart by interfamily conflict over ancestral lands. Land among the Yorubas, as workers like Bohannan have indicated, cannot be alienated or
sold. In a community like Gasparillo, where the high fertility rate creates
an increasing number of "heirs of the ancestral owners," intergroup
contention over fair and just distribution or land allocation can lead
to the steady abrasion of community harmony. But land is not a problem area: the extended patrilocal households in this community an-
nually spread over the allocations as married sons bring in their wives to
live on the family plot and farm the agricultural land prescribed for
them by the lineal "older heads." No matter where the Gasparillo Negro
may migrate, he finally returns to the family lands, rejoins his kinsmen,
and worships at the Yoruba shrines erected by his ancestors to Ogun,
Shakpana, and Shango. It is apparent that the moral rules implicit in the
rituals and the explanatory myths constitute for these people a regula-
tory and spiritual maintenance system, which carries the individual

safely through the rigors of modern technological and cultural change by cushioning him against the anomie and social drift seen at work deteriorating community life in other rural villages in this country at present.

The "Myth of the Singing Skull" is only one of a complex of supportive literary explanations associated with the Yoruba rituals. Some of these legendary narratives are even more direct in the moral imperatives they contain. The Shango cult has been attacked by the Christian churches as being idolatrous; many Negroes, too, in their aspiration to social status and upper-class "decency," reject these relics of African culture, pronouncing them backward and even primitive. The most vociferous critics of this cult have deemed it immoral or, at another extreme, amoral. But careful diligent research has shown not only that the fundamental practices are genuinely "religious" (defined in the strictest sense of that word) but also that the religion of the Yorubas, as Bohannan pointed out about all African religions, is truly moralistic. While there is no body of religious dogma to which one may point, and even though it must be admitted that the devotees of this cult may not be able to present tidy codes of credos neatly written down on parchment, the living repertory of myths and the actual ritualistic somatics of sacrificial dance and music are the media for dispensing moral commands that must be obeyed by all members of the cult. Whatever is the experience of other Yoruba communities in other localities on the island of Trinidad, it can safely be concluded of these Gasparillo votaries of Shango (the old iron workers' patron divinity from Nigeria) that the moral strength of their religion has not been dissipated by enculturation or weakened by secularism. As a moral force making for personality integration and community stability in a transitional society, the cult of the *orishas* has withstood empirical examination. What this examination shows is that it is not in the declared tenets and written commandments that the existence of practical religion and morality can be identified, but in the quality of the interpersonal relationships between those who practice the religion and obey its moral imperatives. The ritual record of the "Myth of the Singing Skull" not only says to all who come into the palais, "Thou shalt not kill," but also demonstrates spiritual and social exclusion of those who shed the blood of a consanguine. This is practical morality in a world where the struggle for power generates envy and hatred even among members of a community of kinsmen.

NOTES

1.   Paul Bohannan, *Africa and Africans*, p. 22.

2.   This study has been made possible by a UWI Research Fellowship awarded under the community studies program of the Institute of Social and Economic Research, University of the West Indies, Jamaica.

3.   Joachim Wach, *Sociology of Religion*, pp. 54–107.

4.   Bohannan, *Africa and Africans*, p. 226.

5.   George Simpson, *Cult Music of Trinidad*; Melville J. and Frances S. Herskovits, *Trinidad Village*.

6.   Kenneth W. and Mary W. Clarke, *Introducing Folklore*, pp. 136–139.

7.   Melville J. Herskovits, "Problem, Method and Theory in Afro-American Studies," *Afro-America* 1 (1964): 21.

8.   Francis J. Child, *The English and Scottish Popular Ballads*; Stith Thompson, *Motif-Index of Folk-Literature*, and *The Folktale*.

9.   Robert H. Lowie, *Primitive Society*, p. 402.

10.   See Ian D. Suttie, *Origins of Love and Hate*, pp. 87–88.

BIBLIOGRAPHY

Bascom, William R. "The Sociological Role of the Yoruba Cult Group." *Memoirs of the American Anthropological Association*, no. 63, 1944.

Bohannan, Paul. *Africa and Africans*. Garden City, N.Y.: Natural History Press, 1964.

Child, Francis J. *The English and Scottish Popular Ballads*. 5 vols. New York: Dover Publications, 1965.

Clarke, Kenneth W. and Mary W. *Introducing Folklore*. Appendix, pp. 136–138, "Singing Bones," Selection G. New York: Holt, Rinehart and Winston, 1963.

Elder, Jacob D. *The Yoruba Ancestor Cult in Gasparillo: Its Structure, Organization and Social Function in Community Cohesion*. St. Augustine, Trinidad: University of the West Indies, 1969.

Fortes, Meyer. *Oedipus and Job in West African Religion*. Cambridge: At the University Press, 1959.

Herskovits, Melville J. "African Gods and Catholic Saints in New World Religious Belief." *American Anthropologist* 29 (1937): 635–643.

———. "Problem, Method and Theory in Afro-American Studies." *Afro-America* 1 (1964): 5–24.

——— and Frances S. *Trinidad Village*. New York: Octagon Books, 1964.

Kluckhohn, Clyde. "Myths and Rituals: A General Theory." *Harvard Theological Review* 35 (1942): 44–78.

Lloyd, P. C. "The Yoruba of Nigeria." In *Peoples of Africa*, edited by James L. Gibbs, Jr., pp. 575–576. New York: Holt, Rinehart and Winston, 1965.

Lowie, Robert H. *Primitive Society*. New York: Harper and Brothers, 1961.

Simpson, George. *Cult Music of Trinidad*. Ethnic Folkways Library Album FE/4478.

Suttie, Ian D. *Origins of Love and Hate*. New York: Agora, 1966.

Thompson, Stith. *The Folktale*. New York: Dryden Press, 1946.

———. *Motif-Index of Folk-Literature: A Classification of Narrative Elements in Folk-Tales, Ballads, Myths, Fables, Mediaeval Romances, Exempla, Fabliaux, Jest-Books and Local Legends*. 6 vols. Indiana University Studies. Bloomington: Indiana University Press, 1955–1958.

Wach, Joachim. *Sociology of Religion*. Chicago: University of Chicago Press, 1944.

Notes on the Contributors

Gerald L. Davis, assistant professor of Africana studies, Livingston College, Rutgers University, New Brunswick, New Jersey, is a native of New York City. A graduate of Fisk University (B.A., 1963), he received his M.A. in Folklore from the University of California at Berkeley (1973) and is working for the Ph.D. in Folklore and Folklife at the University of Pennsylvania. His special interests are Afro-American expressive materials, Afro-American material culture, sociolinguistics, and cultural anthropology.

Jacob D. Elder, of Port of Spain, Trinidad, is chairman of the Trinidad and Tobago National Cultural Council. A native of Tobago, he has studied in Trinidad, London, and Cambridge and at the University of Pennsylvania, where he received his Ph.D. in 1966. He is the author of *Singing Games of Trinidad and Tobago* (1962), *Song Games from Trinidad and Tobago* (1965), and *Song and Struggle: The Politics of Traditional Song*. He is at present engaged in preparing a handbook of Caribbean folklore.

James L. Evans is a native of Missouri and associate professor of English at Pan American University, Edinburg, Texas. He received his education at Central Missouri State College (B.A., B.S., 1950), the University of Colorado (M.A., 1955), the University of Texas (M.A., 1964), and the University of Texas at Austin (Ph.D., 1967). His special fields of research interest are the history and sociology of the American West, especially the part that minorities have played in Western settlement.

James Marston Fitch, of New York City, is professor of architecture at Columbia University, where he is director of the graduate program in restoration and preservation of historic architecture. A native of Washington, he studied at the University of Alabama, Tulane University School of Architecture, and Columbia. His books include *American Building* (1948, 2nd ed. 1972) and *Architecture and the Esthetics of Plenty* (1961). He is a member of the International Commission on Sites and Monuments and the Advisory Council on Historic Preservation.

293

Henry Glassie, of Bloomington, Indiana, is associate professor of folklore at Indiana University. A native of Washington, D.C., he received his education at Tulane University (B.A., 1964), Cooperstown (M.A., 1965), and the University of Pennsylvania (Ph.D., 1969). He is the author of *Pattern in the Material Folk Culture of the Eastern United States* (1968).

Ward H. Goodenough is professor of anthropology at the University of Pennsylvania, Philadelphia. He is a native of Massachusetts and a graduate of Cornell (B.A., 1940) and Yale universities (Ph.D., 1949). He is a specialist in the ethnography of the Pacific. His books include *Property, Kin, and Community on Truk* (1951), *Cooperation in Change* (1963), *Explorations in Cultural Anthropology* (1964), *Description and Comparison in Cultural Anthropology* (1970), and *Culture, Language and Society* (1971).

Leslie P. Greenhill, of State College, Pennsylvania, is professor of education and assistant vice-president for academic services, Pennsylvania State University. A native of Australia, he is a graduate of the University of Melbourne (1940), and was on the staff there before coming to Penn State in 1948. He is the director of the American Archive and member of the Editorial Board of the Encyclopaedia Cinematographica, Göttingen, West Germany; editor of the *Psychological Cinema Register*, 1955–1957, 1959–1960, and 1965 to the present; and a member of the Editorial Board of the *Journal of Educational Technology Systems*, 1972 to the present.

Fred B. Kniffen is Boyd Professor emeritus, Louisiana State University, Baton Rouge, Louisiana. A native of Michigan, he received his B.A. from the University of Michigan in 1922 and his Ph.D. from the University of California at Berkeley in 1930. His special fields of interest are material culture of the United States, particularly folk architecture and other folk arts and crafts, settlement patterns, and the ethnography of the American Indians. Among his books are *Culture Worlds* (with R. J. Russell, 1951) and *Louisiana: Its Land and People* (1968).

William B. Knipmeyer, of Natchitoches, Louisiana, is professor and chairman of the Department of Social Sciences, Northwestern State University of Louisiana. A native of New Orleans, he is a graduate of Louisiana State University (B.S., 1947, M.S., 1950, and Ph.D., 1956). His special field of interest is settlement geography.

Walter L. Robbins is an N.E.H. Fellow in Residence in German at the University of Cincinnati for 1975–1976. He is a native of Massachusetts. He received his B.A. from the University of South Carolina in 1955 and his Ph.D. from the University of North Carolina in 1969. His special interests are American-German cultural history and folklore, especially that of the Germans in North and South Carolina.

Warren E. Roberts, of Bloomington, Indiana, is professor of folklore, Indiana University, Bloomington. A native of Maine, he received his education at Reed College (B.A., 1948) and Indiana University (M.A., 1950, Ph.D., 1953). His special research interests are folk literature, folk architecture, and folk crafts. His books include *The Tale of the Kind and Unkind Girls* (1958), *Types of Indic Oral Tales* (1960), and *Norwegian Folktale Studies* (1965).

David J. Winslow, of Oswego, New York, is associate professor of English, State University College, Oswego. A native of Massachusetts, he received his B.A. at Goddard College, 1966; his M.A., University of Pennsylvania, 1967; and his Ph.D., University of Pennsylvania, 1972. His book *New York State Folklore and Folklife* is to appear in the Monograph Series of the New York State English Council.

Don Yoder, of Philadelphia, Pennsylvania, is a graduate of Franklin and Marshall College (B.A. 1942) and the University of Chicago (Ph.D., 1947). He has taught at Union Theological Seminary, New York; Muhlenberg College; Franklin and Marshall College; and (since 1956) the University of Pennsylvania, where he was chairman of the Graduate Program in Folklore and Folklife, 1966–1970. He is the author of *Songs along the Mahantongo* (with Walter E. Boyer and Albert F. Buffington, 1951) and *Pennsylvania Spirituals* (1961) and has been editor of *Pennsylvania Folklife* since 1961.

INDEX

Abrams, Charles: on Eskimo living conditions, 36
Abu Simbel, 31
"Ach wie laufen doch die jahre" (hymn), 266
advertising: on tollhouses, 224–225, 229
aesthetics: and community, 177–179; definitions of,
    176–177
"affecting things/events": defined, 152–153
Africa: folk vs. contemporary architecture of, 39–42
Afro-American art: attitude of scholarship toward, 182;
    and definitions of cultural system, 152, 153; oral
    vs. material in, 151; and "performance con-
    stituency," 177, 180
agriculture: vs. basketweaving, 181–182; and forma-
    tion of Rio Grande society, 240. *See also* peasant
    agriculture
Algeria: desert dwellings of, 38; folk architecture of,
    40, 41
"Allein auff Gott setz dein vertrawn" (hymn), 266
Alston, Peter: acquisition of weaving skills by, 178; on
    basket trade, 154–155, 156; on farming, 181; on
    gathering of sweet grass, 162–163; on saline
    immersion of baskets, 176
ambosschiesse, 261
American Archive: film prints of, 103
American Dictionary of Superstitions and Popular
    Beliefs (Hand), 11
American Farmer: on turnpike weighing machines,
    221
Americans: migration of, to Lower Rio Grande Valley,
    242, 243; usurpation of Mexican lands by, 243,
    246
American Southwest: desert dwellings of, 38
American Swedish Historical Foundation, 12
ancestor cult: cultural pressures on, 282; ethnographic
    study of, 281–282; moral/ritual complemen-
    tarity in, 288–290; mythical content of,
    285–287; preservation of tradition in, 282, 290
animal necessities: effect of, on human occupancy
    patterns, 52
animism: vs. realism, 182 n.5
Annals of Tryon County (Campbell), 222
anthropology: social/moral obligations of, 23–25
—, cultural: and folklife studies, 19–20
Antoinette, Marie: interest of, in vernacular architec-
    ture, 29
anvil: firing of, by New Year's shooters, 261
archaeology: method of, 28; upper-class bias of, 29,
    47 n.8
architectural past: appreciation of vernacular in,
    29–30; discovery of, 27; preservation of,
    44–46; scientific scrutiny of, 31–32. *See also*
    folk architecture; primitive architecture
architecture, contemporary: alienation of, from
    environment, 32; response of, to social environ-
    ment, 40–42
architecture, preindustrial: compatibility of, with
    environment, 32
Archive of Swedish Folklore, 9

Armstrong, Robert Plant: on aesthetics, 176–177; on
    "affecting things/events," 152–153
Arnhem Congress of 1955, 5
art history: method of, 28; upper-class bias of, 29,
    47 n.8
artistic past: appreciation of vernacular in, 30; con-
    temporary pressures on, 30–31
"Art of the South Seas" (exhibition), 47 n.12
arts and crafts: and aesthetic community, 177–179;
    study of, by folklorists, 151–153
Aschmann, Homer: folklife monograph of, 66
Aufseher Collegium: action of, against New Year's
    shooting, 257
avant-garde, Paris: influence of folk art on, 47 n.12
awl/punch: use of, in basketweaving, 166, 167

Backhof, Ludolf, 261; on New Year's shooting, 257
Baffin Island Eskimos: igloos of, 34, 35, 36
baking: film documentation of, 99
Balch Institute, 12
banditry: myth of, 239–240; retaliatory nature of, 252
barn: construction of, 202–204
Barnwell, B. B., 160
Baroque: architectural influences on, 27
baskets. *See* coil baskets
basketweaving: and attendant cultural modes,
    179–180; as expression of community, 177–
    179; vs. farming, 181–182; film documentation
    of, 91; handle construction in, 172–173, 174–
    175; and industrialization, 163, 166; materials
    used in, 159, 160–165; origins of, in South
    Carolina, 154–156, 159–160; saline immersion
    in, 173, 176; sewing stage in, 167, 168–171;
    tools used in, 166, 167; trade from, 154–156
bateau: design of, 142, 143; distribution of, 144;
    etymology of, 142, 144, 148 n.27; use of, 144,
    146
—*plat*, 144, 146–147
Bausinger, Hermann: and urban-industrial folklife, 9
bayous: culture associated with, 106–107
Beam, J. C., 259
Beam, "Uncle Sid": "speeches" of, 262
Bienville, Jean Baptiste Le Moyne, Sieur de, 109
Black Creek Village, Ontario, 11
blacks, American: attitude of scholarship toward, 182;
    cultural self-esteem of, 23; ethnic conscious-
    ness among, 3. *See also* Afro-American art;
    Negroes
Blegen, Theodore, 12; on democratizing of historiog-
    raphy, 6
boats: *bateau*, 142–144, 146; *chaland*, 130–133, 142;
    construction characteristics of, 107, 147 n.4;
    existing studies of, 105; flatboat, 145–147; in
    Louisiana water culture, 106–107; pirogue,
    108–130, 142; skiff, 133–142; suitability
    of, for folkloristic study, 105; types of, 107–108

Index

Bohannon, Paul: on disposition of land among Yorubas, 289; on morality in African religion, 281, 290; on myth, 281

Boland, Daniel: on New Year's/Christmas shooting, 273

Boone Hall Plantation (South Carolina), 156, 159

Boyer, Ruth: on folk art, 151–152

Boyer, Walter E., 262

Branchport and Penn Yan Plank Road: charter of, revoked, 214

Brannon, William: on New Year's shooting, 258, 259, 260, 261

bread: baking of, 99

Brewington, M. V.: on Chesapeake boating, 105

bridge, covered: diffusion pattern of, 61

Bringéus, Nils-Arved: on folklife research methods, 9–10

Brown, William: "wish" of, 262

Brownsville, Texas: American/European migration to, 243, 246; Cortina raid on, 246, 248; racial tension in, 246, 252

Brownsville Flag: on Cortina raid, 246

Bruner, Jerome: on basketweavers, 182, 183 n.43

Buchanan, James, 248

Buffington, Albert F., 262

Burgess, John, 224

Burrill, Meredith: place-name study of, 65

Cabrera, Tomás, 248

cajeu, 108

Cameron, Ewen: execution of, 244–245; filibustering expeditions of, 242

Campbell, F. M.: on destruction of property, 251

Campbell, William, 222

Canada: folklife studies of, 3, 4

canoes, bark: use of, by French, 109–110

canoes, dugout. *See* pirogue

canotte, 148 n.20; design of, 135, 140

Caribbean islands: folklife studies of, 4

Carpenter, "Aunt Violet," 259

Catawba River region, North Carolina: migrant settlement in, 257; New Year's shooting in, 258–259, 261, 262, 268

Catholic Church: opposition of, to Shango cult, 282

Center for Comparative Folklore and Mythology, 11

Center for Migration Studies (U.S.A.), 12

chaland: design of, 130–131; distribution of, 132; and *jongs*, 142; use of, 133

chaloupe, 134

Chapelle, Howard I.: boat studies of, 105

chapelles, 288

Chapman, John A.: on Christmas shooting, 273

Chardin, Jean Baptiste Siméon, 29

Charleston County, South Carolina: African influence on material culture of, 153–154; landownership in, 180, 181–182

"Cherryville New Year's Shooters," 258, 259

Child, Francis J.: on "Myth of the Singing Skull," 287

chimneys: in log house construction, 190, 191

China: peasant agriculture of, 42

Clark, John, 214

Clarke, Kenneth W.: uncovers "Myth of the Singing Skull," 282, 287

Clarke, Mary W.: uncovers "Myth of the Singing Skull," 282, 287

"Classical Town Names in the United States" (Zelinsky), 65

coil baskets: African/American contrasts in, 163; African origins of, 153–154; handles of, 172–173, 174–175; introduction of, into South Carolina, 159–160; saline immersion of, 173, 176; sewing of, 167, 168–171; style of, 167, 172–173

colonialism: devaluation of ethnic identity by, 22; repercussions of, in folklife studies, 21

Colonial Williamsburg, Virginia, 11

community: and aesthetics, 177–179

"Comparative Studies of North American Indians" (Driver/Massey), 66

complexes: recognition of, by cultural geographer, 61

Congo tribe, 281

Cooperstown and Fort Plain Plank Road: gatekeepers' dwellings on, 217–218

Corbin, Cage: violence of, against tollgate, 211

corn cribs: design of, 42–43

Corpus Christi, Texas: rumored attacks on, 248

Cortina, Juan N.: Anglo hysteria over, 248–252; Brownsville raid of, 246, 248; photograph of, 247; as popular hero, 252

courtship: and wishing in/shooting in, 260

Coxsackie Turnpike Company: construction of tollhouses by, 224; and counterfeiters, 213; payment of employees by, 215, 216

crafts. *See* arts and crafts

cultural anthropology. *See* anthropology, cultural

cultural focus, 287

cultural geography. *See* geography, cultural

culture: effect of, on human occupancy patterns, 52–56; simple vs. complex, 56

— area: as geographical concept, 56; scrutiny of, by cultural geographers, 63–64

Culture Survey of Pennsylvania, 12

culture types: recognition of, by cultural geographers, 61, 63

Curry, Isaac, 217

Curtis, John, 213

Dabbs, Edith: on basketry, 159, 160

dance: film documentation of, 78–81

DAR: and artistic preservation, 30

dating: methods of, 204–205

Delaware Turnpike: payment of employees by, 216

Description of Greece (Pausanias), 30, 47 n.14

Dialect Archive, University of Uppsala, 9

"Disaster and Reconstruction in Cameron Parish" (Kniffen/Wright), 66

documents, written: and dating, 204

dogtrot house: variants of, 58–59

Index

Index

peasant agriculture: response of, to environmental pressures, 42–44

Pease, Andrew, 282

Peate, Iorwerth: on barbarism, 8

Peeke, Phil: on Afro-American material culture, 152

peniche, 126, 134

Penn Center, South Carolina: basketry of, 159–160

Pennsylvania: Halloween customs in, 96–97; bake oven from, 101

Pennsylvania Farm Museum, 11

Pennsylvania Folk-Cultural Index, 7

Pennsylvania German Society, 12

Perdue, Robert: on coil baskets, 153, 182

Perry, Oliver Hazard: on American soldiers in Mexican War, 243

Peter the Great: use of architecture by, 27

Picasso, Pablo: influence of folk art on, 47 n.12

pikes, 229

pine needles: use of, in basketweaving, 163, 164–165

Pinus palustris, 163

pirogue: construction of, 111, 115, 116–121; distribution of, 125, 129; etymology of, 147 n.5; and *jougs*, 142; maintenance of, 115, 124; manufacture of, by French, 110; manufacture of, by Indians, 108–109; modern decline of, 125–126; modern design of, 111, 112–114; navigation of, 122–123, 124–125; postfrontier decline of, 110; use of, 115; use of, by French, 109, 110; use of, by Indians, 108. *See also* plank pirogue

place names: studies of, 65; and tollgates, 232–233

plank pirogue: construction of, 127–128, 130; design of, 126–127, 129–130; distribution of, 128, 129; and *jougs*, 142; names associated with, 126; uses for, 127, 128–129

plates: in log house construction, 191, 194

Plimouth Plantation, Massachusetts, 11

Polish Americans: cultural self-esteem of, 23

Polk, James K.: orders capture of Matamoros, 243

"popular culture": relationship of, to traditional culture, 10

Porter, James: on Afro-American art, 151

Porter's Cave (Morgan County, Indiana): source of building stone, 190

Portugal: peasant agriculture of, 43

potter's workshop: film documentation of, 84–85, 88–89

pottery decoration: film documentation of, 87

prayer-story, 179–180

"preacher": in New Year's shooting, 258, 259

preservation, historical: artificiality in, 45–46; importance of, 44–45;

primitive architecture: cultural milieu of, 33; defined, 47 n.15; environmental considerations in, 32–33; examples of, 33–38; preservation of, 44–45; and social environment, 38, 48 n.19

psalms: influences of, in "shooting" chants, 270–272

Psychological Cinema Register, 102

Pueblo Indians: rejection of cultural domination by, 22

Pugin, A. W. N., 30

quantification: use of, by cultural geographers, 64

questionnaires: and folklife research, 9

radeau, 147

rafters: in log house construction, 194

rake oven: film documentation of, 101

ranching: development of, near Rio Grande, 241

realism: vs. animism, 182 n.5

Rebekahites: violence of, against tollgates, 211–212

rechtliche Volkskunde, 6

Redfield, Robert: on "great" vs. "little" traditions, 21, 33

Reformed Church: attitude of, toward New Year's shooting, 258; in North Carolina, 257; use of English by, 270

regional ethnology, 3, 4, 5

religious folksongs: diffusion pattern of, 65

Renaissance: architectural influences on, 27

Revett, Nicholas, 28

Reyburn, W. P.: on Cortina raid, 250

Ricketts, James B.: on Cortina raid, 250

Rio Grande: Spanish settlements along, 240

— Valley. *See* Lower Rio Grande Valley

Rockefeller family: impact of, on historical preservation, 45

Rococo: architectural influences on, 27

Rome and Oswego Plank Road: and employee dishonesty, 214–215

roof: in log house construction, 197

Rostlund, Erhard, 64

Rouse, Edna: on origin of basket stands, 154

Rousseau, 29

Rumania: flute carver of, 83; folk dance of, 78–81; potter's workshop in, 88–89

rushel grass: use of, in basketweaving, 154, 158, 159

Ruskin, John, 30

Russell, Isaac, 216

St. Helena Island, South Carolina: basketry of, 159, 160

Saur, Christoph, 261

Sauvolle, ———, 109

Schenda, Rudolf: on folklife research methods, 9

Schenectady-Utica Turnpike: toll charges on, 220–221

schneckilies, 273

Schnëggli, 273

scholarship: racist bias of, 182

Sellers, Vance, 259; "wishes" of, 268–269, 271–272

Seneca Turnpike: computation of tolls for, 221

Serenoa repens, 163

"sermon": in New Year's shooting, 258, 259

"Settlement Succession in Eastern French Louisiana" (Knipmeyer), 105–106

Index